AYES TO THE LEFT

For my Neath constituents

ALSO BY PETER HAIN

Don't Play with Apartheid (1971)

Radical Regeneration (1975)

Mistaken Identity (1976)

Community Politics (edited, 1976)

Policing The Police Volume One (1979)

Policing The Police Volume Two (1980)

Crisis and Future of Left (edited, 1980)

Political Trials in Britain (1984)

Political Strikes (1985)

Proportional Misrepresentation (1986)

A Putney Plot? (1987)

The Peking Connection (1995)

AYES TO THE LEFT
A FUTURE FOR SOCIALISM

Peter Hain

LAWRENCE & WISHART
LONDON

Lawrence & Wishart
144a Old South Lambeth Road
London SW8 1XX

First published 1995 by Lawrence & Wishart
Copyright © Peter Hain, 1995

ISBN 0 85315 832 0

British Library Cataloguing in Publication Data.
A catalogue record for this book is available from
the British Library.

Typeset by Jan Brown Designs
Printed and bound in Great Britain by
Biddles Ltd, Guildford

Contents

Introduction	1
1. Libertarian Socialism	5
2. Democracy	42
3. Equality	76
4. Economic Renewal	119
5. A People's Europe	155
6. The Global Economy	181
7. Charter for Change	218
Selected Bibliography	243
Index	245

ACKNOWLEDGEMENTS

I am grateful to Isobel Larkin for her research, hard work and advice; to Sally Davison, Walter Hain, John Underwood and Phil Wyatt for their detailed observations on the whole book; and to Andy Batkin, Roger Berry, Colin Hines, John Denham, Andy Erlam, Hywel Francis, Geoff Hodgson, Tim Lang, Ann Pettifor, Michael Phelan, Nick Samuels, Mike Watts and Phil Woolas for their comments – though none is responsibile for the views and content. Staff at the House of Commons Library efficiently and diligently provided and checked many of the facts and figures. I am also grateful to Jill Hays, Howard Davies, Adelaine Hain, Donna Easter and my wife Pat for absorbing the extra pressure resulting from work on the book.

Peter Hain, Resolven, Neath
May 1995

Introduction

As Britain approaches the millennium £750 is spent prosecuting an unemployed South Wales father who stole £2 of coal to keep his wife and new baby warm, while share options worth £100 million are handed out to directors and senior executives of the privatised utilities.

What has become of us? While the tinsel of digitalisation brings an aura of modernity and progress, we worry desperately that our youngsters may be condemned to a life without hope on the dole, and that our parents will not be comfortable in frail old age. And those of us in work wonder whether we will be so for much longer. Ubiquitous crime and violence means we constantly look over our shoulders: are we safe on the street at night, can our children be left alone to play, will our home be secure, will our car still be there?

The worship of market forces has created an ugly 'me-firstism' which is destroying community cohesion and poisoning social relations. Family stress, isolation in old age, loneliness, couch potato illiteracy, the relegation of courtesy and inter-personal respect as irrelevant and 'old fashioned' – these are not signposts to an 'opportunity' society, they are evidence of a decaying one. As are growing poverty amidst affluence; a widening class divide; mass unemployment; racial violence; the collapse of once-cherished services in health, education, transport and caring; a harsh, casualised world of work; and the spectre of both global warming and global economic instability.

So too is the brazen celebration of institutional immorality as company bosses help themselves to telephone number increases while their workers take cuts in real wages; as millions on low incomes are incited by government to switch out of occupational or state earnings-related pensions; as government lies to parliament over illegal arm sales to Iraq and Iran; as MPs take bribes; as Ministers leave the Cabinet straight for the corporate board rooms they had favoured in office; as privatised utility chiefs pocket millions on the back of the cut-price flotations that short-changed the nation; as politically packed quangos are riddled with corruption; and as high-living City fraudsters get a ticking off or escape scot-free while those who supplement meagre benefits with a bit of gardening or labouring are jailed.

So too is the attack on people who are the backbone of any civilised society. Teachers are derided and assaulted – either physically in the classroom, or professionally by the Tory government. Nurses take second place to pen-pushers. Doctors are transformed into 'managers'. Engineers, instead of topping the career stakes for aspiring youngsters, find themselves lagging in social status and incomes behind accountants and bank managers. Scientists similarly cannot approach anything like the earnings of brokers. Architects must take second place to estate agents. Of course we need people to do jobs in finance and property; of course we need managers; of course we cannot do without bureaucrats. Their work should be respected and appropriately valued. But ours has become a topsy-turvy world in which the people who are creative, who actually generate wealth through inventing and making things, the people who care for us and the people who educate our children, are treated with contempt while respect is reserved for those who could not survive without them.

This is a society, if not in clichéd 'crisis', then incontrovertibly in deep structural trouble. The next generation is going to be morally and socially poorer. And economically too. Now that the cushion of North Sea Oil revenues and privatisation proceeds has deflated, there is no other way forward than to make a break with the suffocating conventional wisdom of Thatcherite and post-Thatcherite economics; it is time to overturn a long tradition of failure, systemic to Britain.

Under-producing corporate Britain, militaristic industrial Britain, over-indebted household Britain, parasitic financial Britain, impoverished public Britain and inept governmental Britain – this is a recipe for long term disaster. It cries out for a socialist alternative, including radical institutional reform. To make such a plea is not to peddle partisan political dogma. It is simply to counsel common sense.

Unless Britain makes a fundamental change of direction there is no prospect of reversing the remorseless decline into a nasty, brutish, inefficient and increasingly deprived society.

By the early 1990s the new right's project had stalled. In Britain the Tories, ideologically washed up, their economic policy in disarray, found forlorn disunity replacing their bullish 1980s confidence. The monetarism of the European Union had generated mass unemployment and fanned right-wing extremism and racism. Eastern Europe was experiencing growing popular disenchantment at the consequences for employment and public welfare of the headlong rush for privatisation which followed the ignominious collapse of communist regimes. World poverty and poor country debt was rising in a global economy favouring the rich and powerful. Exclusive reliance upon market forces was also discredited by successful collaborative arrangements between state and private sector, such a key feature of the fast growing economies of the Pacific Basin.

But if these developments indict the new right, they are not cited in praise of the old statist left which so disfigured and discredited socialism. Instead they strengthen the case for an alternative, decentralised, 'libertarian socialism' which can win popular support. Now that the ghost of authoritarianism and command economics has been exorcised, socialism has the best opportunity for fifty years to win popular support in the democratic world.

Nevertheless if it is to win in a way that will enable it to regenerate Britain, the left cannot rely solely upon the obvious failure of the new right. Antagonism to the Tories might bring Labour victory, but unless the Party arrives with a clear programme of fundamental structural change for which it has marshalled popular support, it may only be a one-term government. The left in general and the Labour Party in particular has to win the *battle of ideas*. People have to be convinced positively about the credibility of the socialist alternative.

Despite the glaring failure of the right, many Labour Party members and others on the left have not felt comfortable in engaging in the battle of ideas, because they have not been equipped to do so. For far too long the left has relied upon old slogans rather than serious policies. A case in point was the 1994-95 debate over replacing Clause IV of Labour's constitution: despite striking at what many members felt

3

was the very soul of the Party, Tony Blair easily won a mandate for change. One reason for this was that the left had not translated the stirring old poetry of Clause IV into modern language and modern policies.

This book is a modest attempt to fill a gap – to give confidence in the commonsense of contemporary socialism. It does not claim to be comprehensive or to cover every policy area. Neither is it a dispassionate academic treatise: it is an unapologetic polemic written by a busy MP. Intended as a call for the regeneration of the left, it aims to present a radical new socialist agenda for a new century.

CHAPTER 1

Libertarian Socialism

In the Spring of 1993 the French socialist leader committed suicide following election defeat, the Italian socialist leader was on a corruption charge and the German socialist leader resigned in despair. For some this unhappy constellation symbolised the exhaustion of the European socialist project. They sought world-wide confirmation in the collapse of the Soviet empire and the people's destruction of the Berlin Wall. Commentators pointed to a series of defeats across Europe, including the collapse of the SPD government in Germany in 1982, the loss of office by socialist parties in Scandinavia in the 1980s and the demise of the French and Italian socialists.

The left's retreat had been epitomised by the ascendancy of Reaganism and Thatcherism in the 1980s. Their new right ideology had become intellectually fashionable, with the writings of Friedman, Hayek and others, previously relegated to the fringe, suddenly accorded centre stage legitimacy. It seemed unsurprising that in Britain, Labour could not win general elections between 1979 and 1992. Meanwhile in the Party it became fashionable to claim that the left-right battles were dead and buried and that the *real* argument was between 'traditionalists' and 'modernisers'.

In fact the 'modernisers' found themselves singing from an old hymn sheet. After the third consecutive Conservative victory in 1959, it was fiercely argued by the then Labour 'revisionists' – followers of the Labour Leader Hugh Gaitskell - that the left had had its day, that socialism should be ditched, and that Labour must become a social democratic party. That Gaitskellite agenda has a familiar ring: Labour could not win without abolishing Clause IV of the constitution (which committed the Labour Party to support a very loosely defined form of democratic social ownership), cutting links with the trade unions, renaming the Party and so on. (Of course Labour did win in 1964, and by a landslide in 1966, without making any of these changes.)

The Gaitskellites asserted that unions had become 'old fashioned' and that strikes would 'wither away'; this on the very eve of a long period in which trade union membership in Britain expanded rapidly (especially amongst the middle classes) and in which there were more strikes than at any time since 1926. There was also excited discussion around the rise of the so-called 'affluent worker', identified by sociologists such as Goldthorpe and Lockwood, and interpreted as justifying a rejection of class politics and socialist policies. The intellectual fashion was to turn up a nose at socialist ideas, to claim that political choices were restricted to the best way of managing capitalism. Big clashes of ideology were redundant, as the old left-right battles had exhausted themselves. Capitalism had 'won': where Francis Fukuyama's *The End of History* claimed to speak for the 1990s, Daniel Bell's *The End of Ideology* made similar claims in the early 1960s.

This is not to make a simplistic equation between modernisers and Gaitskellites (the latter for example were far more committed to equality). Neither is it to suggest that conditions in the 1990s replicate those of thirty or forty years ago. There have been massive changes in these decades. Drawing up the iron curtain and breaking down the Berlin Wall has dramatically altered the world ideological climate. Capital has restructured and, with finance, has Europeanised and globalised. Community has been undermined by privatised culture and consumerism. The class structure has changed: the proportion of manual workers has dropped sharply and women have formed an increasingly significant share of the labour force. A flexible labour market with a great deal of casual, temporary and part-time work has replaced the post-war certainty of relatively stable full-time male employment. A growing 'underclass' with no stake in the mainstream of work and family, and no allegiance to parliamentary politics or even trade unionism, has emerged. Party ties have waned and political activism has declined. Trade unions are substantially weaker. Trades Union Congress affiliated membership, which fluctuated from 8.1 million in 1960 to an all time high of 12.1 million in 1979, was back down to 7 million in 1995.

Clearly, re-thinking is required. A left which simply marched behind old banners chanting yesterday's slogans would indeed consign itself to history. A left which relied on windy rhetoric and did not engage seriously in the debate over both long-term vision and short-term policy would become marginalised. But that does not mean a classic revisionist response dressed up in modern clothing is the only option.

In the 1990s the central ideological challenge for the left is no longer the new right's agenda. (As will be persistently demonstrated in later chapters, its failure has never been clearer.) Neither is it the need to adopt a vacuous middle way. Today's challenge is to overcome a persistent identification with one particular socialist tradition, which has been and remains a curse for the left: the socialism of the centralised state, whether social democrat or Marxist-Leninist, is indeed an ideology of the past. But that is very far from the end of the story.

TWO TRADITIONS OF SOCIALISM

In the history of socialism, discussion usually focuses upon the division between social democrats and Marxist-Leninists, between reformists and revolutionaries. This was at the heart of the struggle between Mensheviks and Bolsheviks in the run-up to the 1917 Russian revolution which had such a profound impact. The Bolshevik triumph did not simply act as a model for revolutionary socialists. The policies of Lenin and his successors also influenced thinking amongst left reformists in Western democracies, including in the Labour Party where central planning and nationalisation became a touchstone of socialism, and where for some on its left Leninist tactics were adopted.

But although the revolutionary/reformist (or Marxist-Leninist/ social democrat) axis is the conventional one for socialist theory and practice, it is not the only one. Indeed it has served to obscure another, and in my view, equally – if not more – important, axis. This is between statism and libertarianism. To chart a clear and credible way forward for the left today, the history of socialism must be viewed in a different way.

Such an alternative approach identifies two principal strands of socialist thought. The dominant one has involved a statist or top-down vision of socialism, with Marxist-Leninists at the revolutionary end of its spectrum and social democrats at the reformist end. The subsidiary one has involved a libertarian or bottom-up vision of socialism, with anarchists at its revolutionary end and democratic socialists at its reformist end. These two strands cut across the conventional axis and have been in more or less constant conflict.

STATISM

Although in the statist tradition, Marxism-Leninism and social democracy have been poles apart in practice, both envisaged change being brought about through the state: dictatorially imposed in the case of revolutionaries, or bureaucratically introduced in the case of reformists. Both saw change being introduced *on behalf of* the working class rather than *by* them (this may have contradicted Marxist-Leninist theory, but it was the practice of Stalinist states; it may have contradicted social democracy's reliance upon an electoral mandate, but it was the practice in office). Such centralism left little or no scope for individual empowerment and local control; on the contrary, these were seen as obstacles to the grand design of a better society and its noble ideal of equality. Yet it was the very absence of individual empowerment that thwarted or corrupted the grand design. In western democracies, the huge popular legitimacy for socialist reformism after the Second World War was also undermined by its attachment to remote and insensitive bureaucracy and a careless disregard for efficacious management of the public sector.

In the East, the 'actually existing socialism' of the old Soviet bloc, China and their satellites, was rightly condemned for its tyrannical denial of freedom, its bloated, self-serving bureaucracy and its innate inefficiency. This form of socialism became a powerful bogey with which conservatives could successfully scare voters in the West: 'what about Russia?' became a typical charge directed at democratic socialists. Indeed the very fact that it became necessary to describe oneself as a '*democratic socialist*' showed the extent to which the West European left lived in the shadow of Soviet 'socialism' and why it is now so necessary for the left to revisit its origins.

8

LIBERTARIAN ORIGINS

For socialism was discredited only because another important strand in its history had always remained subordinate. The 'libertarian socialist' strand has a strong pedigree. At the revolutionary end of its spectrum were Russian thinkers like the 'gentle anarchist', Peter Kropotkin, who preached the virtues of a society based upon mutual aid and mutual cooperation unburdened with the 'oppressive yoke of the state'. At the democratic-reformist end were 'cooperative' socialists such as William Morris. Libertarian socialism experienced something of a revival following the upsurge of a 'New Left' in the 1960s and socialist feminism in the 1970s.

In the ferment of Russian revolutionary debate during the late nineteenth and early twentieth centuries, Kropotkin fiercely denounced state socialist notions like the 'dictatorship of the proletariat', and anticipated all too ominously the rise of Stalinism. He advocated a society based upon mutual aid and mutual cooperation – a federation of self-governing communities. His book *Mutual Aid* was written specifically to refute Huxley's interpretation of Darwinism. Instead of a 'war of the fittest', he argued that evolution depended upon a 'state of nature' in which conflict did exist but mutual aid and cooperation were dominant. For humankind this 'natural' state was only denied by the injustice of capitalism. Although in 1887 he insisted that 'representative government corresponds to capitalism', as his self-described 'libertarian socialism' evolved, he came to accept more democratic-reformist ideas, including representative government and a federation of regional parliaments for Russia.

However, Russian politics in the late nineteenth and early twentieth century, with a backward rural society and oppressive Tsarism, hardly provided fertile soil for such decentralised socialism; it seemed utopian. Conditions in Russia did not even support the immensely more practical social democracy of the Mensheviks. 'Jacobin communism' triumphed: a tradition fiercely egalitarian and proletarian, associated with conspiratorial political action and distinguished by a revolutionary elitism in which a single vanguard group or individual became the sole repository for leadership and ideological correctness. This Jacobin communism has been traced back to the followers of

Babeuf in the French Revolution of 1789, through to Auguste Blanqui's insurrectionist creed in the 1848 turmoil in France and the Paris Commune of 1871. Lenin's adaptation of Marxism gave the theoretical rationalisation for Jacobin authoritarianism to become synonymous with communism as it was catapulted into power in the 1917 October Revolution. Statist, rather than libertarian, socialism, had won and the legacy for the left was momentous.

The libertarian spirit still erupted from time to time in the industrial working class. For instance, in the 1890s syndicalists fought for their ideas in the emerging trade union movement, stressing workers' control and social transformation by general strike, rather than nationalisation and violent revolution. The late nineteenth-century French 'anarcho-syndicalism' of Proudhon and Saint-Simon – with their emphasis on decentralisation, mutualism and their hostility to authority – was explicitly antagonistic to state socialism. Proudhon also advocated a form of federalism: breaking up France into self-governing units similar to Swiss cantons, and in industry encouraging democracy in workplaces which would federate together for common industrial purposes. But although these movements were anti-authoritarian, they lacked an appreciation of the relationship between economic power and the state.

In the communist world, the eclipse of libertarianism, or indeed any politics based upon individual rights, was perhaps predictable. The need for rapid change to abolish the poverty and destitution wreaked by capitalism became a priority. Countries like Russia and China which wanted to industrialise quickly substituted state action for private enterprise in order to achieve their initial shift from an agrarian economy to an industrial one – to make the historic leap which Britain experienced by evolution. The fragmented and incoherent nature of the libertarian alternative made it seem what it became: peripheral. But this was to return to haunt the whole of the left. In the countries of the Soviet bloc, the mass of people, for whom 'communism' was designed, finally overthrew its dictatorial yoke, appearing in the process to turn their back on socialism when in fact they had rightly rejected a grotesque perversion of it.

Another important factor in the historic triumph of state socialism was the failure of liberalism. As a contemporary libertarian socialist,

Noam Chomsky, has pointed out, classical liberalism's most appealing features – its stress on individual freedom, its insistence upon tolerance and its respect for human rights – were perverted by its failure to address the demand for equality, especially at the critical juncture following the French Revolution of 1789 and the long process of industrial revolution which so ferociously transformed the lives of the ordinary people of Europe. As Chomsky has argued:

> With the development of industrial capitalism, a new and unanticipated system of injustice, it is libertarian socialism that has preserved and extended the radical humanist message of the Enlightenment and the classical liberal ideas that were perverted into an ideology to sustain the emerging social order... [classical liberal thought] is in its essence profoundly, though prematurely, anticapitalist. Its ideas must be attenuated beyond recognition to be transmuted into an ideology of industrial capitalism.

Socialism, a term which first came into general use in France and Britain around 1830, sprang essentially from a critique of capitalism and an indictment of its political alibi, liberalism. Socialists were prepared to accept the industrial revolution and to tame it by eradicating the consequent torture and poverty inflicted upon the masses; communists, by contrast, were more radically egalitarian and proletarian and wanted violently to overthrow capitalism. Socialists also wanted democratically to build upon the elements of civilisation which had been established in Europe, especially Britain; communists wanted none of this, favouring instead a transitional revolutionary dictatorship.

BRITISH FORERUNNERS

Whereas the direction taken by revolutionary socialism was a millstone for the left for so long, in Britain the libertarian socialist tradition was more strongly rooted. And because it was more democratic it has direct relevance for the future of the left. Its antecedents are very mixed and they are not cited in a pretence that there was something coherent called 'British libertarian socialism': very far from it. Many who can be identified in its supporting cast did not use the term as such; the contributions of some are partial and contradictory. But the point is that the crucial elements of libertarian socialism – decentralisation, democracy, popular sovereignty and a refusal to accept that collectivism meant subjugating individual liberty – were present in their writings and activist advocacy. Together they stand in a line which provides a robust alternative to statism.

Fenner Brockway, a longstanding member of the Labour left, linked himself in *Britain's First Socialists* to a tradition dating back to the mid-seventeenth century and the English Civil War. He pinpoints the radical activists of that age: the Levellers, Agitators and Diggers. For Brockway, socialism is about democracy and liberty or it is about nothing, and he shows that the ideas motivating the three groups were pre-cursors to socialism:

> The Levellers were pioneers of political democracy and the sovereignty of the people; the Agitators were the pioneers of participatory control by the ranks at their workplace; and the Diggers were pioneers of communal ownership, cooperation and egalitarianism. All three equate with democratic socialism.

As historians have noted, the Levellers were the first democratic political movement in modern history, presaging by at least a century the demands for democracy which erupted in America, France and Britain. They demanded a democratic parliament, the abolition of the House of Lords and democratic reform of the whole state, including even the judiciary and the army. Their insistence upon decentralisation of government and the army, coupled with their proposals for public health, education services and the right to work, showed they were indeed premature libertarian socialists. So were the Agitators with their stress upon workplace democracy. The Diggers' advocate, Gerrard Winstanley, should rightly take his place as a socialist pioneer, with his proposals for common ownership. He urged the poor to seize the common lands and establish egalitarian communities.

During the late eighteenth and early nineteenth centuries, the foundations of the British labour movement in the emerging proletariat shared similar libertarian socialist affinities (albeit not at the time described as such). Trade unions and political organisations evolved from a series of self-governing societies, groups and institutions established in Britain during the late eighteenth and early nineteenth centuries. Local craft-based trade clubs, friendly societies, early trade unions and (later) cooperatives, were all examples of the way in which working people organised and combined collectively from the bottom upward. These were models of local self-organisation not dependent upon some central apparatus, and led some towards local socialism as a model for society.

There were also libertarian socialist elements to other initiatives at the turn of the century. Tom Paine's *Rights of Man* in 1791 was for that period a radical democratic manifesto. Mary Wollstonecraft's *A Vindication of the Rights of Women* in 1792 was even more so given the neglect of women's rights. Later, abolitionists protesting against the racism and oppression of slavery added an important and again neglected dimension. These precursors were part of a radical democratic tradition later joined by the Chartists and still later by the suffragettes.

Significantly, the term 'socialist' was first used in the British *Cooperative Magazine* in November 1827. The chief British exponent of socialism at this time was Robert Owen, a founder of the cooperative movement in 1844. Although his democratic credentials are suspect (he opposed the 1832 Reform Bill for example), Owen's ideas on common ownership and industrial democracy through cooperatives coincide with those of modern libertarian socialism. Meanwhile groups of workers such as the Rochdale Pioneers in 1844 were putting into practical effect local socialist ideas for workers' shops, insurance societies, credit unions and companies. Through such initiatives, these early trade unionists and socialists invented and practised what the historian A. H. Halsey described as 'the social forms of modern participatory democracy'.

Significantly, some Owenite socialists also developed early feminist ideas, as Barbara Taylor shows in *Eve and the New Jerusalem*. One Owenist convert, Anna Wheeler, co-authored *Appeal to one-half of the human race*, a pamphlet which first put a socialist feminist case: 'All women and particularly women living with men in marriage … are more in need of political rights than any other portion of human beings.' She also argued that women could only achieve happiness through general cooperation, not selfish competition. Another Owenite feminist, Frances Morrison, insisted that the only way to end women being treated as property was to abolish private property itself. Two more Owenites, Margaret Chappellsmith and Eliza Macauley argued for reform of financial institutions. And by the early 1830s, Owen's Charlotte Street Institution was sponsoring large meetings of working women who formed cooperatives and trade unions, not just in London but in towns like Manchester and Leicester too.

Later, William Morris made another important contribution. First, he was not simply a 'producer socialist' (in the sense of focusing on the means of production). His was an ethical socialism, concerned about the way people related to each other, the moral values underpinning these relationships, and unusually for the time emphasising sexual equality. His was also a cultural socialism, a sharp counter to the seductions of materialistic consumption: 'Have nothing in your home which you do not either believe to be beautiful or know to be useful,' he said. Second, he stressed the importance of the quality of life and of protecting the environment. His was a green socialism. Third, he was deeply sceptical about the notion that the 'forward march of labour' was scientifically inevitable. He considered this to be almost the reverse side of the coin to religion and a similar threat to individual autonomy. Fourth, he was critical of state socialism – what he called 'semi-demi-socialism', believing that it would result in upholding the status quo of a centralised, unequal society. It is interesting to note that Peter Kropotkin, whilst he was in exile in London in the 1880s, was amongst Morris's close associates and friends. And, over fifty years later, Morris' contribution was acknowledged by the guild socialist advocate, G.D.H. Cole: 'It was Morris who made me a socialist,' he said.

Trade unionism provided a continuing conduit for non-state socialism, especially through the syndicalists. From 1910 Tom Mann started introducing ideas about workers' control, gleaned from French and American syndicalists, in his journal *The Industrial Syndicalist.* Especially in the period before the First World War, syndicalist ideas were widespread in the trade union movement. For example, the South Wales Miners in 1917 put forward a programme for industrial democracy of the coal industry under public ownership.

On the eve of the First World War, anti-statism was rife. Within the left there was a revolt against Fabian 'administrative socialism' because it designated a pre-eminent role for the state. As the historian Ernest

Barker noted, this was because it was believed that 'the governing class under State-Socialism becomes a bureaucracy, regimenting and controlling the life of the citizen'. Instead, many on the left were attracted by the ideas of syndicalism and guild socialism. However, the demands of war quickly prevailed. The need for collective action and the use of state machinery to mobilise for war appeared to vindicate the arguments of the Labour Party for government intervention and control. Sidney Webb wrote in 1917: 'we have had... a great deal of control of capital... *can we afford to relinquish that control when peace comes?*' (his italics). This was reflected in post-war Labour policy statements and in the Party's famous Clause IV, part 4 of which was drafted by the Webbs and inserted in the Constitution in 1918.*

THE RETREAT FROM LIBERTARIANISM IN THE LABOUR MOVEMENT

After the war there was a retreat in the labour movement from radical ideas for direct action and industrial democracy, culminating in their virtual abandonment following the defeat of the miners in the 1926 General Strike. In the 1930s there was increased interest in planning and nationalisation; but although there were admiring comments on the Soviet model, from the Webbs amongst others, this interest was by and large untheorised. Nationalisation was automatically adopted as a model, with the emphasis upon planning and state ownership of still hierarchically run enterprises, rather than turning them over to the workers and the people. This turn was magnified by the shift away from the turn-of-the-century 'municipal socialism' of Fabians such as George Bernard Shaw and young Sidney Webb. They had seen local government as an important source of socialist change. As Webb wrote in 1910, it was a form of 'democratic organisation on the basis of the

---

* Although it was replaced in 1995 because it was felt to be an old fashioned charter for mass nationalisation, the text of the Clause is actually capable of a more libertarian interpretation: 'To secure for the workers by hand or by brain the full fruits of their industry and the most equitable distribution thereof that may be possible upon the basis of the common ownership of the means of production, distribution and exchange, and the best obtainable system of *popular administration and control* of each industry or service'. (my italics)

association of consumers for the supply of their own needs'. Municipal socialism can be seen as standing in the libertarian or decentralist school; its supporters had always been concerned however that it would be extinguished by the growing power of central government.

These worries proved valid. Labour's increasing strength at a parliamentary level led to a retreat from municipal socialism: instead, Labour local authorities became, to quote John Gyford, 'handmaidens of parliamentary socialism'. With the growth of working-class representation in local government, there was a parallel anxiety from the dominant class that Labour local government was a troublesome threat to the state, and that it must be made subordinate to central government. This was perhaps best symbolised by the clashes between Whitehall and the Labour controlled Poplar Council in the 1920s. Under George Lansbury, Poplar refused to implement cuts in unemployment and poor relief, and thirty of its councillors were imprisoned in the fiercest rebellion against central government of the century. In the early 1930s, over twenty councils, mostly Labour, refused to implement means testing for unemployment assistance, until the government was forced to 'nationalise' assistance by transferring the administration to a central board. But 'Poplarism' was as much a threat to the Labour Party establishment as to the Conservatives.

It became common ground between the leaderships of both Parties that, instead of autonomous agencies for 'bottom up' democracy, local authorities should be conduits for the state to disperse services efficiently. Partly in response to this concern for administrative efficiency, Sidney and Beatrice Webb had meanwhile developed a theory of 'administrative socialism', in which experts, professionals and bureaucrats played a key role. Such administrative collectivism may have addressed the need for socialists to run the machinery of government in a different way, but it offered little hope to notions of empowerment, as G.D.H. Cole, the principal advocate of 'guild socialism', was quick to point out. In 1921 he wrote of the importance of building mechanisms for popular participation into local government. In 1947 he sought to reconcile the importance of local democracy with the centralising pull of efficiency in a modern state by proposing both larger and smaller authorities, at 'regional' and 'neighbourhood' levels. The latter would be powerful agencies for local socialism (and Cole can be seen as anticipating the 1990s debate over unitary and regional government).

GUILD SOCIALISM

From 1912, the guild socialist movement had taken up the themes of industrial democracy and decentralised socialism. In 1917 G.D.H. Cole distinguished the guild socialists' belief in *decentralisation* from the syndicalist or anarchist belief in *federation* (i.e. power delegated upward from below) and the state socialist belief in *centralisation*. Decentralisation, he argued, sees society in the national terms which characterise the modern state, and devolves power from the centre. Nevertheless, he insisted, 'it is the essence of the Guild idea that it means government from below'. He believed that 'capitalist supremacy can only be overthrown by a system of industrial democracy in which the worker will control industry in conjunction with a democratised State.' Cole argued 'that there can be no guarantee, except democracy, that the resources of production will, in fact, be used for the benefit of all'. Hence, socialists should seek 'to bring about the widest possible diffusion both of political and economic and social power and of the knowledge needed for putting such power to effective use.'

Three main forms of Guilds were proposed: industrial, distributive and civic (the latter being, for example, the professions, educationalists, lawyers). These would be federated up to a national level and come together in the Guild Congress. Workers would participate at all levels in the direction of the Guilds, which would cooperate with other Guilds but be sovereign within their own sphere (except insofar as their polices affected consumers, for example, on prices). Ownership would be vested in the Guilds, with nationalisation being advocated only selectively where it seemed to be the most rational approach.

Situated in the democratic, reformist tradition of socialism, Guild Socialists were nevertheless sceptical about parliamentary action, believing that the transformation necessary was primarily economic, not political, and that trade unions were therefore the principal agencies for socialist change. In Cole's words, 'The Guild Socialist contends that the internal management and control of each industry or service must be placed, as a trust on behalf of the community, in the

17

hands of the workers engaged in it.' As Walter Kendall wrote in 1969: 'Guild Socialism thus denied head-on the state socialist view, common to both social democrats and communists, that state administration could be equivalent, albeit by proxy, to workers self-administration.'

As Anthony Wright argues, Cole was a 'leading theorist of a school of participatory democracy and socialist pluralism.' It is not necessary to uncritically accept the tenets of guild socialism for Cole's importance in the libertarian socialist tradition to be recognised. In 1960, shortly before his death, he used words later to be echoed (albeit seldom, if ever, acknowledged) by contemporary libertarian socialists:

> I am neither a Communist nor a Social Democrat, because I regard both as creeds of centralisation and bureaucracy, whereas I feel sure that a Socialist society that is to be true to its equalitarian principles of human brotherhood must rest on the widest possible diffusion of power and responsibility, so as to enlist the active participation of as many as possible of its citizens in the tasks of democratic self-government.

This means that every area of social activity – the workplace, neighbourhood, educational institutions, interest groups – must be democratised. Otherwise individuality and citizenship would be suffocated by capitalism and state socialism alike. Cole helps us to retrieve the tradition in socialist thought which does not accept the prevailing orthodoxy that the real choice for the left is between statist revolutionaries and reformists. Instead, he rightly insisted, both revolutionary communism and parliamentary social democracy 'regarded increasing centralisation of power as an unmistakable characteristic of progress, and regarded themselves as the destined heirs of capitalist concentration and of the centralised power of the modern state.'

Socialism is about *empowering* the citizen or it is about nothing. Although this verity has often been downgraded, it is another reason for Cole's significance. In 1917, when asked what was the greatest evil in society, he responded that most people 'would answer POVERTY, when they ought to answer SLAVERY.' In other words, powerlessness is the overriding problem. Equality, freedom – neither of these cherished goals can be achieved without empowerment. Paternal government, however well intentioned, is no answer because it breeds dependence and is ultimately authoritarian. Liberty cannot be handed down, it must be confidently claimed, as of right. Cole believed in 'a participatory definition of freedom'. As Anthony Wright comments:

> Cole's commitment to activism... provided the foundation for his democratic theory... To Cole, men [sic] were born active; it was capitalism which rendered them passive. This attachment to participation as a fundamental human good in its own right, as a school of political education and personal development, places Cole in the mainstream of... a theory of participatory democracy designed to provide ample scope for that active exercise of will which was seen as intrinsic to the definition of a human being, and which was negated by capitalism and state socialism alike.

Individual empowerment through collective action and assisted by egalitarianism is the essence of socialism.

CENTRALISED COLLECTIVISM

By 1942 Joseph Schumpeter wrote: 'what may be termed Centralist Socialism seems to me to hold the field so clearly that it would be a waste of space to consider other forms'. He defined socialism as 'an institutional pattern in which the control over means of production and over production itself is vested with a central authority'. In the process he deliberately excluded 'guild socialism, syndicalism and other types'. Socialism equalled state control and centralised planning. Socialisation equalled nationalisation. Common ownership equalled state ownership. Collectivism equalled centralism.

The experience of the Second World War finally eclipsed any residual libertarian socialism within the British labour movement. It shaped a consensus for centralised collectivism which went far beyond socialists. With the success of wartime centralised planning of production and resources, and the imperatives of post-war reconstruction, statism became all-dominant. From 1945 onward nationalised coal, gas, electricity, transport (and later steel) became the paradigm for public ownership. The nationalised industry model, promoted by Herbert Morrison, led to a total break from libertarian socialism: when poverty, inequality, unemployment and capitalist inefficiency were so widespread, libertarian considerations seemed irrelevant to the need for free health services, for full employment and modern public utilities. Decisive action and planning by central government was necessary, and indeed was successful, as new public health education and social services were delivered for the first time.

As society was reconstructed after the war, R.H. Tawney, for example, stressed that socialism was also about the distribution of power. In 1952, Aneurin Bevan recognised the shortcomings of nationalisation and the need for democratic participation. Although this did not figure prominently in his socialism, he argued: 'industrial democracy is the counterpart of political freedom. Liberty and responsibility must march together. They must be joined together in the workshop as in the legislative assembly.' In 1956 Anthony Crosland noted public dissatisfaction with the public corporation model and expressed some interest in a plurality of approaches to ownership and control.

State socialism came under increasing attack after the Hungarian revolution of 1956 had been brutally suppressed by the Soviet regime. The subsequent departure of key intellectuals from the British Communist Party helped launch a 'New Left'. Writers such as Raymond Williams and E.P. Thompson stressed that democracy and socialism should be indistinguishable. By the late 1950s, the Campaign for Nuclear Disarmament was on the march, encouraging a new radicalism amongst a new political generation.

LIBERTARIAN REVIVAL

But a serious libertarian socialist revival had to wait until the 1960s. The struggle of black Americans for civil rights had been growing remorselessly. As direct action protests increased, black activists and their white allies began to articulate a confident libertarianism. A New Left began to emerge, not just in Britain and America but across Europe.

Part of the reason was disillusionment with the social democracy of the post-war settlement. Although it brought peace, stability and rising living standards, it did not decentralise power or eradicate inequality. In Britain there was a growing left-wing critique of 'labourism' – of the

Labour Party and trade union association with bureaucratic rather than empowering politics, and its conservative identification with pragmatic parliamentarianism.

The Vietnam War came to symbolise all that seemed wrong, especially in the eyes of radicalised youth in the West. The New Left's emphasis upon direct action – confronting racism, boycotts, demonstrations, student sit-ins – stressed anti-authoritarianism and popular participation. This, coupled with a fierce antagonism to Stalinism and the Soviet bloc, led naturally to ideas for a decentralised, popular socialism. Similar ideas took root in Britain, following a rising tide of youth radicalism, expressed through student power, Vietnam War protests – including against the Labour Government's support for US intervention – and campaigns against apartheid. The direct action protests which disrupted the racist South African rugby tour of 1969-70 and stopped the summer's planned cricket tour were very much a product of that distinct period. Widespread squatting campaigns by the homeless and radical activists to occupy empty homes were another. Amidst growing trade union militancy and especially shop steward power, a revival of interest in workers control also occurred and the Institute for Workers Control was launched in 1968.

Across Europe, libertarian socialist ideas spread fast, especially amongst the young. Direct action blurred into revolution in the streets of Paris in May 1968 when the idealism of student radicals merged with the frustrations of shop-floor workers. The resulting alliance shook the very foundations of the state. The 'extra-parliamentary' left grew rapidly. There was a revival of Marxist revolutionary socialism too. Above all there was a ferment of popular radicalism. It spread from trade union syndicalists to Young Liberals (like myself) who in 1967-73 specifically called ourselves 'libertarian socialists'.

The growth of feminism also nurtured such ideas because women's groups stressed their local autonomy from male dominated, centralised institutions, including those within the left. They emphasised personal politics and that socialism's historic concern with class as a source of inequality and oppression ignored other forms of oppression, especially patriarchy (the economic, social and political forces which produce male supremacy). In 1979 a seminal text for socialist feminism, *Beyond the Fragments*, presented a devastating attack on the Leninist left, Sheila Rowbotham specifically urging a recovery of the libertarian socialist tradition. Her co-author, Hilary Wainwright argued 'Much of the oppression of women takes place in "private", in areas of life considered "personal"… this has radically extended the scope of politics.' She also stressed the importance of links between the women's movement and trade unionists who were developing their own 'workers plans', for example at Vickers and Lucas Aerospace. In 1987, the third co-author, Lynne Segal called for 'a renewal of that more democratic and participatory vision of socialism which reaches out to include all social relationships and to give people a sense of greater control over their own lives.'

THE IMPACT UPON LABOUR

The Labour Party in the late 1960s largely stood aside from this upsurge. Under Harold Wilson it held office from 1964-70, and was criticised, among other things, for its failure to stop the illegal racist rebellion in Rhodesia, its support for the Americans in Vietnam, and, in 1969, for confronting the trade unions with ill-fated proposals for legislation to curb unofficial strikes. But, after Labour's defeat in 1970, more radical socialist ideas began spreading through the Party. A prominent 1960s Cabinet Minister, Tony Benn, published a Fabian pamphlet in September 1970, *The New Politics: A Socialist Reconnaissance.* In it he took account of the growing 'grass-roots socialism' and put forward ideas for decentralisation, workers' control and popular participation.

Decentralised socialist ideas started to gain more credence in the wider labour movement. There was a growing critique of Morrisonian nationalisation and increased support for industrial democracy. In 1977 the Labour Government's Bullock Report recommended worker participation at company board level. Although its proposals were dissipated under a twin attack from trade unionists, who saw it as a threat to traditional collective bargaining, and employers, who saw it as a threat to their power, the fact that it was sponsored by government was testimony to the growing interest in workers' participation. So too were several high profile (though short-lived) workers' cooperatives at Meriden and Kirby, and 1978 legislation to place worker directors on the Board of the Post Office.

Meanwhile there had been a growth of community action and demands for popular participation by council tenants associations and radical groups, who saw local socialism as an alternative to parliamentary politics. Partly as a response to this, there was a revival in 'municipal socialism', especially by the Labour left which, during the 1970s, was a growing force in the Party, absorbing many of the 'extra-parliamentary' activists who were children of the New Left. This revival – symbolised by the 1981-86 Greater London Council under Ken Livingstone – was both a challenge to the capitalist state and a rejection of bureaucratic labourism. As David Blunkett (then leader of Sheffield City Council) wrote in 1982, Labour local authorities had an admirable commitment to spending on public services, 'but they tended to be authoritarian: doing the right thing *for* people rather than with them.'

However, it is notable that as the Labour Party came increasingly under the control of its 'modernisers' during the latter stages of Neil Kinnock's leadership and then under that of John Smith and Tony Blair, this critique of labourism has been sidelined. 'New Labour' has not stressed the importance of popular participation and decentralisation. On the contrary, whilst readopting some tenets of post-war social democracy – for instance, parliamentarianism and a centralised Party organisation – it has gone further and given pre-eminence to market forces over industrial democracy. This is a mistake because modern libertarian socialism is not merely altruistic. To be sure, it stresses democracy and liberty. But it is also rooted in a very practical analysis of how modern society operates.

GOVERNABILITY

There is a crisis of legitimacy in advanced industrial states, both political and economic. Political cynicism and disaffection is probably greater than ever before in the democratic age. Membership of and positive support for mainstream political parties has been falling for many years (though Labour's membership experienced an upsurge after Tony Blair's election as Leader in 1994). Electoral turnout, especially from the poor and the young, is no longer certain. (In the USA it is scandalously low, with about half the adult population not voting and therefore having no stake in the conventional democratic process.)

The fragmentation of democratic politics has created increasing problems of governability. In Britain, democratic accountability has been undermined at the national level by a powerful global economy and international integration on the one hand, and on the other by the centrifugal impact of policies for privatisation, contracting out, Quangos, Next Step Agencies and market testing. As a result popular legitimacy for the representative system has been undermined because, for the ordinary citizen, Parliament no longer seems in charge.

The response to this from the right has been still further centralisation and bureaucracy, in the belief that a strong state can somehow assert authority over the disaffected. Hence attacks on local government financial independence and political autonomy, including the abolition of metropolitan authorities like the Greater London Council. Over 80 per cent of local government finance comes from central government compared with 60 per cent in 1979. Independent trade unionism is severely curbed. Potentially draconian legislation like the 1994 Criminal Justice Act is rushed through. Official secrecy is tightly policed. The intelligence services 'come out' in an ominous switch of priority from foreign to domestic activity. The Civil Service is forced to abandon any claims to neutrality and, for career advancement, to follow the thought police of the new right. Health and education are subjected to a bureaucratic jungle of contracts and monitoring. Controls over immigrants are even more rigidly enforced, targeting black people.

As Karl Polyani pointed out, the extension of 'free markets', as in the nineteenth century, is very likely to lead to greater powers for the central state:

> The road to the free market was opened and kept open by an enormous increase in continuous, centrally organised and controlled interventionism. To make Adam Smith's 'simple and natural liberty' compatible with the needs of human society was a most complicated affair. Witness the complexity of the provisions in the innumerable enclosure laws; the amount of bureaucratic control involved in the administration of the Poor

Laws... The introduction of free markets, far from doing away with the need for control, regulation and intervention, enormously increased their range. Administrators had to be constantly on the watch to ensure the free workings of the system. Thus even those who wished most ardently to free the state from all unnecessary duties, and whose whole philosophy demanded the restriction of state activities, could not but entrust the self-same state with new powers, organs, and instruments required for the establishment of *laissez-faire.*

Free market capitalism requires an authoritarian state to police its victims and organise its conditions of existence. Although a welfare net is also needed to ameliorate its destructive consequences, this must be trimmed back to the bare minimum so as not to constrain the market. A further contradiction for capitalism is that, as competition widens income inequalities, the poor and other losers start protesting violently or resorting to crime to secure their share of the spoils. As morality is subjugated to individual self-interest in the competitive race, well-off winners bend the law through tax dodging, insider trading, City fraud or Maxwell-type pensions rip-offs.

The strong state does not work. It cannot curb mushrooming crime. It is unable to deliver responsive services. The poor get poorer and the rich richer. As communities disintegrate and family life collapses, its heavy hand cannot bind society together. It is supposed to hold the ring for the invisible hand of competition and the market to work their wonders, but it cannot even deliver a successful economy. A radically different approach is necessary to escape from this crisis of ungovernability which otherwise beckons increasing social disintegration coupled with growing authoritarianism.

An alternative is necessary for another important reason. Throughout the world, but especially in western Europe and the US, the market and privatisation have triumphed over planning and public ownership during a period of significant change in the system of production. Corporate ownership has become even more concentrated and has centralised beyond the nation state, making it difficult if not impossible to apply the nationalisation model. At the same time new forms of production have arisen (sometimes called post-Fordist).

These forms are flexible and specialised, and have moved industry away from mass production on one site. Heavy, labour-intensive industry with large-scale workforces was the dominant feature of industrialisation in the past, and fitted more comfortably with the notion of command economics. But it is rapidly being superseded by capital intensive, smaller and more diversified industry, and this trend is likely to be maintained as information technology not only permits but encourages economic decentralisation and specialisation. The development of broad band cable will allow an information superhighway into every home and workplace which will empower consumers and permit more individualised services, localised manufacturing, neighbourhood employment and decentralised economic activity.

These changes have occurred in a market-led context, partly because statist forms of economic organisation have become obsolete. But in fact this form of production can only succeed by more cooperative relationships between employer and employee, between government and enterprise. To function efficiently it requires decentralised structures of government and close regulation. It needs government to promote key sectors, to sponsor investment and to ensure the provision of high quality infrastructure and skills. It also depends upon the active participation of employees who become the principal agents for innovation, high quality and therefore market performance. If state socialism was the product of an earlier industrial age, so was state capitalism. The new industrial age requires an alternative.

A PARTICIPATORY DEMOCRACY

Today's libertarian socialists place a high premium upon the objectives of democracy and freedom, and the decentralisation of control, ownership and decision-making necessary to achieve these objectives. Socialism cannot in practice be achieved unless it springs from below by popular demand. The task of socialist government is an enabling one, not an enforcing one. Its mission is to disperse rather than to concentrate power. A pluralist notion of democracy is at its heart.

For libertarian socialism, the question of power is the key one.

Without decentralisation of power, not just individual liberty but also social equality is impossible. No ground should be surrendered in the quest for a broadly egalitarian society. On the contrary, economic justice and the greatest possible social equality is impossible unless each citizen has the power – at work, in the home, in the neighbourhood, over services, as a consumer – to demand it for herself or himself.

In place of the limited form of democracy inherent in the British system, the objective should be to create a 'participatory democracy' in which there is the greatest possible involvement of citizens. This will require two principal changes: making representatives much more accountable; and decentralising decision-making as far as is compatible with wider interests. It will also involve not just the democratisation of government but the whole of society. If decentralisation were to be confined to government structures alone, it would simply reproduce the existing patterns of elitism and inequality at lower levels. The result would be a dispersal of administration, in which popular participation would still be blocked by the obstacles resulting from class, sex, race and disability inequalities: the face of government would be more local, but it would not be more representative and would still be constrained by extra-parliamentary forces favouring the interests of dominant groups in society. Participatory opportunities and localisation of power should therefore spread into every area of social activity.

However, power can only be spread downwards in an equitable manner if there is a national framework where opportunities, re-sources, wealth and income are distributed much more equally, where democratic rights are constitutionally entrenched, and where there is equal sexual and racial opportunity. Effective decentralisation will require concentrations of private ownership and wealth to be broken up and spread more evenly throughout the population. It will mean national redistribution of resources from prosperous to poor regions of the country, from the suburbs to the inner cities, from the dominant to the subordinate classes, from rich to poor, from men to women, from whites to blacks and from able to disabled. There will need to be nationally established minimum levels of public provision. Minimum levels should be set for housing provision, public-transport subsidies, social services, nursery schools, day-care facilities, home helps and so on. The extent to which these would be 'topped up' and different priorities set between them, would then be a matter for local decision. Similarly, there should be a statutory minimum wage, above which pay levels could be negotiated by independent agreement.

But this need not mean the 'statist' approach, according to which inequalities of power are overcome centrally, rather than the people involved taking control. However worthy its intentions, this has led in practice to centralised bureaucracies suffocating local initiative and reproducing hierarchical structures. Policies and programmes implemented through the state are necessary to clear away obstacles to democratic participation and freedom, but unless pressure is actively maintained through new democratic avenues from below, a participatory democracy will not take root.

There are severe limits on what can be achieved by a 'top down' focus on spreading power. National and local government can facilitate wider democracy. They can assist people to take greater control over their own lives. But government cannot force a participatory democracy onto people. Unless citizens have themselves participated in the process of gaining influence and pressing for greater control, they will not be prepared to take the new opportunities or exercise the extra responsibilities that go with increased decentralisation.

The state is not dismissed by libertarian socialists; it is prescribed a crucial role as an agency for asserting the public or national interest, a means of reconciling different groups and associations in society, an instrument for decentralised socialism rather than for the imposition of state socialism. Through active devolution of power, a pluralist conception of democracy emerges in which the state, though pivotal, is not suffocatingly dominant over other associations in society. This stress on pluralism is a key tenet of a modern libertarian socialism. A Labour Government, for example, should not be afraid to promote countervailing sources of power – whether through an elected second chamber to replace the House of Lords or regional government which might not all be Labour controlled. Unless democratic power is dispersed, socialism cannot take root. The state in this conception assumes an enabling role, though it will retain an enforcing role through upholding individual rights and restricting the influence of the rich and powerful.

'POPULAR' CAPITALISM

Although the new right might make parallel claims for curbing the
state's role,* their vision is of individual empowerment through
extensive ownership of private property – this was the 'popular
capitalism' of Thatcherism which for a time seemed to capture the high
ground and was electorally effective. Through heavily discounted
council home sales and cut-price share offers in privatised utilities, its
rhetoric promised each individual a stake in capitalism. But there is a
difference between personal ownership and social power. Despite the
fact that home ownership is more widespread, housing is in crisis:
widespread homelessness, negative equity from falling prices, and
problems over re-selling former council houses all trap families against
their will in unsatisfactory accommodation. Although more individuals
own shares than ever before, two thirds of individuals who bought
privatisation shares cashed them in almost immediately: the motive was
profit rather than any illusions about having real power under popular
capitalism. Individual share ownership has declined in proportion to
institutional share ownership – power over, and ownership of, shares,
capital and industry is now more centralised than ever before, whether
at a national, European or global level. It may benefit the few but for the
many empowerment cannot be realised by standing alone in such a
marketplace.

Most individuals need active government which intervenes to curb
market excess and market power. They need a social context to
ownership. They need the assistance of strong communities. They
need the solidarity which comes from acting collectively to exercise
influence over the decisions which shape their lives, and to experience
the fulfilment of active citizenship. They need power to be decentralised. This 'popular socialism' is the *real* alternative to the new right
'popular capitalism' which has ideologically exhausted itself.

---

* The term libertarianism has also been appropriated by some on the new
  right and in America is almost always associated with extreme
  individualist and pro-market views.

SOCIALIST MORALITY

In contrast to all this, a strange perversion which can be laid at the door of Marxism-Leninism was the anti-political insistence that socialism is a 'scientific' theory. The proposition that capitalism would transform itself through socialism into communism, as a process possessed of some higher scientific inevitability, gave it a powerful attraction. But it also gave its followers a mechanistic rather than a moral imperative. Indeed they often derided as mere sentimentalism the idea of morality as the basis for socialist activity. Working-class self-interest would accomplish capitalism's transformation because capitalism was inherently unstable, structurally unable to satisfy mass popular aspirations and ultimately doomed – provided of course there was the requisite revolutionary intervention by the chosen few. This scientific inevitability rendered a quite spurious justification for the elitism of the Party and later the state. Once under Marxist-Leninist control, these institutions could float free of democratic and popular accountability because they were acting 'scientifically' (that is to say, 'objectively') in the interests of the working class. Thus were sown the seeds of dictatorship.

Socialism springs from individual morality and is sustained by a moral vision of an alternative society. Deny this elementary truth, that socialists are pre-eminently motivated by moral concern for their fellow human beings, and the whole project is sunk in a mechanistic pseudo-scientific morass. Socialist politics drained of its moral imperative becomes Machiavellian, however noble may appear the objectives which drive it. In 1994 Ralph Miliband, a long time supporter of a participatory socialism whose essence is democracy, egalitarianism and socialisation, wrote that the socialist enterprise is sustained by

> a belief, inherited from the Enlightenment, in the infinite perfectibility of human beings; or, to put it in more contemporary terms, the belief that human beings are perfectly capable of organising themselves into cooperative, democratic, egalitarian and self-governing communities, in which all conflict would certainly not have been eliminated, but where it would become less and less frequent and acute.

Underlying libertarian socialism is a different and distinct notion of politics. In the words of the 1962 *Port Huron Statement* from the American New Left: 'politics has the function of bringing the individual out of isolation and into community'. Its mission is to find a meaning to life that is 'personally authentic'. Much as in the Greek *polis*, this view of politics rests on the belief that it is only through interaction with others in political activity and civic action that individuals will fully realise their humanity. This contradicts classical liberalism (and modern new rightism) which sees the individual in isolation, not in community. It helps to explain why the objective of socialists should be to create not simply a participatory government but a participatory economy and participatory *society*. Politics, as the Italian socialist Antonio Gramsci stressed, is not confined to parliament or town hall but extends throughout 'civil society': the local communities, groups and institutions which are the foundations of active citizenship. Democracy should therefore extend not simply to government but throughout society: in industry, the neighbourhood or any arrangement by which people organise their lives. Politics also extends to the personal. It is not simply a vehicle through which people govern themselves. It springs from the way citizens behave privately toward each other, from notions of mutual respect and tolerance for individual diversity.

The focus on state power – by capture for Marxist-Leninists or by election for social democrats – actually negated the spirit of collectivism and community which ought to be the essence of socialism. The absorption of all social functions by the modern state, whether capitalist or communist, led to what Kropotkin had predicted as 'the development of unbridled narrow-minded individualism' – which should be antithetical to the socialist instinct. Through centralised public provision, individuals' obligations to the state increase, and they lose their obligations to their neighbours. They become individual clients of the state rather than autonomous citizens, passive recipients rather than active cooperators with each other.

Although public provision remains a vital priority for socialism, historically its centralised character and delivery made people dependent upon the state, in the process jettisoning reliance upon communal identity, collective organisation and personal relationships, which are the foundations of citizenship and a good society. Statism may have achieved important social objectives both in the Soviet bloc and in the West, but its incapacity to transform itself with economic and democratic progress meant socialism could be interpreted as an alternative, rather than a complement, to individual autonomy.

EXTRA-PARLIAMENTARY ACTION

The transformation from capitalism to socialism cannot be accomplished exclusively through parliament or the town hall. It is a process which must be rooted locally in each citizen, as worker, consumer, neighbour, relative or acquaintance. Everyone who chooses to should have the opportunity to empower themselves.

This has important implications for socialist strategy. Electoral politics are self-evidently crucial to win support for change and to implement it democratically. But the 'extra-parliamentary' arena is also important because that provides the springboard for 'bottom-up' change by involving people directly in the process. Unless people have themselves been directly involved in building socialism from the bottom up, the result will not be socialism at all, but a mirror image of the centralised capitalist state. Consider, for example, industrial democracy. Legislation can put in place a requirement on employers to establish new structures for workers' participation. But unless workers and their trade unions are enthusiastically involved, such structures could become empty shells and power relations will not alter: participation will be a device for co-opting dissent rather than empowerment.

However, according *extra*-parliamentarianism such importance should not be confused with the *anti*-parliamentarianism of Leninist and anarchist left groups. Their insurrectionist politics is authoritarian, and so corrupts the very socialist values of democracy and liberty in whose name it claims to act. Furthermore, insurrectionism is irrelevant in Britain where the parliamentary system is almost universally seen as the legitimate mechanism for democratic change. Indeed it was the left which historically fought hardest for the universal franchise and for strengthening the power of parliament. Insurrectionist politics is also fatally flawed because it has no theory of change. It is unable to bridge the gap between escalating agitation and capturing state power. 'Confrontation' and 'struggle' become slogans which substitute for a serious strategy for change, because the preeminence they are accorded by the far left leaves a chasm which can only be filled by a leap in the dark toward some distant but never properly explained 'socialist transformation'.

An extra-parliamentary dimension is necessary because it facilitates an intervention in the layers of society which surround or are below state institutions. It is in this 'civil society', as Gramsci wrote, that the ideology of capitalism establishes its 'hegemony', that is to say a hold over popular ideas and behaviour. Whether in the media, education, culture, leisure or voluntary associations, the dominant class is able to establish its ideas as 'commonsense' ones. In this way capitalism has been able to establish and maintain an 'invisible army' of support. The left needs to project an alternative 'socialist commonsense', with its supporters leading by example and arguing for their ideas in the school governing body, the playgroup, the residents' association, the professional body, as well as by working in groups committed to change, for example women's groups, anti-racist campaigns or environmental organisations.

Such a perspective illustrates another dimension of socialist change. In 1994 Ralph Miliband wrote: 'I think of socialism as a new social order, whose realisation is a process stretching over many generations, and which may never be fully "achieved". Socialism, that is to say, involves a permanent striving to advance the goals that define it.' There will be no sudden point at which a socialist society 'arrives'. It will be a gradual process of achievement, building from the present. Whether or not this process is successful will depend upon the extent to which the socialist society of the future can be 'pre-figured' under contemporary capitalism. That is why, for example, even limited forms of worker participation or employee share ownership are desirable as staging posts toward full industrial democracy or popular ownership.

The lessons for the left in government are crucial. A Labour Government needs to introduce legislative change. But it must also do something not previously attempted. It must generate support through popular mobilisation and campaigning for socialist ideas. The problem is that, in liberal-capitalist democracies like Britain's, the left finds itself in office but not in power. A Labour Government will be considerably constrained by hostile 'extra-parliamentary' forces in the City, the currency markets, the civil service and other parts of the state apparatus including, on past form at least, the judiciary, the intelligence services and the military. It needs to negotiate with these forces; but, to strengthen its hand, it also needs to reach out to the electorate to bring its own supporters together, and embark upon a consistent and continuous programme of discussion, highlighting the nature of power in a capitalist society, and working together for an alternative. It must also govern without being identified as the establishment. As it happens, Margaret Thatcher was rather adroit at this, where the Wilson-Callaghan Labour Governments were not. They came to be seen as representing an established order which had failed (notably in 1979) because they lacked a clear strategy for change and, buffeted by short-term events or pressures, they drowned in a sea of pragmatism.

MARKETS

Democracy can only be extended if there is social ownership and democratic control of the economy, because this is necessary to ensure that capital serves the interests of the majority of people and not the other way around. Government intervention is essential in order to channel investment into manufacturing, into skills and into infrastructure, and thereby to overcome the vagaries and injustices of market forces, to plan, and to secure economic progress in the interests of the majority. One example is a legal obligation upon employers to invest in their employees through training. Another is a tax on pollution, adopting the principle that the polluter pays, in order to require to companies to invest in processes which ensure a clean and safe environment.

But although such strategic intervention or, where appropriate, planning, is needed at a national level, it too cannot succeed without decentralisation. Quite aside from being a bureaucratic nightmare, it would be mathematically impossible to process the sheer quantity of information needed for statist planning, covering such matters as varieties of product, differences of quality and the minutiae of consumer choice. Although computers might conceivably be capable of handling such vast quantities of information, it is the *character* of much information – tacit, uncodified, knowing 'how' rather than 'what' – which makes it difficult if not impossible to gather and process by a central authority. Furthermore, as Geoff Hodgson wrote:

> To handle and process all the information it is necessary to create localised planning structures which can relate to their sphere of influence on a more direct and informed basis. In addition, it is necessary to give each enterprise considerable autonomy to plan its production and work out its requirements. Some degree of centralisation and coordination is necessary under socialism. But central planning cannot function without considerable decentralisation at the same time.

Equally, the decentralisation of the economy requires a market mechanism: there is literally no alternative. To that extent the proposition, part of the traditional baggage of the left, that markets equal capitalism and the absence of markets equals socialism, is utterly simplistic. This is both because capitalism cannot in practice be equated with markets, and because markets can be enabling mechanisms which allow consumers to influence production. Capitalism has never operated solely according to market theory. It has always existed within a governmental framework which has allowed capital the freedom to distort markets according to the demands of the financial elite, or the dominance of large corporations. The way in which the global economy operates against the interests of the poor South and in favour of transnational companies based in the rich North is a case in point, and will be demonstrated in Chapter Six. Capitalism has a tendency for a small group or class to control or even rig markets. People do not always get the goods and services they want, which in theory a perfectly functioning market mechanism might deliver. On the contrary, they frequently get thrust upon them – through monopolistic distribution or centralised determination of choice – the products which suit the interests of private capital. The new right notion that free, unregulated markets automatically deliver some optimal equilibrium is nonsense, as Will Hutton demonstrates:

> Markets turn out to be unstable, irrational and quite capable of

producing perverse results... Yet they are also quite capable of producing great wealth, productivity and sponsoring innovation. The problem is to tease out why they go wrong and how they can be corrected. The answer is not to let them do what they like.

In its anger at inequality and its understandable impatience to establish collective provision to overcome this, state socialism neglected the importance of individual choice and individuality which markets can help to be exercised. But for choice and individual aspiration to be real for the many, and not simply for the privileged few, people must have the *power to choose*. In a libertarian socialist society, egalitarianism will be promoted and market forces would be curbed and their power reduced by regulation, democratic control and popular ownership in favour of strategic or social interests. The free market mania wreaked upon Britain since 1979 cannot be allowed to continue except at huge strategic and social cost. Market forces are a useful mechanism, but under socialism they should not be dominant. Properly regulated and subject to planning, markets have an important role, but as the servants, not the bosses of society. Locally regulated markets and consumer choice can be agents of empowerment, a key ingredient of socialism. As Bryan Gould wrote in 1989, 'Where market provision is the preferred alternative, this requires a conscious effort to empower and enable each citizen so that market power is fairly distributed and choice becomes a practical reality rather than a chimera.'

This is not to concede the case for 'market socialism', which sees markets as the predominant mode and is sceptical about social ownership or public planning. A key objective of socialism is to create an economy which is democratically accountable to its citizens. As Michael Meacher wrote in 1992, 'state versus markets is not so much an irreconcilable antithesis as a continuum where different trade-offs are possible... between... a much more flexible state regulation, and... a much more constrained market system.' Where markets offer the best way, they should operate. The extent to which they are regulated or subject to strategic intervention by government is not a matter of theoretical dogma, but a practical matter to be judged on its merits.

REGULATION AND OWNERSHIP

However, casting the state as an 'enabler' rather than a domineering 'enforcer', does not mean a passive role in the economy. On the contrary, government should be highly active, intervening in partnership with industry to train the workforce and to create high quality infrastructure. It should intervene in markets to steer economic activity towards social or strategic objectives, as has been the case, for example, in Japan and the recently successful 'tiger economies' of the Pacific Basin. It should also promote industrial democracy and popular ownership of industry.

In 1991 the biggest 29 manufacturing companies produced 27 per cent of UK output and the biggest 100 companies 45 per cent of output. Only socialists are willing to tackle these concentrations of wealth, caused by the inexorable tendency of capitalism to centralise wealth, power and control into a few hands; thus it is only the left that can offer a prospectus which genuinely liberates the individual and guarantees freedom for all. The question of ownership of industry is not one which can be wished away. It is essential to have policies for social ownership and democratic control of the economy. For example, pension funds need democratising, as do life insurance funds and building societies. Together they account for about 80 per cent of equity in British companies, and they are controlled by a tiny elite of around two hundred people in the City. Yet these institutions are holding money on behalf of the millions of ordinary citizens who have pension and life policies, mortgages and savings. Pensions, for instance, represent postponed income to attain security in old age and they should be controlled by employees and retired employees, not by a few fund managers. This is not simply a matter of justice and democracy. It is also a question of economic policy, because these financial institutions have completely failed to use their enormous leverage to create a system of finance geared to the long-term interests of the population rather than the short-term avarice of shareholders.

Ownership remains a pivotal issue. It has altered in character of course: managers acting on behalf of institutional shareholders are now the key elite rather than the individual capitalists of the nineteenth century. But the essential contradiction of capitalism remains: the dividends of private shareholders receive priority over the interests of the community or the workforce. Between 1979 and 1990, for example, the market value of UK shares rose in real terms by 214 per cent. This was *twenty times* more than the rise in manufacturing investment which was 10.6 per cent in real terms over the same period. Shareholders have been rewarded at a rate which is not just morally iniquitous but is economically unsustainable. The British economy – especially the City – is structured in such a way that asset-holders rather than wealth creators are rewarded.

Re-distribution of ownership must remain a principal objective for socialism. And this includes public ownership of some nature at national level for the delivery of key utility services, whether (as discussed in Chapter Four) this is through nationalisation or a combination of regulation and a 'golden share' type ownership stake. It can also be appropriate in industries or services where government seeks, for strategic reasons, to kickstart growth and innovation, or maintain activity which would otherwise be closed down. New right fundamentalism which insists on privatisation of all enterprises is just as absurd as old left fundamentalism which insists upon blanket nationalisation.

But this argument is not confined to the national level. There is a strong case for regional public ownership, regulation and intervention, especially in a Europe which is the sum of its regions, and not just its nations. There should also be municipal ownership, regulation and intervention, again not rigidly pre-ordained according to some socialist master-plan, but locally, organically and democratically driven. In parallel, popular ownership should be spread and deepened through promoting cooperatives, employee share ownership, profit sharing, and 'wage earner' ownership whereby (as with the Swedish model) workers' pension funds gradually assume ownership of their industries. There should be variety rather than uniformity, with government at all levels providing incentives for democratising and socialising the economy, granting employees the opportunity to empower themselves through taking ownership for themselves rather than having it exercised in their name through some abstract state ownership which is neither efficient nor democratic.

Similarly, industrial democracy is a key plank of a socialist economic strategy: not merely as an agency for socialising industry in a popular way, which centralised nationalisation could never be, but as one more likely to produce the high productivity, investment and wealth needed for economic success, as various studies have confirmed. The experience of works councils in Germany suggests they lead to high product standards and also help generate greater teamworking and commitment, which is such an important requirement of complex modern production systems.

SOCIAL DEMOCRACY?

The failure of new right policies has created a vacuum which needs filling – but not by social democracy which has also failed. The idea – frequently advocated in the modern Labour Party – that it is desirable to seek a 'middle way' between capitalism and socialism, between markets and nationalisation, entirely misses the point. Modern socialism will not survive or prosper as a fudge. It will only succeed by being seen in its own right as a distinct, confident, alternative vision. Social democracy – the system widely subscribed to by socialist parties in post-war Western Europe, whereby private capital and the market economy are regulated and welfare services provided by a democratically elected state – is not that alternative. It may have appeared successful in the post-Second World War era when it was the product of a particular settlement between capital and labour, between the market and representative government. And certainly it *was* successful compared with pre-war monetarism: it delivered three decades of welfare services and economic stability which seemed a godsend. In Sweden, extensive government interventionism without nationalisation and a high quality welfare state was perhaps the model for social democracy.

But as an ideology it too is exhausted. No longer economically underpinned by sufficient growth to sustain a settlement acceptable to all parties, it has lurched into monetarism, with a European Union which puts the single market before democracy. With no priority given to creating decentralised mechanisms for popular participation and ownership, it has been beached on the wreckage of statism. The social democratic parties (some calling themselves 'socialist') which have followed this path across Western Europe have lost their way. Disintegrating Italian socialists, imploding French, value-less Spanish, and drifting Germans hardly provide the model for the British Labour Party. In the last decade the left in Europe has found it very difficult, if not impossible, to win on a social democratic platform – indeed, worse than this, it has all but self-destructed, its working-class base dangerously alienated and vulnerable to racist and fascist appeals.

Yet some in the Labour Party have appeared to pursue this kind of agenda for Britain. Embracing Euro-monetarism and timidity over macro-economic policy – spurning demand management in favour of supply side policies – could land a Labour Government in exactly the same predicament as European social democrats. An anxiety to demonstrate at all costs that Labour is not against entrepreneurial innovation and enterprise has led to excessive emphasis upon the virtues of a 'dynamic market economy' whilst neglecting its vices: large income inequalities, instability, unemployment, over-consumption, under-investment and authoritarian employee relations, together with the social problems created by poverty and inequality.

Denying the importance of class, and instead proclaiming a new approach based upon tackling 'vested interests' (with the implication that these include trade unions), does not stand serious scrutiny. Trade unions, for example, reflect the legitimate self-interest of workers who would otherwise have no protection or representation. Some 'vested interests' are defensible, others are not. On pension fund assets, for instance, which 'vested interest' is the more acceptable: that of current pensioners to get the highest, safest short-term return, or that of industry to get the long-term finance without which future pensioners will be sold short? The vested interest framework may produce good sound-bites but does not stand up to serious analysis and, indeed, ducks key issues.

Another fad was the 'Clintonisation' of Labour. Bill Clinton's 1992 election triumph was deployed, amongst other things, to vindicate the view that the unions should, as in the USA, be constitutionally separated from decision-making influence in the Party. It was claimed that the Democrats' 1992 success confirmed that Labour should re-cast itself as a modern, social democratic party. Whilst there were indeed lessons here for Labour – notably Clinton's effectively aggressive response to negative campaigning, his focus on economic issues and his promotion of positive polices – the fact is that he won with a vote below that of the much derided 1988 loser, Dukakis, and may even have been beaten if Perot had not stood as a strong third candidate. His subsequent performance in office hardly became a model for Labour.

After a dreadful 1983 performance putting Labour barely above the SDP/Liberal Alliance, the case for 'Americanising' British politics was put with a flourish. Reflecting the views of the business world, the *Economist* advocated 'a non-socialist, or barely socialist, opposition as the main alternative to the Tories'. Citing the USA as an ideal, Margaret Thatcher herself told the *Director* magazine that she favoured two major British political parties operating 'within the same framework of free enterprise'. After returning from the 1984 Republican Party Convention, her national Tory Chairman, John Selwyn Gummer, told the BBC: 'It is very valuable to have two sensible parties that both support capitalism. We have suffered in Britain from having the Labour Party.' In 1994 the *Sunday Times*' Political Editor reported a private conversation with Lady Thatcher: 'her ultimate ambition was to destroy a socialist Labour party and replace it with a British-style Democratic party. Britain would then have two parties committed to the success of capitalism: the Tories in the anti-state role of American Republicans, opposed by a Labour Party backed by the unions but free of left-wing dogma.' Thatcherism's project was never purely an economic one. Its strategic ambition was to destroy the post-war social welfarist consensus and replace it with a market consensus by restructuring British politics.

To an extent it has succeeded. By 1993, Professor David Marquand, the former Labour MP who defected to the Social Democrats and later joined the Liberal Democrats, was able to argue: 'the Labour Party of the 1990s has become the social-democratic party which Hugh Gaitskell tried and failed to create in the 1960s.' A year later he proclaimed: 'The mission the SDP's Gang of Four set themselves in the early eighties has been accomplished – by the party they left. Britain now has a social-democratic party rooted in the labour movement.'

But abandoning socialism for a modernised social democracy is not the answer. Offering a clear libertarian socialist alternative is.

41

CHAPTER 2

Democracy

Although Britain is often said to be the 'mother' of parliamentary democracy, it is in fact a highly elitist, backward society with a centralised, secretive state and a class system which thwarts its potential. But Britain's political system does not simply fail to achieve high democratic standards. By discouraging participation throughout society, and particularly through discouraging industrial democracy, it stifles individual initiative and energy and thereby acts as a brake on the country's ability to adapt to change, on its economic performance and ultimately on its prosperity. Fundamental reform is needed, not just to guarantee individual freedom and extend democracy but as a necessary condition for a strong economy.

If there was a persuasive case for reform before 1979, it is now unassailable. Virtually all the principles under which Britain's so-called constitutional democracy is supposed to function have broken down during the elective dictatorship of the 1980s and early 1990s. The increasing use of the Royal Prerogative has brazenly short-circuited the Parliamentary process. The use of the state apparatus, in the name of 'national security', to attack particular groups or pursue particular policies in secret is another example. Revelations surrounding the Scott Inquiry of an official conspiracy to export arms to Iran and Iraq in open defiance of publicly stated government guidelines, and the role of the intelligence services in the 1984-85 miners' strike, are just two cases which show how state agencies and operatives have slipped completely free of parliamentary accountability. And when they are exposed there is hardly an apology from a government minister, let alone a resignation, even when Parliament has been lied to or Cabinet Ministers have broken the law. Meanwhile the whole legitimacy of the

British state has been increasingly threatened by the resistance to demands for devolution of power to Scotland and Wales in particular.

Within the national system of government, power has been centralised to a considerable degree on the Prime Minister. In recent decades, the tendency towards 'prime-ministerial' rather than 'cabinet' (let alone 'parliamentary') government has increased. A significant aspect of this power is exercised through prime-ministerial appointments, from Cabinet Ministers and top civil servants to the head of the BBC, and by patronage both inside Parliament and through the honours system.

Between 1945 and 1995, for example, ten prime ministers made 2,490 ministerial appointments (500 in the Cabinet, 1,990 outside); created 922 hereditary and life peers, 119 baronetcies and 533 knighthoods for political and public service; appointed 174 chairs of nationalised industries and 65 chairs of different sorts of royal commissions. During this fifty-year period, these same ten prime ministers also appointed hundreds of civil service permanent secretaries, ambassadors, chiefs of staff, and heads of the security services. Given that there may be two or three hopefuls for every successful candidate for an honour or appointment, direct prime-ministerial influence extended to over 10,000 senior people in public life: a medieval monarch would have been envious of such powers of patronage.

One of the major tools of the Prime Minister in particular, and ministers and civil servants in general, is extensive secrecy. British government is one of the most secretive in the world, catch-all official secrecy legislation being manipulated and frequently abused to control the flow of information vital to a healthy democracy.

This cumulative democratic deficit, and many consequent abuses, can be directly attributed to the ancient structure of British democracy. Instead of resting on a clear and modern constitution, it operates according to a series of customs and common law precedents, with no serious check upon absolutist power.

The first reason for extending democracy is that individual freedom cannot be protected if power is concentrated in a few hands. Second, each citizen has a fundamental right to a say in decisions affecting him or her. Third, the absence of democracy thwarts the development of human potential. Fourth, it affects the capacity of a society to prosper: in industrially advanced countries, democracy is a necessary condition for sustained economic progress and for efficient use of resources. Therefore, contrary to the views of many on the right and some on the left, democracy is not simply a means to an end, but an end in itself: it is essential on moral, political and economic grounds. Indeed, the deeper democracy penetrates throughout society, the better it is for everyone – not just in government, but also in industry, the City, large corporations and the financial institutions. As Ralph Miliband argued in 1994: 'socialism incorporates the vision of a society immeasurably more democratic than any capitalist society could ever be. Socialism seeks to give real meaning to the notion of citizenship and popular sovereignty, well beyond universal suffrage, regular elections, political rights and other features of capitalist democracy.' The only major constraints on democracy should be those of practicality, and the balancing of the general interest against those of specific groups, local concerns or minority views.

The main reforms necessary to modernise British democracy are outlined in this chapter. The objective should be to empower citizens, to enable them to take greater control over their own lives and to bring decision making as close as possible to those affected. The relationship, central to British democracy, between Parliament and the people, must be modernised. Reforms are necessary, internally in Parliament's structures and procedures; and externally, in its relationship to civil society, to its citizens, localities and regions. There is a strong case for electoral reform, for state finance of political parties and for compulsory voting. The *ancien regime* which, so uniquely, lingers within Britain's government and makes it so anachronistic and ineffective must also be dismantled as part of a new constitutional settlement which entrenches individual rights.

MONARCHY

As a modern country nearing the end of the twentieth century it is extraordinary, not simply that we have a monarch who de facto believes in her divine right to reign over us, but that we accept such nonsense. Its political significance is not underestimated by the Tory right for whom the cloak of the Crown is clearly a handy legitimising force. The Conservative Cabinet Minister Michael Portillo, in a sycophantic speech in January 1994, argued that the Royals should remain a criticism-free zone and, most revealingly, insisted that the point of the monarchy 'is that it is the source of the authority and legitimacy of Government'. Whilst it may be argued that the Monarchy does not in practice exercise its potential power, Portillo correctly pinpoints its constitutional importance.

The Crown reinforces an undemocratic instinct in Britain, that of obsessive secrecy and unaccountability. Whitehall and the executive establishment exercise power in the shadow of the Monarchy's mystique. Loyalty and secrecy are the twins which bind civil servants and cabinet together. The Queen's Privy Council consists of current and former Cabinet Ministers and senior politicians of all parties. Allegedly a mechanism for 'non-partisan' government decisions or actions, its sole genuine function is to preserve secrecy: this function is reinforced by requiring Privy Council members to take oaths of allegiance. Civil Servants' guidelines issued by Lord Armstrong stated that 'Civil servants are servants of the Crown... For all practical purposes the Crown means the Government of the day.' Clive Ponting, a civil servant dismissed because he challenged a Minister's decision on the grounds that it was not in the public interest as defined by Parliament, was in theory acting in a treasonable fashion because he did not obey a Government Minister. MPs are not even permitted to refer to the Monarch in an adversarial manner in the Commons; when I asked in 1991 whether the Queen had been consulted over proposals to privatise the Royal Mail, I had to refer to 'a certain person whose head appears upon the stamp' in order to avoid the Speaker cutting me short.

The Royal Prerogative gives massive, unaccountable powers to the executive. Acting in the name of the Crown, it allows the government to take decisions without parliamentary consent. By invoking it governments can even introduce primary legislation which may not be subject to court challenge. Under Britain's 'unwritten' constitution it is not clear what (if any) are the constraints upon exercise of the Royal Prerogative by the Prime Minister and other Ministers.

Some 1400 orders were made under Royal Prerogative during the 1980s. Some of them were harmless, such as amending Royal Charters.

However, some were most certainly not, for example the ban in January 1984 on trade union rights at GCHQ. The Prerogative can also be invoked to go to war or to make treaties. Mrs Thatcher used it secretly to permit America the use of English air bases for the bombing of Libya in April 1986. In December 1990 she went to war in the Gulf; although this was subsequently debated in the House where she had majority support, the debate was upon a procedural motion which could not be amended. As Tony Benn said in January 1991 during this Commons debate: 'This is the first time in the history of this country that British troops have been sent into battle under foreign command, using the Royal Prerogative of war-making to do so, without the House having had an opportunity to express its view on any motion other than that we adjourn.' At least the American Congress debated and voted upon a specific motion supporting military intervention. The Maastricht Treaty was signed by John Major in 1991 under Royal Prerogative and, despite its immense economic and constitutional significance, could have been implemented without parliamentary approval, save for the almost incidental fact that it increased the powers of the European Parliament which did need a Parliamentary Bill.

However, powers exercised in the name of the Monarch are not the whole story. The Monarch also has the power to dissolve Parliament and call an election. By custom and practice this power is exercised with care and in concert with the Prime Minister. Nevertheless it remains an important discretionary power which could also be used, for example, to avoid an election in the event of a government losing its majority, through the Monarch's invitation to an alternative Party Leader to form an administration. It should also be noted that the Prime Minister is not constitutionally bound to seek the agreement of the whole Cabinet for a dissolution, or even on his or her own resignation, which automatically results in the resignation of the rest of the Cabinet. The real indictment of the Royal Prerogative is not simply that it is a pre-democratic hangover from rule by the Crown, but that it enormously concentrates power in Prime Ministers and the unaccountable state apparatus behind them. It must be abolished.

It is almost impossible to reform Britain's constitution without tackling the royalty question. The monarchy is the British equivalent of the USA's Bill of Rights – the glue that binds the whole thing together. Because the concept of monarchy is at the heart of the constitution any proposed structural changes would have a direct impact on it. For example, removing hereditary peers from the House of Lords would leave the monarch exposed as the sole hereditary element in the constitution. How could such an exception possibly be defended? Disestablishment of the Church of England is also linked to reforming the monarchy because the head of the Church is also the head of state, and the two institutions, together with the House of Lords, are closely entwined as part of the seamless web of Britain's *ancien regime.* For instance Bishops automatically have a seat in the House of Lords.

Why should the Prime Minister acting in the name of the Monarch decide who should be appointed Archbishop or Bishop any more than Chief Rabbi? Surely that is a matter for the Church alone to decide? The Church should also be divided from State to achieve genuine spiritual and intellectual freedom for all people whether they are Christians, Muslims, Jews or atheists, for Britain in the 1990s is a secular state in all but name. It appears that there would be only three losers should the Church be disestablished: the Clerk of the Closet who vets any religious book passed to the Queen in case she strays from the true path, the Lord High Almoner who used to be in charge of washing the feet of the poor on Maundy Thursday but who now keeps his hands dry and looks after administrative arrangements and the Prelate of the Order of the Garter who would be deprived of his entitlement to wear a blue mantle whilst officiating at garter ceremonies.

Republicanism is not a new idea – it's rooted in the British left tradition with such major figures as Milton, Paine, Cobbett, and H.G.Wells arguing its case down the centuries. But there is a serious argument that focusing the constitutional debate around the royals would divert attention and perhaps alienate support for other aspects of a radical reform agenda, including a Bill of Rights and devolution. This is an important consideration and, given much more pressing priorities, it would be hard to justify an incoming Labour Government immediately getting bogged down in abolishing the monarchy. But this does not mean that the subject should disappear from the left's agenda.

There is argument for a slimmed-down Scandinavian style monarchy with ceremonial rather than constitutional functions. But even this would not meet the demand for full modernisation of the British state which can only be achieved by getting rid of the monarchy. And although it is often countered that abolition would mean opting for an American-style executive Head of State, that is not the case. Europe provides better guidance. A President need not have executive powers on the US model and need not be a party figure. The Czechs elected a playwright and the Poles a shipyard worker. The Irish plumped for a president who was better known as a civil rights lawyer and women's issues campaigner than a back-bench parliamentarian. As Irish President Mary Robinson is an excellent advertisement for the head of state of a modern democracy. Her blend of dignity and political sensitivity has shown just how much Britain could benefit from a similar elected head of state to replace the monarch.

As part of a strategy for reforming and modernising the British constitution, the left should adopt a policy of 'pragmatic republicanism'. Increasing democratisation, including abolition of the Royal Prerogative and the House of Lords, would steadily reduce support for the monarchy which would be progressively exposed as not merely quaintly anomalous but constitutionally obsolete. As this process continued, a Scandinavian style monarchy with no constitutional functions could be a staging post to the ideal of a non-executive, elected Head of State.

ABOLISHING THE HOUSE OF LORDS

The House of Lords is another hangover from the pre-democracy days, a constitutional dinosaur. No other Parliamentary democracy rewards individuals with a seat at the centre of power on the basis of who their great-great-great-great grandparents were. There are 759 such hereditary Peers, discreetly labelled 'peers by succession', of whom just 17 are women and 13 Labour.

Additionally, over the last 35 years there have been created 388 life peerages (only 60 of whom are women). They owe their position to Prime Ministerial patronage rather than to democratic election. Adding in 26 archbishops and bishops, 16 hereditary peers of first creation and 19 life peers under the Appellate Jurisdiction Act 1876 – and the total numerical power of the House of Lords is over 1,200 –

almost double that of the Commons. Not surprisingly they are overwhelmingly male (just 77 are women) and Conservative. In 1993, 478 took the Tory whip, compared with 116 Labour, 59 Liberals and 272 cross-benchers.

Fewer than half bother to turn up on any regular basis. Though many are hard-working, many are the backwoodsmen who remain at home on their huge estates, awaiting the clarion call of the Tory whips summoning them to overturn the will of the working Peers: at crucial votes, like fungi in the dark, the number of Peers mushrooms. And this practice has not diminished with the creation of life peerages, as can be seen, for example, in Lords votes in the 1960s on the London Government Bill, the Southern Rhodesia Sanctions Order, and in 1985 the Abolition of the GLC. Successive Tory Governments have used the House of Lords in the same way that a drunk uses a lamp-post – for support rather than illumination. Self-interest plays an important part too in determining the voting patterns of the peers. In May 1988, after years of absence, many hereditary peers turned up to vote for Mrs Thatcher's notorious poll tax, saving themselves on average about 90 per cent on their previous rates bills. The third Baron Cranworth, a Suffolk farmer who had inherited his title in 1964, turned up for the first time in 24 years to take the oath so that he could vote.

But abolition without any replacement is not the answer. There is a need for a second Chamber which scrutinises legislation and acts as a constitutional check. It should be similar to Senates in other mature democracies, such as Australia and the USA: a check and balance on the excesses of the Executive, but one which doesn't duplicate the responsibilities of the Commons. It could also draw on the experience of Germany's Second Chamber, the Bundesrat, which provides a direct regional input from the regional Governments, the Lander.

The Lords should be replaced with a new second chamber – or Senate. One proposed model, which I favour, would be based on around 400 members and elected from Party Lists according to the size of the regional vote each party polled at a general election. The same vote given to a parliamentary candidate locally would be allocated to that candidate's Party in a regional pool. The percentage of that pool received by each party would determine its allocation of Second Chamber members from the region concerned. This is a form of proportional representation based on the 'List' system. As is argued later in this chapter, the objection to the 'List' principle for elections to the House of Commons is that it would break the vital link between the MP and his or her constituency, undermining accountability. That valid objection does not apply to members of a Second Chamber who do not have any constituency duties or local representative responsibilities.

Such a List system would not only give a voice to the regions of Britain, it would also allow positive action to secure a fair representation of women and ethnic minorities. For example, each Party could select its Regional Lists for the second chamber by democratic vote of either regional members or conferences. It could build in quotas, thus satisfying legitimate claims for equal representation in a way that cannot be enforced whilst retaining the local autonomy which is such an important tradition for MP and councillor selections.

The result would be to meet in full aspirations for proportional representation in at least one half of Parliament. The new second chamber could also genuinely claim legitimacy as a constitutional check since it would contain a fair spread of almost all political opinion. Such an approach could retain the advantages of single member seats in the Commons – with or without electoral reform there – and the prospect of being able to form a single-party Government, while the reform of the second chamber could satisfy the demand for fairer representation.

CENTRALISATION

Britain's highly centralised system of government has become much more so since Mrs Thatcher won office in 1979. Democratic accountability has been fatally injured by a plethora of hived-off agencies, market testing, contracting-out, deregulation and privatisation. These are not decentralising measures – on the contrary they centralise power by removing decisions from direct democratic accountability. Services are now delivered at arms length by officials who retain considerable discretion. On present trends, the 'civil service' will soon be a rump of 25 departments with around 2000 staff in each (a total of 50,000 compared with 730,000 in 1979): instead there are over 300 executive agencies, over 4000 Quangos (quasi-autonomous non-governmental organisations) and thousands of rolling contracts.

Local government in particular has found its powers, previously limited enough, massively reduced by direct Whitehall controls over expenditure and the hiving-off of functions to Quangos. Local councils elected to improve public services (for instance, by subsidising public transport) have found local democratic wishes overridden by central government. Their role has also been diminished by privatisation, opting out, contracting out and compulsory competitive tendering. In this environment, the desire for greater public participation has been thwarted: while 'town hall democracy', already remote enough from local communities, is itself undermined, there is no hope of extending it downwards through neighbourhood councils, participatory mechanisms and community groups.

Because the process of hiving off has occurred piecemeal, the public have not appreciated the extent to which government in Britain is now fragmented. The process has spread so far that the scope for socialist administration is called into question. How can such a highly disaggregated system be effectively managed by Ministers or held accountable to Parliament or local councillors? And there is a further consequence. British public life has historically been relatively free of corruption. But the extent of the fragmentation and the close proximity between public bodies and private contracts means that this is likely to end. Indeed, scandals uncovered by the Commons Public Accounts Committee in the early- to mid-1990s demonstrate that corruption and a collapse in ethics are already with us. As the PAC scathingly observed in 1994, there has been a decline in public standards unprecedented since the Northcote-Trevelyan reforms to establish integrity in public services one hundred and fifty years ago. Confirmation of this came in 1994 with the establishment of the Nolan Committee to examine public ethics following revelations that a number of Conservative MPs had taken bribes to table parliamentary questions. Its reforming recommendations amounted to a belated acknowledgement of the extent to which the rot had set in.

A 'governance gap' has emerged in the last sixteen years. Quangos have mushroomed: by 1996 7700 new Quangos will have been created. There is a new, unelected, Quango state which operates according to ill-defined, contradictory and opaque rules and covers almost every aspect of public policy and service delivery. Almost £55 billion of public money (or 20 per cent of all public spending) is in the velvet-gloved hands of Quangos. Of this almost £6 billion was directly controlled by elected local government.

The result is a growing democratic deficit. Whereas local Councillors are elected, Quango members are appointed either by government ministers (as in Urban Development Corporations) or in the main self-appointed (as in Training and Enterprise Councils or TECs). Whereas most council meetings and documents are by law open to the public, there is no similar legal obligation on many Quangos – such as Housing Action Trusts and NHS Trusts. Whereas councillors are liable to surcharge, Quango members are not. Whereas councillors must declare an interest and cannot vote on a matter having done so, this does not apply to Quango members who have been involved in conflicts of interest. Local government is also subject to much stricter audit.

Quango members additionally have the advantage of being much better remunerated than councillors. For example in 1993 the Chair of Liverpool Housing Action Trust was paid £37,000 a year whereas the Leader of Liverpool City Council only received £8500 despite having a much greater range of responsibilities. The great and the good in the blue-rinsed Shires have cottoned on to this too. In a damning radio interview, the former Conservative Chair of the Association of District Councillors, Lady Anson, said: 'You can spend one day a month on a district health authority and you get £5000 which is more than any councillor will get in a whole year unless they're leader of some massive big authority...I know many people who've been a councillor for four years and they say "we can't afford it any more – do you know any Quangos we could get on?"'.

Surveys show that Quangos have become a refuge for Tory placemen and women unseated via the democratic process as councillors or MPs. There is a clear bias toward Tory appointees amongst the 40,000 strong Quango army across Britain. Moreover, a 1994 study covering 13 departments of State and 100 Quangos, found 157 individuals appointed to these bodies who simultaneously had ties with firms which donated to Tory Party funds. Baroness Denton, an Industry Minister said: 'Of course you don't put people in who are in conflict with what you are trying to achieve. It's no good going on an NHS Trust Board if you don't believe in the policy that the Department of Health is pursuing.' She added: 'I can't remember knowingly appointing a Labour supporter.'

Quangos must be rigorously pruned and their functions and powers should be either subject to direct parliamentary accountability or returned to elected local or regional government. Where Quangos remain they should be subject to local government-type disciplines, including surcharge, and new appointments to senior posts should be subject to ratification by Commons Select Committees or regional authorities.

A NEW CITIZENSHIP

The Conservative unelected state has been the product of a new right agenda to destroy independent local government, centralise power and undermine democratic accountability whilst subjecting public services to the dictates of the market. Coupled with continued violations of civil rights, not least by Government, it has strengthened the case for a new citizenship in Britain underpinned by a Bill of Rights.

The first stage would be to incorporate into British law the European Convention on Human Rights; this would give each citizen basic civil rights such as freedom of speech and privacy. It would also shortcut the existing time-consuming and expensive procedure of petitioning Strasbourg. The next stage would be a full-blown Bill of Rights creating a new culture of citizenship and entrenching a range of rights from consultation and information to welfare benefits. (For an excellent guide to comprehensive reform of government see Graham Allen's *Reinventing Democracy*.) The Bill should however be framed so as to limit the power of the judiciary to 'make up' law by interpreting it in a reactionary way.

Accompanying this should be a new framework for industrial relations which abandons Britain's historic attachment to voluntarism and to 'negative' rights. Even at the height of union power in the late 1970s, British workers have only ever achieved the 'right' to immunity from prosecution if they formed unions or went on strike. In other words, workers have never had the positive right to strike or to union recognition, only the right (subject to varying constraints) to avoid being taken to court if they took industrial action or formed unions. There should be positive rights to join a union, to have it recognised, and to take industrial action after a ballot; there should also be legally guaranteed protection against unfair dismissal, and positive rights over such matters as health and safety, equal opportunities, maternity leave and consultation and information.

A new contract between the state and citizen also depends upon access to information. The principle of open government should be enshrined in a Freedom of Information Act giving the public basic rights to information. This would replace the now discredited official secrecy legislation.

PARLIAMENT AND CIVIL SOCIETY

Uncritical support for the British political system is often based on two main assumptions which are mistaken. The first of these is that Parliament sits at the apex of real power.

In fact, although it is very influential, it is only one actor on the stage. It is severely constrained by a series of 'extra-parliamentary' forces, the most important being national and international private capital, which exercises massive power and shapes the whole nature of society. Parliament cannot easily resist the pressures of the industrial and financial elites which control private capital.

A second assumption underpinning Britain's parliamentary democracy is that the state itself is a neutral body which can be steered in any direction according to the policies adopted by the party in office. In fact, in a capitalist society such as Britain's, the state operates within a wider division of power imposed by the class structure, and cannot remain neutral as between these conflicting class interests: it usually tends to reflect the interests of the dominant class. The various agencies which make up the state - the civil service, judiciary, police and military – also reflect this class bias and, in addition, have their own interests to defend.

This is why even the most progressive reformers will end up failing if they assume – as, for example, all Labour governments have done – that the exclusive purpose of political activity is to win elections and secure office, without actively engaging the support of sympathetic extra-parliamentary forces to resist the hostile forces of financiers, speculators, bureaucrats and technocrats.

However, notwithstanding its limitations, Parliament is the principal, legitimate vehicle for democratic change in Britain and is seen as such by the vast majority of the population. Although the democratic process in Britain is inadequate, any attempt to override it will be rightly rejected as authoritarian and elitist. Libertarian socialists, though critical of the limitations of parliamentary democracy, defend uncompromisingly the electoral process and the principle of government by consent.

Achieving the radical changes necessary in Britain will require the adoption of a 'third road' strategy, fusing parliamentary initiatives with the pressure which can be brought by the activity of progressive extra-parliamentary movements, including trade unions, single-issue pressure groups and community organisations. This means that Labour both in opposition and in government at all levels should work closely with such groups, linking them into its structures, supporting their struggles and maintaining an ongoing policy dialogue. The aim is to create an 'invisible army' of persuaders for socialism throughout civil society. An organisation like Greenpeace, for example, should be seen in positive terms as pursuing a common objective to protect the environment, since it is often up against the very vested interests which will also resist a Labour government's green agenda. Similarly anti-racist groups should be encouraged, since their activism on the ground is an important counterpart to policy initiatives in Westminster or the town hall. In the 1980s the Labour Greater London Council showed how groups in the community could be involved and therefore feel part of the process of government; in the process it transformed initial public hostility to its left-wing stance into popular enthusiasm for its general work.

However, even progressive pressure groups will not always agree with Labour administrations: they have different interests to advance and different roles to perform. But there ought to be a stance by Labour ministers and councillors of openness, creative dialogue and tolerance. That stance will not only empower such movements, it also has the advantage of creating greater grass roots legitimacy for Labour in government, and of building a popular consensus for socialist policies.

Implicit here is a concept of political representation distinctly different from the conventional one associated with parliamentary democracy. Socialist MPs and councillors should not be Burkean-type representatives in whom is reposited the public will, and who act independently, free from tiresome nagging by the rank and file of their Party or their constituents. Rather, they should be accountable. This is not an argument for merely rubber stamping the swirling prejudices of populist opinion or sectional interests: representatives will of course exercise their own judgement, act according to their principles and provide leadership. They should be bound by their consciences and reflect their Party's policies. But they should be linked like an umbilical chord to their grass-roots base. This is not simply for democratic reasons. Only by such accountability can socialist representatives avoid being sucked into the system and avoid acting according to the pressures of the dominant class rather than in the interests of their constituents. Elected Labour representatives should constantly be aware that they operating in a system which is ultimately hostile to their socialist values.

DEVOLVING POWER

That is a further reason why, according to libertarian socialism, very little will be achieved if reforms are only concentrated at the centre. The overriding objective must be to devolve decision-making down through the structure of government, in order both to enhance democratic rights and to produce the better decisions which are likely to follow when the people most closely affected are involved.

Within such a framework, directly elected Parliaments should be established in Scotland and Wales, not only with significant political powers but with significant industrial and economic ones as well. They would have important functions of economic planning and industrial intervention, as well as responsibility for strategic areas of policy such as town and country planning, the environment, health and transport. In England, a parallel system of regional government should be established.

Devolution should be approached as an evolving process in which power is increasingly taken from the centre, rather than one in which legislation establishes an immediate and final blueprint. Wales is a case in point. The Welsh Office was established thirty years ago with a relatively narrow remit, but has since gradually accumulated more and more powers and responsibilities, so that it now covers almost every aspect of public policy. A Welsh Parliament would begin by having its own legislative powers confined to matters which are Welsh specific such as the Welsh language; it would oversee local government and take over responsibility for areas which are currently dealt with by Quangos. It would initially be financed through a block grant, according to the already established formula. But, in time – and as Britain moved towards a federal structure – greater legislative and revenue raising powers could be obtained.

As with other forms of decentralisation, control should be exercised through elected and accountable authorities, sweeping away the whole gamut of Quangos and quasi-public institutions (now run by Whitehall appointees) and either taking over their functions or making them democratically accountable. Regional government in England, for example, would take over and make democratically accountable Integrated Government Regional Offices. In establishing these, the Conservatives have conceded the principle of a regional tier whilst continuing to thwart pressure to make it democratic.

Local councils, too, should be given greater powers. Within district boundaries, they should have extensive powers of intervention in commerce and industry, and should be able to sponsor local economic initiatives, including taking ownership stakes. They should also be given control over spending their own revenue provided they achieve minimum national standards. The centralised controls over revenue-raising and expenditure introduced by the Tories must be replaced, with much greater scope for local councils to raise income according to local needs and local wishes.

Local authority facilities should be opened up for more active use by local people, and community groups should be given greater information and access to the decision-making process. In this respect, the style of local government pioneered by the Labour Greater London Council in 1981-6 would repay study. By opening up policy making to greater popular participation, it won much greater identification with local government amongst different layers of people including women, the young, black people, the arts world and trade unionists. There should also be a systematic decentralisation of services to administrative units outside the town hall. For example, neighbourhood housing offices should be established on council estates and tenants' associations given some control over their operations.

AN 'ALTERNATIVE STATE'

In keeping with a pluralist vision of democracy, and in order to create structures through which participation can occur from below, the idea of an 'alternative state' should be pursued: a publicly resourced yet independent network established specifically to pressure (and where necessary agitate against) the dominant structures, whether these be traditional national structures or new local ones, and whatever political party happens to hold office.

To some extent this is already in place through a publicly supported network of voluntary or independent groups. But it should be positively extended. Resources should be provided for community groups, tenants' associations, residents' groups, consumer groups, workplace committees and so forth, enabling them to organise better and sustain their activity. Pressure on conventional structures – even if they happen to be controlled by the left – should be welcomed and indeed encouraged, not thwarted.

A priority should be given to establishing 'community resource centres'. These would offer certain local authority services at neighbourhood level, such as housing advisers, welfare rights workers, health workers, community workers. They would also offer facilities for local groups. These community resource centres would be managed by local groups and could become vehicles for local people to exert their own political leverage and to deliver services which are best handled at this level. Their management committees could be answerable to elected 'neighbourhood councils' (see my *Neighbourhood Participation*). It is important not to impose standardised, pre-ordained structures upon local communities which are diverse in so many ways. It is also important not to suffocate community groups with official finance and the bureaucratic procedures which usually come with it. On the other hand, neighbourhood councils must not become mere talking shops. They need access to resources if there is to be any real decentralisation of democracy. And this is why local authorities must be prepared to fund new structures such as community resource centres without insisting on the kind of bureaucratic control which so often alienates people who wish to become more involved in local issues.

ACTIVE CITIZENSHIP

To underpin such reforms of the structure of government and public administration, a sea-change in individual attitudes and aspirations will be needed. Otherwise, even the best-designed participatory system will founder on the rocks of apathy and public passivity.

An important measure of the health of a democracy is the extent to which its citizens *actively* play a part in the decision-making process. In Britain, citizen participation is confined to relatively few people. Part of the reason for this is widespread political apathy and ignorance. Civic education hardly exists and, where it does, 'politics' is avoided, except for anodyne descriptions of the structure of parliamentary government. Socialisation for work, for family responsibilities, for adult life, takes place – but our culture does not socialise people to participate in political activity. Politics is seen as something undertaken on behalf of others by professionals (i.e. politicians). The citizen's role is a passive one, focused on casting a vote at periodic elections.

The argument here is not that people should be forced to 'participate'. Nor is it suggested that their lives should be turned into an endless series of committee meetings. Instead, society should be consciously organised so as positively to promote and encourage popular participation by opening up the structures of power and by equipping people with the confidence and knowledge to take advantage of the new opportunities thereby created. At present they have little choice: only the most dedicated and confident can participate effectively.

Official encouragement should be given to families to educate young children about their civic rights and their opportunities to participate. The National Curriculum should include 'civics' or 'political education' so that citizenship can be taught from birth. Instead of socialising for apathy, the socialisation process should encourage people to expect that they will be 'participators', that the positive exercise of their democratic rights is an important duty in their role as citizens. Experience suggests that a more participatory society is not merely more democratic, but is also healthier, since it has greater popular legitimacy.

School pupils should have much greater rights over the management of their schools, students over their universities and colleges, consumers over the services they receive and the goods they purchase, pensioners over how and when they retire and the issues which affect them. This should apply to work as well, with industrial democracy encouraged by government legislation. Significantly, the evidence shows that workers are not only more content, but that their productivity is increased when they are given more control and a more direct say in the organisation and objectives of their work.

This is the practical route to establishing a new concept of active citizenship in Britain. And it is as much about building a modern economy as a modern democracy. Both require collaborative relationships rather than ones subordinated to either shareholder or statist dictat. Both require creativity and consent from below rather than centralised control from above. As Will Hutton has written: 'Britain must complete the unfinished business of the seventeenth century and equip itself with a constitution that permits a new form of economic, social and political citizenship.'

COMPULSORY VOTING

Active citizenship is however a two-way process, involving not just rights but also responsibilties. The freedom and opportunity it creates should be complemented by the duty to vote. Compulsory voting would not be an attack on individual freedom – which is at the heart of libertarian socialism. It would place voting alongside other civic duties and obligations. People are rightly required to pay taxes, go to school or wear seatbelts in vehicles. They have to obey laws and are compelled to behave as responsible citizens. Such duties are not seen as denials of freedom, but an acceptance that to be a member of a civilised society requires the voluntary relinquishing of 'rights' which could doubtless be exercised in a state of raw nature. Individualism is subordinated to community and citizenship; but nobody seriously suggests their freedom is thereby threatened, because everyone gains collectively. The same principle should apply to the process of democracy.

Democratic politics is fundamental to society, and the obligation to vote should be part of our civic duties. The Australians do not complain of their rights being denied through their system of compulsory voting and nor should the British. Anyone who wished to abstain would have the right to do so, either through an abstention box in the polling station or through the familiar device of spoiling the ballot paper. Other reforms would make compulsory voting relatively painless. General election day should be made a public holiday. There should be much easier voting arrangements, including access to postal voting for anyone who can give good reason for needing it.

Voter turnout would, of course, increase. This would place a greater premium upon parties to win the argument about policies, rather than simply to concentrate upon turning out their vote. It would also require the main parties to address the needs of the 'underclass' which is increasingly alienated from the conventional political system and tends not to vote as a consequence. Mandatory voting would also require much greater civic and political education in the broadest sense: from guidance on the mechanics of voting (about which there is still surprising ignorance, as anybody who has canvassed young voters can confirm) to information on party policies.

PUBLIC FINANCING OF POLITICS

As part of a new relationship between Parliament and civil society there should be public funding for political parties. Although many on the left point to the dangers of making a socialist party dependent upon the state for finance which could be withdrawn, there is no logical reason why the arts, sport, leisure and voluntary action in general can be publicly financed, but the very cement which binds together civil society – politics – cannot. The argument against is a relic from an earlier age when there was virtually no public funding of any activity in civil society. It is a product of the 'amateur gentleman' spirit of

British parliamentarianism in which politics was financed from private income. Today, we need to decide whether democracy is worth supporting and the answer must surely be self-evident.

The principle was first conceded in 1975 when funds were allocated to each parliamentary party to help run its offices: in 1993-94 these totalled £2.2 million for all opposition parties. The 1993 overhaul of, and substantial increase in, the Commons Office Costs Allowance, which releases funds for MPs' staff and equipment, including local constituency offices, further highlighted the link between state finance and politics: it totalled over £27 million in 1995. As with most areas of the British Constitution, state aid has evolved down the years in an ad hoc fashion. It includes free public meeting rooms at election time, a free delivery of parliamentary candidates' election addresses by the Post Office (which cost the state about £12 million in 1992) and favourable tax treatment. The free time for Party Political Broadcasts and Party Election Broadcasts has been estimated to be worth £3 million and £10 million respectively for each major party. Around £9 million annually is also provided to British parties in the European Parliament for political education purposes (and, since Britain is a net contributor to the European Union, this in effect amounts to state financing). Consequently public funding for political parties would merely be an extension of an existing practice.

At the heart of the liberal democratic tradition is the principle of political equality. Voters shouldn't just have the right to vote but the right to do so in elections where parties compete on roughly equal terms. Politics should be played on a level-playing field. There are two ways by which it can be ensured that parties have equal access to the electorate – either by making sure the parties have roughly the same public resources (as in Germany) or by limiting the amount that can be spent on elections (as in Canada). It seems that, as in many other areas of public life, Britain stands almost alone, in adopting neither of these systems.

As Martin Linton observed in *Money and Votes*, 'people are unequal in the market place but they should be equal in the polling booth'. A representative democracy doesn't function well without political parties, and they can't survive without money. Although nobody disputes the right to donate money, the process must be transparent and accountable rather than concealed and corrupt. The case for reform is made stronger by gross discrepancies in party income: the Tories have consistently enjoyed up to three times Labour's election finances. At the 1992 election, the Tories had a fighting fund of over £20 million, well over double that for Labour. Only a fraction of the fund came from local party donations. The source of the rest was deliberately kept secret.

The Tories have relied for a long time on funding from wealthy business people, yet, unlike trade unions who ballot members on whether they want to make political donations, company directors don't have to ask their shareholders for permission. An opinion poll by MORI in November 1994 found that 86 per cent of individual shareholders did want a say. There should be a change in company law to enforce shareholder ballots. The source of any donation to any political party over £5000 should be published with the parties' annual accounts which themselves should be publicly available. The Tories have benefited enormously from the cloak of secrecy surrounding foreign donations in particular. Until everything is above board, suspicion will persist that there have been trade-offs between foreign donors and Tory government policies; examples of such donors are Hong Kong banker Li Ka Shing and the Sultan of Brunei.

There is a definite link between political donations and honours bestowed on industrialists. Between 1979 and 1993, 18 life peerages and 82 knighthoods were given to industrialists connected with 76 companies which between them over the same period donated £17.4 million to the Tories and their front organisations. Of the top ten corporate donors, including United Biscuits, Hanson, Taylor Woodrow and Glaxo, only two had managing directors who weren't honoured: one a Canadian and the other an hereditary peer. Public financing of parties would help to ensure that in twenty-first century Britain you can't buy preferment or buy votes.

PARLIAMENTARY REFORM

Parliament also needs radically reforming. A combination of prime-ministerial control, the bureaucratic power of the civil service, institutional anachronisms in the House of Commons, and the undemocratic blocking powers of the unelected House of Lords, means that Parliament does not properly fulfil its democratic function. Constitutional theory about the legislature having control over the executive does not describe reality in Britain. Parliament usually rubber-stamps the wishes of government. The average backbench MP has very little power – the Conservative MP, Edwina Currie, for instance, confirmed that she now has less power than she had as Chair of the Housing Committee on Birmingham Council. Quite apart from dutifully trooping through to vote for legislation on pain of offending the Party Whips and thereby losing all sorts of privileges and career opportunities, backbenchers are powerless before the Executive steamroller in another respect. There are normally around 2000 Statutory Instruments each year which are the equivalent of 10,000 pages of legislation and can almost never be amended or altered. They are 'minor laws' – normally consequential regulations or mechanisms for implementing European directives - and they mostly pass through by 'Negative Procedure': unless someone shouts 'object', they become law. It is not suggested that they should be abolished (for that would mean so much extra legislation, it would bring Parliament to a standstill); rather they emphasise the acute constraints upon backbench power.

Reforms should be directed at increasing the accountability of the executive to Parliament. A system of fixed-term parliaments, for example a term of four years (subject to a majority being eroded by by-election defeats) would remove the ability of the Prime Minister to manipulate the electoral cycle and ensure greater democratic responsiveness. The powers of the Commons need strengthening in other ways. The normal practice with a majority government is for Bills to be whipped through with government MPs silent voting fodder and opposition amendments brushed side. Once a Bill is introduced it becomes almost a test of government virility to get it through unscathed. This can produce bad legislation (the poll tax is an obvious recent example). And it can easily produce flawed legislation (the setting up of the Child Support Agency is an example).

Legislation should be better scrutinised by reforming the procedures. Commons Standing Committees would have the opportunity to examine Bills and call witnesses before they were put before the floor of the House. After the Report Stage and before the final vote, a special Revision Committee could take another look, to check for drafting errors and accommodate other improvements. Additionally, the executive needs to be made more accountable by enhancing the system of Select Committees, giving them more powers, greater access to information and much better facilities and back-up resources, so that they can really maintain a close eye on the operations of each department of government.

The sheer weight of parliamentary business and the complexity of modern legislation mean that most MPs cannot possibly understand the full implications of the laws they dutifully troop through the lobbies to vote for (or against). Nor can they possibly scrutinise the great tide of European directives which washes through Westminster almost unnoticed. MPs also have a constituency case-load which has increased exponentially since the Second World War, and even more massively in the last ten years. The electorate is simultaneously less deferential to MPs and more demanding of them. They are expected both to be active on local issues and to play a part in national policy determination. Some enjoy a comfortable life, but most are over-worked and over-stretched.

Westminster has become logjammed. Part of the solution is to strengthen the democratic process at other levels of government. The European Parliament should be given more powers over the European Commission and the Council of Ministers. Devolution to Scotland, Wales and the regions of England would decentralise much decision-making to a more appropriate level where it can also more effectively be scrutinised.

Additionally, there should be an end to the culture of the amateur English gentleman MP of independent means which still stalks the corridors of Westminster. This culture plays into the hands of the establishment because it leaves MPs without the resources effectively to monitor government. It also lies at the heart of the crisis of public ethics which the Nolan Committee examined in 1994-95. It influences not only MPs' resources but also their pay and has created an environment in which Conservative MPs in particular feel free to more than treble their salaries and provide extra funding for their offices from outside consultancies, directorships and jobs. Modernisation of the Commons is very long overdue and would help maintain a proper check on the executive. Although the resources MPs receive have been improved in recent years, they are still totally inadequate. MPs should have larger secretarial and research staff who should be paid properly. There should be much improved facilities, including new technology, and separate adequate resourcing of constituency offices. And – in return for a bar on outside jobs, remunerated directorships and consultancies – the rate for the job should be paid so that there is no excuse for those who treat it as a part-time profession.

MPs should further be discouraged from having other paid jobs by introducing more regular working hours for the Commons. This would have the great virtue of enabling MPs to live more normal lives. Both these moves would bring MPs closer to the people who elect them. Women would benefit particularly, though there are many other changes necessary to achieve equality, such as introducing child-care facilities at the Commons and scrapping the various antiquated routines which are modelled more on a gentleman's club than a genuinely representative parliament of the nation. As a result of the Jopling Committee some changes in hours were introduced in 1994-95 to assist backbenchers – a small though welcome beginning. But the whole culture of British politics must be reformed and *popularised* so that the political parties and national and local government are opened up and linked into civil society rather than being seen as separate, elitist institutions, trapped in a previous age and increasingly remote from the average citizen.

Even more substantial reforms are necessary to act as a counter-weight against the power of Prime Ministers over their parliamentary parties. At present, Prime Ministers and their senior civil servants can prevent open discussion of decisions and policies by controlling the flow of information and invoking the protection of official secrecy; the increased transparency introduced by John Major (such as making public the membership of Cabinet Committees and the name of the head of MI5) is minimal. The objective should be to make ministers much more accountable to Parliament, to their parties and, beyond that, to groups and opinions outside the parliamentary arena. One way of achieving accountability to their respective parties would be to have a system of 'ministerial committees' (consisting of MPs elected by their parliamentary party's specialist groups) to act as advisers to ministers and to provide a channel for support and consultation to and from their parties as a whole, and also to the community outside.

Barbara Castle, in her autobiography, *Fighting all the Way*, gives a salutary description of life as a Labour Cabinet Minister in the 1960s and 1970s: 'I had not realised how completely the civil service was in control.' And she added that to have challenged this in Cabinet 'would have been like blaspheming in Church.' Although not a complete answer to the problem she identified, more full-time political aides are needed in ministers' private offices to provide alternative advice and to act as watchdogs when civil servants are tempted to impede the implementation of radical policies. There is a strong case for a *cabinet* of political advisers to all Ministers. These advisers would strengthen the power of Ministers against the Cabinet office. They should also have a 'campaigning role' in keeping open channels of communication between Whitehall and groups and individuals who have no access to senior policy-makers. Building links with extra-parliamentary forces would enable Labour to challenge and overcome the financial, bureaucratic and political establishments, which would otherwise imprison even the best-intentioned minister.

MINISTER FOR WOMEN

An important mechanism for transforming the culture of Whitehall would be a Minister for Women. In 1992, three sections of the civil service were merged to form a sex equality branch in the Department of Employment, but this has been little more than tokenistic. There should be a new Minister for Women with a seat in cabinet and a remit to range across Whitehall and determine positive policies for women. She should have powers to ensure that equal opportunities are promoted throughout the public and private sectors, setting the agenda for women's rights and drawing upon foreign experience: in other parts of the world there are 28 women's ministers, 12 ministries and over 30 national government offices addressing the needs of women.

Some argue that this would be best advanced through a separate Women's Ministry. Others point out that a 'token' Whitehall Department with no clear mandate and no budget of its own could easily be sidelined within the civil service; they propose a Women's Unit in the Treasury because, situated there, it would enjoy the authority of the most powerful of all the government Departments. Whichever option is chosen, the Women's Minister and her staff would have a 'campaigning' role rather than an administrative one. Her department would play a role comparable to that of the Cabinet Office. It would stimulate, coordinate and chase up government policy and activity across Whitehall. It would have an annual debate in government time in Parliament and publish an annual report, as well as impact statements in the Budget and other legislative measures.

Wherever the Women's Minister is located, there must be transparency and genuine consultation with women across all boundaries – from a national consultative body, and through regional offices for more direct consultation and liaison with local authorities, regional government, academics and grass-roots women's organisations.

Freshly established, it would have a new ethos to challenge and overcome the conservatism and elitism of Whitehall. By reaching out to involve women's groups and women at large, it could promote popular participation in government which would both strengthen socialist forces and mobilise much greater support for government policies. As such it could provide a model for the rest of Whitehall and so for a Labour Government of a different type. There are enormous constraints on any government seeking radical reforms. Preoccupied with the time-consuming process of administration and legislative change, not enough attention has been given to using the machinery of government to mobilise popular support for radical policies.

PUBLIC SERVANTS

Democratic accountability should also be increased over public appointments. Senior civil servants, heads of nationalised industries, senior officers in the armed forces and the police and other major public appointments should require endorsement by Select Committees shadowing Government Departments, with such endorsements submitted for acceptance to the Commons as a whole. And the many other public appointments now made from what almost seems like a list of 'the great and the good' ought to be made in a more open way. Positions should be advertised wherever possible, and nominations openly invited from the appropriate representative bodies.

Positive action including the introduction of quotas is needed to correct the gross imbalance in appointments which has produced a judiciary disproportionately right-wing, upper-class, male and white. For instance, there are no women Law Lords; just seven out of 138 high court judges are women; and there are only 42 women Queens Counsel out of 492. At present, judges are selected by the Lord Chancellor after recommendations from a legal profession which regulates itself and is not democratically accountable. Similarly, magistrates are chosen by the Lord Chancellor acting upon recommendations from local Advisory Committees appointed by – the Lord Chancellor. The system must be opened up and made democratically accountable, with appointments of Judges overseen by an independent Judicial Commission whose membership would itself be subject to endorsement by a Commons Select Committee. The Judicial Commission should also oversee the selection of magistrates by local advisory committees.

The security services should be made much more accountable, not least because – as Peter Wright confirmed in *Spycatcher* – they spent some time in the 1960s and 1970s trying to disrupt Labour Governments they were supposed to be serving. A Select Committee on Security Services was established in 1994, but it meets in secret and all members are appointed under Privy Council secrecy rules by the Prime Minister, not by Parliament. It is staffed from the Cabinet Office and its power is limited, even compared with other select committees.

In the absence of any clear statutory basis for defining their duties and responsibilities, the security services have virtually become a law unto themselves. A Security Act should be introduced establishing the powers under which the security services operate and defining the meaning of terms such as 'subversion' (whose present ambiguity allows far too much discretion to be exercised and has led to serious infringements of individual rights). Parliament should receive an annual report on their operations, and the powers of Select Committee should be beefed up. Other steps include extending the rights of MPs to receive answers to parliamentary questions (which are often blocked at present) and permitting much more scrutiny of expenditure (also currently denied).

ELECTORAL REFORM

Nobody can deny the validity of the charge 'unfair' levelled at Britain's electoral system. First-past-the-post does unquestionably result in all sorts of anomalies and the case for electoral reform is a strong one in principle. But in practice the systems of proportional representation (PR) proposed are very unsatisfactory. In particular they undermine MPs' local accountability to their constituencies, equally if not more important a criterion for democracy as fairness. Another option, the 'Alternative Vote' system, would satisfy the desire for greater fairness whilst protecting the other democratic principles which PR can be shown to undermine (see my *Proportional Misrepresentation*). But to support this argument it is necessary to examine PR in rather more detail than the other democratic reforms discussed in this chapter.

PR options

There are three main PR systems: the Single Transferable Vote in multi-member constituencies (STV), and the List and Additional Member systems.

STV, which operates in Ireland and has been most widely advocated in Britain by the Liberals, would replace our traditional single-member constituency averaging 65,000 electors with massive new multi-member constituencies containing about 315,000 electors, each of which would normally have five MPs. Votes would be cast in order of preference. During the count, bottom candidates would be progressively eliminated and their lower order preference votes transferred until five winners were elected. This would allow a very close approximation of votes cast to MPs elected, ensuring that each of the three major parties had at least some representation in all areas – which is denied under the winner takes all system.

List systems are widely used in Europe. Basically, electors vote for a party rather than an individual, and MPs are then selected from central or regional party lists of candidates, in numbers proportional to their party's total vote and allocated to local areas. They produce exact proportionality.

A compromise between the two is found in Germany. Here, proportionality is achieved by 'topping up' a single-member constituency system with a list system. Each elector has two votes. The first is for the 'constituency candidate', chosen on the same basis as in Britain. The second is for the party. Half the seats are filled by 'constituency MPs' elected on the first-past-the-post basis. The other half are allocated by a computer to candidates on regional party lists' to top up their total number of MPs to an amount that is directly proportional to their overall standing in the second or 'party' vote aggregated across each region.

The drawbacks of PR

Under STV rural constituencies would cover huge areas (in the case of Northern Scotland, thousands of square miles of land and sea.) Because of the problems associated with such large constituencies, a prestigious all-party and pro-PR commission set up by the Hansard Society recommended against the STV system in 1976. Its Report pointed out that in no case had STV been used in a country with a population anywhere near as great as Britain's.

Although they operate widely in Europe, the real objections to List systems are ones which have led most British supporters of PR to reject them. First, the link between the MP and the local constituents is completely broken. Second, power is further centralised by concentrating decision-making over the selection of candidates, and thereby the allocation of seats, into national (or, at best, regional) party organisations. Local community and even local party opinion can be virtually shut out under this arrangement.

In some respects preferable to other List systems, the German one nevertheless suffers from a number of disadvantages. The first-past-the-post constituency element still returns MPs who do not have to win a majority of the local electorate, offending one of the principles most keenly adhered to by PR supporters. And the list element of the system is controlled by party bureaucracies and is vulnerable to patronage: the great virtue of local party control is that the scope for patronage and central manipulation is limited. As one of Britain's leading PR advocates, Enid Lakeman, conceded: 'It is nearly impossible for the German voters to elect a person whom the Party organisation does not want, and quite impossible to reject one whom the party does want.'

When it considered the implications of introducing a German-type system in Britain, the Hansard Society report was especially concerned that the directly elected MPs could claim to be more legitimate than those appointed. It opted instead for the 'Additional Member' system. Under this, electors would vote exactly as they do now, filling three-quarters of the seats (480), except that these would be increased in size by about a third. The remaining quarter (160) would be used to 'top up' these seats, as in the German system, to achieve greater proportionality within each region of the country. In other words, the directly elected MPs would be supplemented by others in order to ensure that the number of seats in the regions corresponded as closely as possible to the proportion of votes cast for each party.

But it is significant that, despite its prestige and its dispassionate approach, the Hansard Report came up with an option suffering from major shortcomings. It still recommended two classes of MPs, those directly elected and those 'additional' members. Some constituencies would have two or maybe even three MPs; other constituencies would have just one MP. The 'additional' MPs need have no connection with the area to which they are allocated. On the basis of doing relatively well in another area, candidates would be allocated as additional members to seats without being endorsed by the local electorate.

In its conclusions the Hansard Commission was caught between a 'fundamental and unanimous' desire for electoral reform, and an honest acknowledgment that when it came to their actual implementation in Britain, all the PR options proposed had major, and in some cases fatal, defects. In that sense it expressed rather neatly the dominant dilemma of those who readily concede that the present system has shortcomings but who remain sceptical that democracy will be enhanced by adopting any of the alternatives so far proposed.

A further version of the Additional Member system was proposed by the Labour Party's 'Plant Report' in 1993 which contained perhaps the most thorough analysis of electoral reform yet attempted in Britain. What it termed a 'Mixed Member System' would have 500 single member constituencies of around 88,000 electors (about 30 per cent larger than at present). The remaining 150 MPs would be selected on a regional basis from the 'highest losers' in proportions to ensure that the overall composition of the House of Commons as closely as possible reflected overall Party votes. Within this system there are various options, including for the 500 single member seats to be elected by transferable vote. But it still suffers from the problem of two classes of MPs: some would have no constituency responsibilities.

PR AND ACCOUNTABILITY

The major defect of PR is that, whatever system is adopted, the scope for local accountability is reduced, and more power is sucked upwards to regional or national levels of the party structure. This undermines the tradition of *constituency* representation which is much stronger in Britain than most countries with PR.

Because of the sheer size of STV seats the influence of the ordinary party member – small enough as it is – would be still further reduced. It would also be almost impossible for the MP to develop a close or informed relationship with his or her constituents and with local issues. There is also likely to be some conflict between MPs in the same multi-member seats in deciding how their roles will differ. Will they seek to represent their own party supporters only? Or will they divide up the whole constituency, and take a section each?

Under List systems candidates will have to be known outside their local areas to be voted onto the party list, and those supported by party officials and organisers would have a head start. And although under the Additional Member system the 'topping up' procedure may preserve many single-member constituencies, these will still be a third larger in order to make room for the additional members in the Commons.

In addition, under PR the ordinary voter will have less opportunity to determine the composition of the government, because coalitions will become the norm rather than the exception. In general, the voter does not vote for a particular combination of parties to form a coalition. This is determined by a post-election political deal done at the centre, not by the people voting in their local polling booths. Coalitions inevitably mean wheeler-dealing behind closed doors and therefore a further concentration of power in the hands of political elites. This was acknowledged by the political scientist Giovanni Sartori, a proponent of an 'elitist' system of democracy. He argued quite unashamedly that PR would be a good thing because it invariably produces coalition governments which make it difficult for the electorate to 'pin down who is responsible' for decisions! Another political scientist, Hugh Berrington, argued in similar terms that STV would encourage a 'moderate leadership' of the Labour Party because it would 'help to protect the parliamentary party from extra-parliamentary control.' In other words, it would undermine the accountability of the political elite to local party members, community groups and trade unions.

Small centre parties usually hold the balance of power under PR, exercising an influence quite out of proportion to their popular support. In Germany, the Free Democrat Party has been described as 'the universal harlot of the German system; always in the governmental bed with the highest bidder.' It has failed to win a single constituency by a simple majority since 1957 yet has been in government for all but three years during this period. In Israel, tiny right-wing parties have held the balance of power. Besides being undemocratic, this can have a de-stabilising effect. In Europe, many countries regularly find themselves in the hands of 'caretaker' governments when it proves difficult to surmount the obstacles to forming a majority government. The Netherlands, Belgium and Italy have all been without effective governments for periods of weeks or months – for as long as seven months in the Netherlands in 1977.

THE ALTERNATIVE VOTE

A better option is the Alternative Vote, which is used in the Australian House of Representatives. The voting procedure is similar to STV: each voter numbers the candidates listed on the ballot paper in order of preference and these are transferred as bottom candidates are eliminated until somebody achieves more than 50 per cent and is elected. But because the AV retains the single-member constituency, it does not have the 'space' to be fully proportional.

The AV has a number of advantages. First, it would be fairer than first-past-the-post: it would stop the kind of 'exaggerated' parliamentary majorities the Tories achieved in 1970, 1979 and 1983 on just over 40 per cent of the vote by being much less biased against the third party. Second, the AV requires winning candidates to secure a majority of votes from their constituencies which is often not the case (in February 1974, for example, nearly two-thirds of MPs won on less than half the vote.) Third, there would be no fear of a 'wasted vote', so electors' first preferences could be more truly stated and would be a more reliable guide to their real views.

Fourth, it would undermine the tendency of the current system to concentrate party representation on a geographical basis, either between North and South or between cities and rural areas. Fifth, it would be easier than under PR to form majority governments, though coalitions would be more likely than under the current system. Sixth, it would be easier to understand than STV and much simpler to introduce. The existing constituencies could be retained, with only the ballot paper, method of voting and counting altered. Seventh, it would be a good system for by-elections, giving a more accurate picture of public attitudes to the government's policies than the existing system. Eighth, and most important, the single-member constituency would remain. This would overcome the central democratic objections to PR and maintain local accountability to the community and to party members. Finally, Parliament would have to determine any change in the electoral system, and the AV is much more likely to get through because each of the PR options would invite MPs to vote themselves out of their own jobs.

The Labour Party has proposed a referendum on electoral reform allowing voters to choose whether they wish to change and, if so, to which system. But electoral reform, like a Bill of Rights and a written constitution, is part of a momentous programme of reform which would take a number of Parliaments to secure. To become a modern, effective democracy, what matters more than anything else is decentralising power: this is the real, practical priority for democratic renewal.

CHAPTER 3

Equality

Although there has been some trendy talk that the longstanding socialist concern with equality has been superseded by new buzzwords such as 'community', 'choice', 'flexibility,' and 'opportunity', Britain remains an elitist society. Wealth and family status are still important tickets to health, education, opportunity, work and high living standards. Senior posts in companies, the City, the civil service, the judiciary, and the military are still disproportionately occupied by people from a narrow upper-class, public school background.

Such elitism flows from the still deeply entrenched class structure which is the main source of inequality. In 1989 Ralph Miliband showed (in *Divided Societies: Class Struggle in Contemporary Capitalism*) that there is a small 'dominant' class at the top, with the vast majority of people in various 'subordinate' classes. At the top of the dominant class is, as C. Wright Mills termed it, a 'power elite' of people who own or control the commanding heights of the economy and the media, and who are in strategic positions in the state apparatus. There are also other important sources of inequality – notably between men and women – which are only loosely connected to the basic class divide, and indeed operate within classes. Inequalities of class, sex, race and disability have placed severe limitations on democratic and individual freedom for the majority of the people.

Britain's class system has also had a deadening impact upon industrial relations. It reinforces old practices and anachronistic cultural behaviour. It blocks opportunities for workers to contribute their own ideas and skills to the running of their enterprises. It breeds conflict between employee and employer. By acting as a barrier against individual advance and self-development, class inequalities have encouraged the 'industrial backwardness' which has been such a marked feature of Britain's steady economic decline.

Britain has for generations been plagued by a unique ethos of inequality buried deep in its social structure: the ethos of Eton, Oxbridge and the amateur gentleman of private means. But this is intertwined with the system of capitalism which is by its very nature unequal. As Will Hutton argues, (in *The State We're In*): 'Without the incentives offered by inequality, either as a reward or punishment, a capitalist economy simply loses its dynamism... There needs to be fear and greed in the system in order to make it tick.' So unless capitalism is fundamentally reformed and replaced by socialism, the prospect of eradicating inequality and creating a classless society is slight.

Since 1979 Britain has being going determinedly in the opposite direction. As was shown by the report of the Rowntree Foundation Inquiry into income and wealth published in February 1995, the legacy of Britain's recent return to reliance upon the free market is a society more divided and more unequal than for over a hundred years, with an increasingly alienated underclass.

This is not simply unjust, it is also grossly inefficient. Creating a more equal society is not only a moral imperative but a practical one. Unless the widening chasm of inequality is reversed, there is no hope of building a Britain that is secure and comfortable to live in, let alone a Britain which, for the majority of its citizens, is free. The new right has no answer to this imperative. Indeed, as the destructive consequences of the free market bite more deeply, there is pressure for still deeper cuts in social security and public spending – precisely the policies which ferment social instability, rising crime and a declining quality of life for the majority. As the Rowntree report argued: 'Just as in the last century it was in the interests of all to introduce public health measures to combat the spread of infectious diseases fostered by poverty, so in this century it is in the interests of all to remove the factors which are fostering the social diseases of drugs, crime, political extremism and unrest.'

As Will Hutton argues, Britain is now a 30:30:40 society. The first 30 per cent are severely *disadvantaged* through being officially or unofficially unemployed. The second 30 per cent are *marginalised* and *insecure*, trapped in low paid, casual or temporary and often part-time work. The final 40 per cent are *privileged* in the sense of being in relatively secure jobs and enjoying rising living standards, although they too are divided between rich and poor. As a result more than half the population are living in poverty or under the shadow of stress and insecurity. A 1993 survey of members of the GMB union found that only 6 per cent felt their jobs were secure. The consequences strike deep into society: as Hutton notes, Britain has the most deregulated labour market and the highest divorce rate in Europe.

So the left's aspiration for equality needs to be restated. It is ironic that during current debates, some of those traditionally regarded as being on the right of the Labour Party have been most persuasively insistent on retaining equality as a goal of policy. In his book, *Choose Freedom*, published in 1987, Roy Hattersley quoted his mentor Anthony Crosland's definition of socialism : 'It is about the pursuit of equality and the protection of freedom – in the knowledge that until we are truly equal, we will not be truly free.' Many of those loudly proclaiming their leftist credentials in the late 1970s and early 1980s have lurched rapidly past Hattersley, losing their ideological moorings, to embrace a sanitised, civilised version of the new right's agenda. Whilst they may well not be caught in public opposing Hattersley's insistence upon equality, in practice their stance on policies, for example in education, denies it. As he argued: 'Socialism is the promise that the generality of men and women will be given the economic strength which makes the choices of a free society have some meaning.' Echoing R.H.Tawney, Hattersley also makes it clear that in its consideration of education, health, welfare or tax policy, socialism cannot defend the privileges of a few if the aspirations of the many for freedom and real opportunity of *outcome* (and not simply of *choice*) are to be achieved. It is not enough to have some theoretical 'choice': equality of resources is a pre-requisite for choice to be exercised in practice and for individual opportunities to be realised.

At the same time the implementation of equality needs to be reformulated. For the statist version of the welfare society bequeathed a social system which, through its weaknesses, opened the door to the new right. The social settlement during and after the Second World War, which brought three decades of unprecedented prosperity, full employment and universal welfare, was based on a centralised, bureaucratic and paternalist system. Public services were top down and often inefficiently delivered. Management of education and health was too centralised and remote. A dependency culture was created: rather than a system of welfare which created opportunity, it tended to trap people. It was over-rigid, too, as in the failure to grant council tenants both a say and a stake in their homes. The political reaction to the unresponsiveness of the welfare state was successfully channelled by the right. They succeeded in turning criticism of the way the system functioned into large scale rejection of its principles, with the embrace of the free market and minimal state.

The left has now found itself facing a different obstacle. Reversing the cumulative legacy of inequality and injustice will require a huge shift in the way society is organised and a positive role for public spending, together with progressive taxation to fund it. Standing in the way, however, is a successful hijack by the right to focus the terms of reference of political debate on low income tax and public spending cuts. Rather than confronting this agenda, the left in general and the Labour Party in particular has appeared to follow behind with its own agenda for a minimalist state. As a result the debate between the main parties is in the common currency of 'promising not to spend what we cannot afford'. This may well be electorally prudent, but risks offering short-term fixes which ignore and ultimately cannot conquer the long-term problems British society faces. The case for a new egalitarianism needs to be made, beginning with the link between social justice and economic success which the new right may seek to deny but which is now clearer than ever before.

THE INEFFICIENCY OF INEQUALITY

Policies which reward the few and abandon the many are economically counter-productive. During fifteen years of Conservative rule the number of people dependent upon means-tested benefits doubled from one in twelve of the population to one in six, and the proportion of total public spending accounted for by social security went up by a third. It is not only tragic that millions more people have been forced to struggle with poverty, ill health, unemployment and homelessness. Their plight is also eloquent testimony to a shameful waste and misallocation of public resources. Whereas public expenditure remained constant, at an average 44 per cent of GDP between 1977 and 1994, its distribution altered fundamentally and in a manner which is an indctment of the huge inefficiency of free market economics. Within this constant total, what has been called 'renewal spending' (i.e. investment in the future of the country, such as in industry, education, research and development, transport and housing) has fallen by £21 billion. At the same time 'rescue spending' (paying for the failures of economic policy, largely through benefits) has risen by £22 billion. This direct switch of spending from renewal to rescue demonstrates the huge economic cost to the nation of social inequalities. The failure of policy means massively subsidising inequalities, to the detriment of investing in infrastructure, industry and skills. Straitjacketed by the dogma of 'low tax, low spend', renewal spending continues to diminish and the wasteful subsidy of rescue spending becomes self-perpetuating.

The tragedy is that the 1980s offered the United Kingdom a financial resources bonanza. The country literally struck oil in the 1970s. Whereas prior to 1979 oil tax revenues hardly featured, by 1981 they accounted for over a quarter of average tax revenues as a percentage of GDP. From 1979 to 1994 the Government received £122 billion from North Sea oil, a unique windfall. When £70 billion of privatisation proceeds are added in, the potential for meeting social and investment need was immense. However, the pot of gold became the Tory Party's swag bag. In effect UK Ltd was subjected to a hostile takeover from Conservative PLC which asset stripped the country, leaving it in the hands of the receiver.

As a result the UK was not able to defend itself when the good times turned sour. The natural immune system a nation builds up, of a comprehensive welfare safety net, a skilled workforce and well educated future generations, a core industrial and manufacturing base, a transport and amenities infrastructure and an accessible health care system had been stripped away.

The costs of paying people not to work are equally massive. By 1994, the cost to the Treasury of those officially unemployed was about £25 billion; additionally the number of people on Income Support had reached 5.6 million (ten per cent of the population) at an annual total cost of £16 billion. Not only does the state financially support the unemployed and their families, but the resources spent on their education and training are totally wasted: billions are blown away as engineers, nurses, miners, teachers, mechanics, technicians and others sign on the dole.

A low wage economy, based on a reservoir of unemployment, and employees living and working in poor and dangerous conditions, is grossly inefficient. For employers, low pay breeds lack of commitment to the job. For employers, cheap labour means there is less incentive to become more efficient and to reduce costs by investing in new techniques and skills. Lack of motivation encourages absenteeism and high staff turnover which in turn places extra burdens upon industry, including sick pay and the costs of replacing an individual. Economically, it is therefore bad for skills, productivity, innovation and development.

The Tories have actively promoted a low wage economy – and then complained at the consequent cost in benefits. They have effectively subsidised low wages through granting family credit to those with dependents who earn low incomes. There has been a dramatic increase in the annual Family Credit bill from £394 million in 1988-89 to £929 million in 1992-93, with a projected rise to £1,600 million by 1996-97. The total cost of all in-work benefits doubled between 1991 and 1995 when it stood at £2.4 billion. It would be more efficient and productive to invest such rescue spending in better paid employment that offers improved job security and working conditions. Subsidising a low wage economy perpetuates a low skill workforce and short-termism in investment and training.

The poor are also the real victims of the soaring crime rate in our dislocated society. The 1992 British Crime Survey found that those households most at risk of burglary had an annual income of less than £10,000. Manual worker households had a higher risk of being burgled than non-manual workers. However, everybody picked up the bill for rising crime. Household contents insurance premiums jumped from an average of £71 to £114 between 1987 and 1993 – a rise of 60 per cent. Motor insurance premiums doubled from £162 to £338 over the same period. In 1988, the total value of property stolen was £1.6 billion; by 1992 this figure had shot up to £4 billion – a rise of 151 per cent.

Home Office funding for victim support schemes rose from £3.4 million in 1988-89 to £7.3 million in 1992-93, with spending forecast to rise to £11 million by 1996-97. Of greater concern, however, is the high rising cost of payments by the Criminal Injuries Compensation Board, up from £89 million in 1988-89 to £152 million in 1992-93 and estimated to rise to £183 million by 1995-96. These are the financial consequences of the social collapse which has seen crime more than double since 1979.

Free market mania is a culprit in another important respect. A report in 1994, by Richard Wilkinson of Sussex University, showed that in Britain, throughout the 1980s, as differentials in income widened, life expectancies for men and women between 15 and 44 began to fall. As Wilkinson explains:

> *Within* countries mortality rates are closely associated with people's social and economic circumstances. But when comparisons are made *between* developed countries they show that average life expectancy is not related to a country's wealth. The apparent paradox arises because health is affected more by relative than by absolute income levels. This is confirmed by the close relationship between income distribution and national mortality rates. Not only is life expectancy longest in countries where income differences are smallest, but data shows that changes in income distribution affect the rate of change in life expectancy.

In Britain Wilkinson identifies 1985 as the time from which differentials widened dramatically and other indicators reacted accordingly. The consistent downward trend in death rates which he monitored from 1975 changed in 1985 when death rates failed to fall nearly as fast as they had done prior to that date. Figures for male suicides also showed an alarming rise from the mid-1980s following relative stability from 1975. In fact rates doubled between 1984 and 1990. (By contrast countries such as Sweden, Norway and the Netherlands, which have narrow income differences, have a life expectancy two to three years higher.)

Accompanying the low wage economy has been a rise in real terms, in living standards for those at the top. Between 1993 and 1994 alone the wealth of the top 500 richest people in Britain rose by 16.8 per cent from £42 billion to £49 billion. One per cent of the population own half the land. Between 1979 and 1992 the poorest 10 per cent of households saw no growth in real income and an 18 per cent fall after housing costs were taken into account; while the wealthiest 10 per cent of households saw their income increase by 57 per cent before, and 62 per cent after, housing costs. Under the Thatcherite 'miracle' wealth flowed one way – to the wealthy.

Trickle-down economics does not work. It has left a nation where one in five 21-year olds are functionally innumerate and one in seven functionally illiterate. In 1974, six per cent of the population (2 million people) had insufficient literacy skills to cope with everyday life. In 1987, 13 per cent of young adults had numeracy and literacy difficulties: a pattern suggesting that 6 million adults (three times the previous number) have literacy and numeracy problems. All this is on top of a skills base which has been falling behind our competitor countries as public resourcing of training and education has declined.

To argue for publicly funded policies to tackle these problems of inefficiency and inequality is not to indulge in soft options. The right has no answer except to seek to contain the divisive and disruptive consequences through an increasingly authoritarian, centralised state continuously plagued by squaring the impossible circle of rising rescue costs on the one hand and low income tax demands on the other. Only socialist interventionism offers a solution.

HIGH QUALITY WELFARE

The Tories have succeeded in creating feelings of insecurity in every nook and cranny of life. At the centre of this is economic insecurity: no job, no stamp, no benefit entitlement, no chance of a hospital bed when you most need it. (With an ageing population, care of the elderly is a particularly thorny problem – and the government response has been to privatise elderly care, forcing those who have paid into the national insurance system all their lives to pay twice by parting with their savings. 176,000 NHS elderly beds have been closed since 1979 and private beds have jumped from 26,095 in 1979 to 134,510 in 1993).

During our lifetimes we all pass through the stages of being net beneficiaries and net contributors to the welfare state: it does not benefit only a minority, of the poor, ill or disabled. For example, most of us receive our education from the state, use the NHS, and, until recently, could expect to receive reasonable pensions. High quality, universal welfare provision is therefore essential. There has been a great deal of seductive sophistry pointing to an abandonment of the left's traditional commitment to this ambition, and its replacement by a programme of 'targeting' selective benefits upon the needy. It is suggested that modern society 'cannot afford' the welfare state, that decent pensions cannot be financed because of the burdens of an ageing population and that universal benefits channel resources to people who don't need them.

Before confronting each of these myths, it is worth identifying common ground. Palpably, the world has changed since the days of Beveridge fifty years ago, and his assumption of full, male, bread-winning employment. Today there is mass, structural unemployment. Women form almost half the workforce. The problem if anything (partly due to the low wage economy) is now *male* unemployment, with one in five able men of working age unable to find jobs. With earnings inequality greater now than at any time since 1886, with one in three children growing up in poverty, and with a huge gulf between poor and affluent pensioners, of course things have changed. There is also quite rightly a refusal to accept the 'big daddy' paternalism of welfare provision delivered centrally, unresponsive to individual wishes or needs. Clearly the welfare state needs to adapt to current needs; however this does not necessitate a departure from the universal principle; nor does it mean that high quality benefits for all are a utopian desire.

Let us start with the question of pensions. The argument that society cannot finance decent state pensions may be instinctively plausible but it is plainly wrong. The UK's population is ageing but not on a scale to justify the panic and alarm whipped up by the right. In 1991, those over statutory pension age made up 16.5 per cent of the population compared with 11.4 per cent fifty years before. Further increases are forecast but, as the welfare academic John Hills argues: 'even if pensions kept up with overall living standards, the total net effects on public finances over the next fifty years would add up to an addition of about 5 per cent of this country's GDP.' This is an amount relatively easily financed, certainly by a country committed to equality, and to the need for security in old age.

Although pensioners' average income rose by 35 per cent in the decade to 1991, this average was skewed by big increases for the richest pensioners. Thirty per cent of all pensioners were among the lowest income fifth of the population in 1991, and, like other sections of the population, the gap between worst and best off has grown since 1979. Despite the widespread belief that most pensioners now have occupational pensions or some other sort of private provision, two thirds of single pensioners and nearly half of pensioner couples receive £20 or less per week from occupational pensions or savings. State benefits remain by far the most important source of income to retired people. In 1991, 70 per cent of pensioners received at least half their income from benefits and 50 per cent received at least three-quarters.

Furthermore, the fact that affluent pensioners receive the state pension is not an argument against its universal provision any more than the fact that the better off can make use of NHS hospitals or state schools is an argument against free schooling or health : a progressive taxation system (i.e. one which increases with higher incomes) can rectify any resulting anomaly or inefficiency in the allocation of public resources. The real problem since 1980 is that we have had an increasingly regressive tax system, which has led to higher taxes for those on low incomes. Thus everyone is concerned about high taxation and this has encouraged the illusion of a fiscal crisis when there need not be one.

Meanwhile the state pension withers on the vine. Since 1980 when the Thatcher government broke the link which triggered pension increases in line with either average earnings or inflation (whichever was the greater), the state pension has fallen behind general living standards. Since 1979, earnings have risen significantly faster than prices: by 270 per cent compared with 175 per cent. By 1994, breaking the link to earnings meant that a single pensioner was worse off by £1130 annually (at 1995 prices) and the gross annual saving to the Government stood at over £10 billion. Such a massive switch of resources away from the retired to the rest was bound to increase pensioner poverty, force more onto income support and bring demands for reform.

In common with the Tories, Labour's Social Justice Commission under Gordon Borrie proposed to maintain the state pension but allow it to continue to shrivel relative to general living standards as reflected in earnings. Provided earnings continue to rise more than prices – as has historically been the case in the long run – then during the next century the state pension will be purely tokenistic: whereas it was worth 20 per cent of male average earnings in 1977-78, it could fall to less than 9 per cent in the year 2020 and 6 per cent in 2040. Unlike the Tories, of course, Borrie proposes other important reforms. He suggests a new 'pension guarantee': a form of tax benefit integration acting as a supplement to raise incomes to a guaranteed level above both the existing retirement pension and income support. He also proposed a new universal contributory 'second pension', perhaps based upon the State Earnings Related Pension Scheme (SERPs).

Done in the name of the left, the motive for policies like these is clearly different from the right's cost cutting agenda. But the result can be very similar, as the internationally respected social policy expert Professor Peter Townsend pointed out in criticising the inadequacy of the proposal. First of all, 'targeting' or 'selectivity' involves means testing. There is no other way of providing something like a 'pensions guarantee'. And means testing inevitably means that the poor get 'targeted' alright, but in the discriminatory fashion which has traditionally been so oppressive – and which means many people are deterred from applying even when eligible for benefit. The second and equally important objection is quite different. If welfare provision – whether pensions, child benefit, health, social services, housing or education – is targeted primarily upon what are deemed to be the deprived, then the great mass of the population is excluded. The middle classes and the better off working classes who constitute the majority of people will no longer have a stake in the welfare system. And, not having a stake in it, they will first have to look for private insurance solutions, then rebel at paying twice and finally refuse to fund it, expressing as J.K. Galbraith warns in *The Culture of Contentment* 'righteous anger over having to pay taxes for services they don't even use'. The result? An inevitable spiral of decline into an under-financed American-style sink welfare system in which a 'safety net' is supposed only to catch (but actually never does) the very poor. The universality principle should be modernised of course, but not jettisoned: we *can* afford benefits like decent state pensions for everyone, financed through a system of progressive taxation.

A universal benefit system could also assist in bridging the gap between welfare and work. The poorest have found themselves increasingly squeezed between a harsher benefit regime on the one hand, and on the other a combination of low paid job opportunities and the replacement of untaxed benefit with taxed wages (which can mean losing up to 97p of every extra pound earned), which do not make it worthwhile to work. There is a strong case for a universal basic income paid to everybody in or out of work. A Citizen's Income paid by the state to everyone as a right of citizenship could eventually replace most of the existing tangle of means-tested benefits. Any income earned on top of this basic sum would be taxable, but earning it would not affect the amount received from the state. The practical implementation of the principle needs further examination. Although it would cost more, this could be offset by reducing the bureaucracy of the social security system at a stroke.

A number of myths about maintaining welfare need debunking. In the 1990s Britain produced more than double the national wealth or GDP of the 1950s (at constant prices). Of course we can afford decent pensions, good schools, adequate housing or a minimum wage, especially if rescue spending on economic and social failure is switched to renewal spending on investment. The idea that an ageing population means too few workers to finance welfare is another myth – there are more people in the labour market than ever before (largely due to the growth of women in work). The so-called crisis in welfare payments is not caused by people living too long, rather by mass unemployment. Another myth is that single parents choose to live off the state. Actually, the vast majority are widowed, divorced or separated. They didn't choose to become single parents. And many can't work because of inadequate childcare support. Universal benefits like child benefit are not wasteful: their value is that they go to the poor without the stigma of means-testing or the obstacles of form-filling, and they create a stake for everyone in the welfare system. Nor are all social security recipients a separate impoverished underclass. Most people who have to claim benefit do so because they have reached a difficult time in their life; unemployment, long-term sickness, industrial injury, parenthood, retirement. It is very easy for people who have become poor to be trapped in poverty – they have spent their savings and can lose benefits if they increase earnings. High quality welfare can help people to escape from the trap.

The case for retaining universal benefits, funded from progressive taxation, has never been more pressing. At a time when economic insecurity plagues a majority of the population we need a modernised and stream-lined system of delivery, with the stigma and bureaucracy of means-testing once more removed, a system no longer based on paternalism, but on the assumption that everyone benefits from high quality welfare. Such a system could be popular with the whole population, and give us all a stake in the well being of the nation.

STATUTORY MINIMUM WAGE

Another critical imperative for social justice is legislation for a statutory minimum wage. Nearly ten million workers in Britain earn poverty wages. The demeaning spiral into poverty pay is illustrated in South Wales where security jobs have been advertised on the basis: '£1.80 an hour – bring your own dog'. A minimum wage must eradicate such pauperism. The level at which it is set is clearly crucial. About 330,000 people earn less than £1.50 an hour and over 1.1 million less than £2.50 an hour. The Labour Party's commitment in the 1992 election to set it at half median male earnings would have meant a rate of £4.15 an hour in 1995. That would help four and a half million workers, 70 per cent of whom are women; a figure of £3 (which is the UK equivalent of the US minimum) would assist three million fewer workers, and again most of the losers would be women.

A figure of around £4 would hardly generate affluence: barely £160 for a forty hour week. But it would boost spending power, raise aggregate demand and thereby create more jobs. There is consequently a strong economic case for a minimum wage. At around £4 hourly it would have other financial benefits. Virtually nothing would be added to the public sector paybill, but extra tax and national insurance revenues would come in and about 300,000 people would be lifted off dependence upon social security. So taxpayers would benefit. Currently, employers of low paid workers are subsidised by the tax-payer through benefit payments. In the private sector the impact would hardly be massive. The CBI has estimated it would add just one per cent extra on the nation's paybill, and still less on prices. A survey by Industrial Relations Services of 527 firms revealed that two-thirds said there would be no increase on their pay bill, with the rest saying it would add less than 5 per cent on paybill. Almost all – 86 per cent – said there would be no consequent job losses.

General economic efficiency would be improved. Low wages are not a productivity incentive. If employers can get away with poverty pay, they have no incentive to invest in better training or modern equipment. On the contrary such investment can leave them vulnerable to being undercut by other companies with even lower wages. Cheap labour is also closely associated with high staff turnover and absenteeism – major inefficiency factors.

Over nearly two decades Britain's record confirms that a low wage, deregulated economy is no passport to economic success. During this period Britain created just 3 per cent more jobs; at the same time France created twice as many, Germany four times and Italy six times as many. The abolition of the 24 main Wages Councils in 1993, withdrawing protection from 2.5 million workers, did not produce the much trumpeted jobs explosion promised by its free market advocates of 'flexibility'.

The right falsely claims that such a policy would result in job losses. (The 1970 Equal Pay Act was also opposed on similar, spurious grounds). In France OECD economists found that a minimum wage has had no disemployment impact on adults and only a very marginal adverse impact upon youth employment. In the US, the evidence shows that rising wages do not cost jobs. In 1991 the US government raised the national minimum wage in two stages to $4.25 from $3.35. Successive academic studies showed no resulting job losses. In the State of New Jersey, the minimum wage was raised additionally to $5.05 whilst neighbouring Pennsylvania kept to the $4.25 national rate. Yet in fast food restaurants employment actually rose in 'expensive' New Jersey and fell in 'cheap' Pennsylvania. Harvard economist Richard Freeman underlines this and points out that the substantial drop in the value of the US minimum wage during the 1980s was accompanied by a rise in unemployment amongst the unskilled workers most affected.

The American experience confirms that workers may actually be priced *into* jobs by a decent national minimum wage because they have more incentive to work than to remain on benefit. As a 1993 London School of Economics study of Britain argued: 'Minimum wages significantly compress the distribution of earnings and, contrary to conventional economic wisdom but in line with several recent US studies, do not have a negative impact upon employment. If anything, the relationship between minimum wages and employment is positive.' Other countries demonstrate that a strong dynamic economy with high levels of investment and skills and modern infrastructure are far more successful than Britain's cheapskate economy. And a 1995 study by the International Labour Organisation showed that there was no automatic link between high wage rates and unemployment levels.

A FREE, UNIVERSAL HEALTH SERVICE

Re-establishing a genuinely National Health Service which remains free at the point of use and where access is based on need and not on the ability to pay, is one of the greatest challenges for the left. This legacy of 1945 is cherished and the left has a genuinely popular mandate to nurture it, by sweeping aside the monstrosity of bureaucratically rigged market forces whilst at the same enhancing the principle of localised management and control that puts patients first and values the work of NHS staff.

The wholesale re-invention of the NHS as a market in 1990 by Conservative ideologues has resulted in massive upheaval, chaos and demoralisation, and an uneven distribution of facilities and services across Britain. The development of a commercialised and competitive internal market, based on contract systems, has destroyed quality and created winners and losers. As the Assistant Chief Officer of the Kent Ambulance Service said in March 1993: 'it would be naive to say (that) working within a budget does not affect quality'. The independent King's Fund recognised that 'in a market, the bottom-line financial viability of an organisation is at risk of becoming more important than patient care.' By making hospitals and doctors compete with each other in an artificially constructed market, the principle of universal access has been undermined. Whilst all patients are equal, some are more equal than others. Valuable resources are also squandered away from patient care as independent trust hospitals build up their corporate image. Southampton University Trust, for example, spent almost £60,000 on identikit uniforms for its secretaries whilst more than 10,000 patients were on the waiting list – the equivalent sum could buy 1,000 outpatient appointments or 22 hip replacements. Additional costs also result from the phenomenon of peripatetic patients, forced by the system to travel to distant hospitals (sometimes literally at the other end of the country) for treatment.

Healthcare has been turned into a financial commodity, and it is this aspect which is the most sinister of the reforms. Placing a *cost* rather than a *value* on healthcare necessitates judgements about the financial rather than the medical worth of treating somebody. Making health equivalent to a business and subjecting it to the market is equivalent to treating patients as company stocks, with the share value of Hospital Trusts reflected in the contracts they have.

Buying care or treatment (the 'purchaser' function assigned to health authorities and doctors who are 'fundholders') has been separated from the delivery of it (the 'provider' role given to Trusts). The new, market-driven NHS has Trust hospitals which operate as independent businesses providing health care, yet competing with each other both for 'consumers' who need care and for 'purchaser' Health Authorities or GPs who have the resources. Health care purchased on patients' behalf by Health Authorities (HAs) and GP fundholders has necessitated a bureaucratic contracts system. It is further complicated by the division between GP fundholders and non-fundholding GPs. Whereas GP fundholders purchase services directly without the HA acting as a go-between, non-fundholders still depend on health authorities to purchase healthcare in their area on behalf of their registered patients.

The result has been nightmarish complexity and all the predictable anomalies and distortions which come with commercialising a caring service. Patients have rightly become deeply suspicious that accountancy rather than medical need motivates doctors and managers when providing for their care. The old 'contract' of trust between patient and doctor has broken down. No-one trusts the Trusts. The market has in-built inconsistencies and discriminations that vary both the access to, and the treatments available to, patients from the same communities. For example, two elderly women living in a street which falls on either side of a HA boundary may receive very different treatment for a similar, relatively straight-forward hip replacement. One HA may have successfully contracted for the operation to include transportation to and from the hospital with follow-up community physiotherapy (thus allowing an earlier discharge and freeing a much-needed bed). The other may not, instead, for commercial reasons sacrificing quality for quantity – say 30 hip operations at £3000 each. Both women will get their new hips but one will probably have to wait longer for it and take longer to recover fully.

The nature of purchasing has created a two-tier system in provision. GP fundholders have had huge capital allowances for investment in management and computing systems to establish contracting mechanisms. Administrative costs for GP fundholders can be as high as £80,000 per practice whereas non-fundholders' costs are met more cheaply and efficiently. Generous budgetary allowances to entice doctors to become fundholders meant that GP fundholders made a 'profit' of £120 million in the three years to 1994 – savings which they were allowed to keep and re-invest. They have therefore had a financial advantage in purchasing for their patients. Trusts see them as more lucrative sources of additional income on top of their health authority contracts. So GP fundholders have been able to strike better deals for their patients with Trusts.

Because in the early years of the scheme fundholders have been in a minority, and a source of additional income to Trusts with separate contracts, exclusive arrangements have been negotiated. These have included shorter waiting times, guaranteed appointments with the consultant (rather than a junior doctor with less experience) and access to better services (such as fast-track pathology results and direct diagnostic X-rays). This system is iniquitous, creating different qualities of service depending on which practice you are registered with, which HA area you live in and which Trust your purchaser is contracted with. The system has encouraged some GP fundholders to dump patients with expensive, chronic, long term conditions like diabetes from their lists. Whether fundholding will have any advantages if, as the Conservatives intend, all GPs are in the system is a moot point: once having cut doctors loose their resources can not easily be trimmed back.

With the abolition of Regional Health Authorities and the government favouring 'light-touch control' at the Department of Health, there is no coordinated strategic planning. The planning of healthcare should not be left to spurious market forces where foresight consists of annual planning rather than the longer forecasting required in a complex, hi-tech service. Authority for strategic planning has been devolved to an inappropriate level – it is too small to have a sufficient overview. With vital specialist services such as organ transplants, neurosurgery and burns and plastics demanded by small numbers of people over large areas, the GP fundholder or HA contracting system is too limited. The regional planning and provision is now at the mercy of local purchasers, who often cannot afford to sustain such regional specialities out of local budgets. Co-ordination between HAs and GP fundholders for purchasing the most sophisticated and expensive healthcare is a massive burden on their resources and expertise, with which the system cannot cope.

The competitive element of the market is stifling innovation and destroying cooperation between providers and HAs or GP fundholders. Where Trusts are competing for contracts there have to be winners and losers. If a Trust wins contracts (which are usually short term, preventing long-term planning), then its services stay in business; if it doesn't they are cut. Equally, if as a patient your purchaser has secured the right contract, then you get the right treatment – if not you receive inappropriate treatment or none at all. Nowhere is this more obvious than with the care of the elderly. It is scandalous that accidents of geography are the determinants of provision. Cases where hospitals are targeting each other as opponents who must be defeated or eliminated reveal the destructive nature of competition: for example the titanic behind-scenes struggle in West London between Hammersmith, Charing Cross and Chelsea & Westminster Hospitals, each trying to knock the other out of the market-place.

Ironically, the market has become a bureaucrat's dream with each purchaser and provider requiring the paraphernalia of contracts departments, business managers and public relations. Family doctors and hospital consultants matter less than spin doctors and PR consultants. Since the reforms, the number of nurses in Britain has been cut by around 27,000 whilst senior administrators' and accountants' posts have increased by 36,000. The associated spending on bureaucracy shows a staggering increase of 286 per cent in England alone (from £156 million in 1989/90 to £602 million in 1993/94). Expenditure on staff cars – half of which are not used by front-line medical staff – rose by 47 per cent over two years to £78 million. Meanwhile management consultants have swooped in for rich pickings (in 1994 the government spent £980,000 for their advice on 'market-testing' – a code for future further privatisation.) The paperchase that has been created is irrelevant to health care need, and is expensive and divisive. The internal market should be dismantled and the NHS renationalised with local management of health encouraged.

Neither should the continuance of a two-tier service in primary care be accepted. GP fundholding should be replaced with joint commissioning – a system under which doctors cooperate rather then compete and which plans ahead for all patients, rather than queue jumps for a favoured few. Instead of competing, GPs would plan their services in line with local needs and in conjunction with relevant local authorities. Freed from huge administrative load and waste, GPs could nevertheless retain the autonomy which came with fundholding.

Privatisation of the NHS by stealth must be stopped in its tracks – and the colonisation of the health system by quango must be re-conquered by accountable democrats everywhere and at all levels from central government to community health councils. This is necessarily a re-active agenda. But there is no alternative to reversing reforms which have inflicted such damage. And there is a widespread consensus on this across the left-right divide. As the Conservative turned Labour moderniser, John Gray, a Fellow of Jesus College, Oxford, wrote in January 1995: 'Labour, which is rightly friendly to markets in many areas of policy, will be entirely justified if it commits itself to reversing the Tory market reforms. Indeed sweeping away the NHS's current managerialist structures and returning power and initiatives to doctors and their patients, may well prove to be a vital element in any Labour modernising project.'

Like education, health has undergone such massive organisational upheaval that the prospect of unravelling it may be daunting. That is why it is important to spell out the scale of the problem and gain the public's support for the scale of the changes necessary. Central to this is understanding why the pre-reformed NHS was so successful in the first place; it was funded from direct taxation, there were very limited payments on a fee-for-service basis and the monopoly employer was both willing and anxious to control wages and salaries whilst applying common employment standards nationwide. And *everybody* benefited from it – including the middle classes who invested in it both financially and emotionally.

The Tory legacy of privatisation and commercialisation is a depressing one. In the first four years following the start of the internal market in 1990, one in eight (a total of 304) hospitals closed and 36,000 beds were lost. Since 1979, one in every three NHS beds has been cut. Meanwhile private beds outside the NHS have almost doubled from 6,671 to 11,391 by 1994. In 1984, 92.5 per cent of all UK spending on health was through the NHS; by 1993 it only accounted for 81.1 per cent Three quarters of all NHS consultants now have earnings from private practice; prior to 1980 less than half did private work. There is also privatisation by stealth through market testing and funding of new hospitals through private finance.

NHS dentists are an endangered species and the system is in crisis. In the three year period from 1992-1995, 830,000 adults and children were 'deregistered' as NHS patients as a direct result of government policy. If you are unfortunate enough to live in Huntingdon you have only a 2 per cent chance of finding an NHS dentist. One result is an increase in sugar-based decay, estimated to cost the NHS £1 billion a year. The restoration of free dental check-ups and the development of a national oral health programme are two minor but essential steps forward. This will also save money in the long run because regular dental check-ups have a preventative effect.

Poor health isn't just costly to the individual, it costs the nation billions of pounds too. This should not just be measured in the obvious ways of avoidable medical treatment, over-prescribing of drugs and sickness and disablity benefit payments, but also in time off work and reduced productivity. In 1994, some 280 million working days a year were lost to sickness – of which up to 70 million were due to mental illness. (By contrast, only 255,000 working days were lost in industrial disputes). This translates to an estimated lost output of £18 billion a year. Socialists should underline the fact that health policy is directly linked to wider economic objectives including targeting social deprivation as the prime cause of ill-health.

A 1995 British Medical Association study confirmed the importance of inequality in health policy. One in four people now lives in a household with an income below half the national average, compared to one in ten in 1979. The bottom tenth of the population are 17 per cent worse off after housing costs than in 1979 and the distribution of income is more unequal today than at any time since the mid-1880s. The health gap between rich and poor has some startling regional variations: ill health is concentrated in deprived areas while the most affluent are invariably the most healthy. Infant mortality is 13.8 per 1000 births in Gateshead compared to 1.1 per 1000 in Huntingdon. The death rate of 15-44 year olds living in deprived parts of Glasgow increased by 9 per cent over the period 1980-1992, while it fell by 14 per cent in nearby more affluent parts of the same city. And some poor people pay the ultimate price for poverty too – suicide rates are four times higher in deprived central Manchester than in comfortable mid-Staffordshire. The unemployed, the low paid and those with poor working conditions, those in poor housing and with poor education have higher risk of ill health and lower life expectancy. They therefore become a much greater burden on public expenditure. The cost of subsidising this waste through increased benefits and health spending is massive.

There has also been a disturbing return of Dickensian diseases of squalor. The Tories got into office in 1979 promising great expectations but have delivered hard times. The incidence of scabies has more than doubled in the last five years. By 1995 tuberculosis cases in the East End of London were running at ten times the national average. Public health authorities have indicated anxiety at the re-emergence of scurvy and diptheria. Poor diet, bad housing and stress are the routine explanations given to these phenomena and are undoubtedly very important. But the attempt to shift the blame back onto individual behaviour neatly dodges the fact that the government is actually the main culprit.

While smoking has halved amongst the better off since the 1970s, there has been almost no change among the poorest; a total ban on tobacco advertising would help redress the balance. Underprivileged social groups receive the least information about their health during doctors' consultations. Cuts to NHS services in critical areas has played a part too. Department of Health funding of Family Health Services has been shown not to be taking into account the rate of deprivation in the area. The number of people taking eye tests fell by over 33 per cent after charges were introduced in 1989. Access to free eye tests should be re-introduced and would help the early diagnosis of diabetes and glaucoma.

Tackling all causes of ill health should be at the forefront of any radical public health agenda. The egalitarianism always at the heart of socialism but recently downgraded must be revived. There is no dodging the reality that conquering ill health means implementing some basic economic measures such as a shift to a redistributive taxation system and a national minimum wage. As Sir Douglas Black, former President of the Royal College of Physicians and no left-winger argued: 'the single measure that could do more to help... would be to reverse the shift from direct taxation (which falls fairly on income) to indirect taxation (which falls unfairly on the poor)'.

The right's homily that the country cannot afford a quality National Health Service is a myth. Another is that the problem can be solved by dividing the cake a little more fairly. Some increase in the cake could be achieved by removing tax exemption on some categories of private health care, thereby saving £85 million a year – that could buy 22,300 hip replacements or 69,000 cataract extractions. And another valuable measure would be introducing VAT on private health care, raising £300 million. But the inescapable fact is that the cake just isn't big enough. According to the OECD, the United Kingdom lags behind all the major western economies in spending on health as a percentage of GDP. The United States spends 13.4 per cent, France 9.1 per cent, Germany 8.5 per cent, Italy 8.3 per cent, whilst the UK commits just 6.6 per cent. There has been serious underfunding of the NHS for some time; the 1988 Tory-dominated Health Select Committee judged it to be nearly £2 billion annually.

The key to reform must be adequate funding, together with an NHS based on cooperation, not the market. There must be equity for patients and potential patients, not for health professionals and health managers. Wherever possible, decisions should be made locally – although placed in a national context with national guidelines, whether covering ethical questions like organ transplantation or strategic questions like public health and overall spending levels.

At the centre, the Secretary of State needs to be accountable to Parliament. An intermediate regional tier should be based on recognisable boundaries – through Scottish and Welsh parliaments and English regional authorities – with strategic, developmental and regulatory functions. Local planning needs would be worked out by using a ring-fenced NHS budget determined by a national formula (taking into account measures of deprivation etc). There should be a compulsion to work within the national framework and to meet minimum quality standards. But management of hospitals and community units should have considerable autonomy. There is no reason why efficiency cannot be achieved by setting clear management targets within available resources. Accountability should be through medical representatives being joined by elected representatives on local health authorities co-terminous with local government boundaries. In this way the advantages of local decision-making can be attained within a properly resourced, renationalised health service run according to patient needs rather than market forces.

EGALITARIANISM THROUGH EDUCATION

Even in its darkest hours, democratic socialism in this century has kept an abiding faith in the liberating power of education. The importance of equal opportunities for academic and vocational attainment regardless of race, creed or class – the *right* to a decent education – was the 'big idea' that motivated democratic socialists, whether of left or right, uniting them even when they disagreed on nationalisation or nuclear disarmament. During Labour's crusade in the 1950s and 1960s to replace the divisive, selective, class-ridden segregation between secondary modern, technical and grammar schools with a system of comprehensive education, Gaitskellite and Bevanite marched as one.

Even if capitalism seemed impregnable, its inequalities could at least be significantly ameliorated by giving the child from the slum the same educational opportunity as the child from the suburb.

But during the 1980s and 1990s the confidence of such thinking has been undermined not only by the new right, but also within the left. Egalitarianism has been derided. Yet what else is 'socialism' about if not the idea that all people, whatever their background or beliefs, should have the right and the opportunity to a good life? This should not be confused with *uniformity* (the historic and tragic mistake of state socialism). But a society which is organised in a broadly equal way must remain a cardinal objective for socialists. Otherwise the 'freedom' which must also remain a principal socialist value cannot be attained, except for a privileged few.

The left today needs to revisit its heritage if it is not to go badly astray. Within the Labour Party there has been some loose talk about parents having the 'right to choose' where to send their children even when the exercise of such a 'right' denies it to other parents and thereby penalises their children. One Labour MP even told her colleagues in Parliament that stopping middle-class parents like herself from sending their children to the best schools was like stopping council tenants from choosing the colour of their front doors. As Roy Hattersley has eloquently insisted, such new philistinism on the left is either ignorant of, or wilfully ignores, John Stuart Mill's distinction between exercising rights that harm nobody else and exploiting liberties which damage others. The socialist dictum articulated by R.H.Tawney that freedom for the pike meant death to the minnow needs to be re-learnt by Labour and re-asserted by the left. Exercising the otherwise admirable right of choice must not mean that a privileged, articulate minority chooses the best at the expense of the majority which is saddled with the worst.

In his book *Equality*, Tawney put in sharp perspective much current educational parlance about 'opportunities' and 'choices', insisting that these are not real for the majority of people without equality:

> opportunities to 'rise' are not a substitute for a large measure of
> practical equality, nor do they make immaterial the existence of
> sharp disparities of income and social condition. On the contrary,

it is only the presence of a high degree of practical equality which can diffuse and generalise opportunities to rise. The existence of such opportunities, in fact, and not merely in form, depends not only upon an open road but upon an equal start.

This framework of principles should inform Labour's approach to the operation of market forces in education, especially to opted out schools or private schools. Just as with health policy, Conservative education reforms in the 1980s and 1990s have sought to introduce to the educational system both the jargon and the reality of competition, on the premise that it widens consumer choice. Instead market forces have failed to improve education, and have widened the inequality gap. Such 'choice' is an illusion. The introduction of a three-tier system – of local authority, opted-out and private schools – has led to a restriction of choice for most parents. The government's claims for diversity amount to a parental scramble for places in over-subscribed 'good schools', trying to dodge the surplus of places in crumbling, under-funded 'bad schools'. By forcing on schools models of competition which apply to businesses, they ignored a central truth that schools (like local hospitals) are community institutions – which belong to all of us and should serve all of us. John Gray identified the root of the problem: 'The need is not – as the New Right has tried to drum into us – for private freedom of exit from public institutions (viz schools) of which we despair. It is for stronger and inclusive institutions in which we have a voice.'

The challenge is to re-create genuinely comprehensive and representative schools, which the middle classes will want to opt into, and whose standards they will thereby collectively help to raise. This principle of egalitarianism should run all the way through educational policy. Far from being a levelling down, as opponents of comprehensive education argue, there should be a levelling up with the removal of any financial advantage for schools which have left local authority control for opted out status, and the removal of subsidies for private schools.

Furthermore it should be acknowledged that it was the failure of top-down, statist, educational policies in the 1960s and 1970s which left the garden gate open for market driven solutions, which appeared to offer choice and local control. There is no need to opt out from local authority control to enjoy the maximum independence from bureaucracy, so that schools can decide locally how best to meet the needs of all their pupils and their wider community. Local Management of Schools (LMS), a measure introduced by the Tories which devolves financial management to the level of the school, can be seen as a response to over-bureaucratic control by LEAs. It applies to all schools and should be distinguished from opting out, which means opting out of any relationship whatever to the local authority. It can be empowering – but only if it operates within a framework of adequate resourcing, with educational authorities able to meet strategic needs and to provide the type of specialist help not possible amidst an amalgam of competing schools. In other words, devolving power to the school is a liberating measure, but cutting it loose from any local strategy for education leads to jungle law. LMS has given heads and governors very substantial budgetary delegation, as well as control over day-to-day decision-making, which should be retained. Indeed, properly resourced, LMS can empower local communities rather than merely delegating to them how they make their own cuts. At present in some authorities, with inadequate resourcing and with the performance of privatised services such as cleaning and maintenance inadequately monitored, LMS's transfer to the governors of responsibilities that are properly the preserve of these authorities provides the government with a convenient means of passing the buck for inadequate resourcing.

LMS also provides the basis for absorbing grant-maintained schools. If decentralisation is retained in line with a libertarian socialist perspective – giving parents, teachers and governors the opportunity to create the best school – then the choice is not between municipal control and local control. It is between a decentralised comprehensive system that protects the interests of all children, through ensuring an adequate level in all schools within a local education authority, and an opted out market driven system which allows the development of 'good' and 'bad' schools and thus benefits a select group. Opting out is incompatible with the egalitarian imperative that should drive education and should wither away. A Labour government should in the first instance withdraw the financial privileges which have generally been the reason for opting out and establish parity of funding for all schools. All state-funded schools should then be placed back within a local democratic framework which would be more accountable to the communities they serve.

By 1995, out of a total of 23,000, about 1000 schools (16 per cent secondary and 2 per cent primary) had opted out. They benefited from about £250 million one-off grants and extra capital spending. In the 1993/4 academic year, over £150 per pupil was spent in the grant-maintained (opted out) sector, compared with just over £100 in local authority schools. By levelling the playing field and removing any financial advantage, these schools will gradually discover that they are losing, in terms of support services, more than they are gaining. This realisation has happened in many schools already, particularly in Wales, where thoughtful debate has preceded parental ballots on opting out. Grant maintained schools disrupt and undermine provision of a fair, integrated stable system. If allowed to grow unchecked they could destroy a locally accountable education system – replacing it with an appointed (rather than elected) bureaucracy, nationally controlled, with no local knowledge, accountability or representation. Transforming schools into business units and subjecting education to competition on the one hand and centralisation on the other is not the way to improve standards.

Ultimately this is the task of teachers whose commitment must be nurtured and whose professional status must be enhanced. The destruction of teacher morale through constantly attacking their professionalism and down-playing their role, whilst subjecting them to constantly changing massive extra administrative burdens, including testing and the national curriculum, is perhaps the most serious educational legacy of modern Conservatism. It must be reversed.

It is also time to grasp the nettle of endemic private educational privilege, which has disadvantaged most children for generations. The British education system has always been partially privatised in order to train a largely hereditary elite to maintain its position of dominance and privilege by perpetuating inequality from one generation to the next. The 'right' to educate your child privately has in Britain historically become a ticket to monopolise power and wealth. Members of this elite have a fast track into the higher civil service, the judiciary, the military and captains of industry. As Will Hutton has shown so compellingly, this fast track has also nurtured and sustained an elite in charge of the City, operating an old school 'gentlemanly capitalism' which has historically and systematically failed the needs of industry and the real economy.

Labour needs to continue to set an example with Labour MPs using state schools. Socialist credibility on education springs from the fact that Labour MPs use the state system themselves and therefore have a vested interest in ensuring it delivers high standards. This is not true of the Tories. In the 1992 intake of MPs, 62 per cent of Tories were privately educated with 45 per cent ex-Oxbridge, compared to 14 per cent of privately schooled Labour MPs and 16 per cent ex-Oxbridge. Virtually all members of the Tory Cabinets since 1979 paid to educate their children in the private sector while in the Labour Shadow Cabinets nobody did. The cost of private schooling is quite beyond the reach of all except an elite. In 1995 annual average fees at a private day school were £4,386 and for boarders £10,245 – the latter almost two thirds of average earnings.

As a *Financial Times* survey confirmed in 1994, private schools dominate the A-level league tables, allowing a fast-track into higher education and better life chances. Private schools educate one child in 15 but account for more than one in four university students. By 1995, the door to higher education had practically been slammed in the faces of children from low income families. The freezing of the value of full student grants, and the relatively low parental income threshold for disqualification from the full grant, coupled with the widespread introduction of top-up loans to supplement student income has left newly qualified graduates with average debts of £4000. This is a massive disincentive for working-class or low income students. There is no compensation for them in the fact that most students have been forced to take at least one (low-paid low-skill) job to help keep them afloat. The student loans scheme is a voucher system in disguise and is entrenching inequality and denying opportunity.

If the voucher system were extended into mainstream schooling it surely would be Armageddon for those schools teetering on the brink. The egalitarian arguments deployed by supporters of vouchers are pure sophistry. Appropriating attractive terminology like 'choice' and 'opportunity' cannot hide the fact that vouchers would accelerate inequalities as the stampede to a few 'good' schools closed the rest. No school can stand out against the corrosive individualism fostered by such a market mechanism. Vouchers are an admission of despair for public education, yet Tory proposals for nursery schools signal their commitment to this market mechanism.

Only 7 per cent of children benefit from private education and the country's resources should be heavily targeted on the other 93 per cent. Socialists should promote policies that create a high quality state-funded system, which means that back-door public funding of private education must end. Ideally there would be no private educational system of the kind which has so distorted British society for centuries. There may be a legitimate continuing role for the private sector to provide some scope for experimentation and for specialisation (such as Summerhill and the Rudolph Steiner schools). But the phenomenon of 'public schools' should be allowed to wither away by choking off all direct and indirect public subsidies, and channelling the resources thereby released into the state system which these schools would be encouraged to join.

The Assisted Places Scheme introduced by the Tories in 1981 applies to 350 schools, which receive more than £105 million a year from the tax-payer. Official figures confirm that the scheme is actually acting as a lifeline for independent schools, which were squeezed in the recession. Middle-class victims of a rising divorce rate are also beneficiaries. The *Daily Telegraph* reported in March 1995 that the scheme had become 'a provision vigorously exploited by middle-class parents (as) only the income of whoever has custody of the child is taken into account'. Research published in 1986 also dispelled the myth perpetrated by some independent school heads that the scheme introduces pupils from all backgrounds into the school, thus providing working-class children with lifetime opportunities that would otherwise be denied them: only 9 per cent of fathers and 4 per cent of mothers of these children could be defined as working-class.

Phasing out the Assisted Places scheme would raise about £100 million. Phasing out private school fees currently paid by government departments such as the Defence and the Foreign Office would raise a further £125 million. Removing charitable status and rich parents' tax relief would harvest another £40 million. This combined state subsidy totalling £265 million should be removed and redistributed at enormous benefit to state schools up and down the country. Ways of ending the private schools' current VAT exemption (worth £600 million) should also be examined to see if it could be achieved without levying VAT on state education.

National public educational standards have fallen under the Conservatives since 1979, while they have been feathering the private sector's nest. International comparisons also show that Britain has been falling behind. OECD figures for 1991 show that the proportion of 18 year olds obtaining A-level/Higher GNVQ equivalents was 68 per cent in Germany, 48 per cent in France and just 29 per cent in Britain. There is a serious problem with 16 year olds too. Comparison with European equivalents to GCSE (grades A-C) in maths, English and science showed that only 27 per cent of children in England achieved this level compared to 62 per cent in Germany and 66 per cent in France. Despite Tory propaganda to the contrary, those educated in the 1960s and 1970s have fared better than those taught in the 1980s. A depressing one in six adults currently has severe difficulties with literacy and numeracy and a 1992 survey revealed that only 17 per cent of the population could spell correctly six commonly used words.

There is failure even before our children reach statutory school age. Britain is bottom of the European league for nursery provision when all the evidence underlines the benefits of an early start, in forging social skills, getting ahead with the business of learning and reducing delinquency in adolescence. There should be free nursery provision for all three and four year olds.

Successful economies depend upon a dynamic, properly resourced education system. Competitor countries – especially those in the Tiger economies such as Korea and Taiwan – have recognised that education forms the basis of national wealth in much the same way that physical resources did in the past. It is not just the numbers of students entering higher education which impresses in the far East, but the value placed on them by their own cultures and the commitment of the individual students to education attainment – whole societies are united in responsibility for the success of the economy. In Japan over 93 per cent of students continue post-16 studies to 18, compared to 29 per cent in the UK. Performance at earlier ages is equally striking. Comparisons between 13 year olds in mathematics and science in twenty countries across the world showed the Koreans and the Taiwanese came out in the top three in both, with China beating them at maths. The UK came 11th. Nations positioning themselves for the future – Japan, Germany and Scandinavia – all have in common an excellent education system, a highly skilled workforce and effective re-training. Although the UK's university system is a world leader, because of the emphasis placed on training an elite, average levels of educational attainment are poorer. Less academic pupils are not given the rigorous technical training available, for example, in Germany. Business managers in particular are poorly educated: only 24 per cent of senior British managers have degrees compared with 85 per cent in both the US and Japan, 62 per cent in Germany and 65 per cent in France.

The competitiveness of nations is now more than ever determined by the skills and talents of their citizens. In the modern economy where capital, raw materials and technology are internationally mobile and tradeable worldwide, it is people's education and skills that will prove a vital determinant of growth. Aside from the destruction of individual life aspirations reflected in this dreadful record, the skills revolution and the demands of both the global economy and rapidly changing technology mean that effective learning takes place at various stages of everyone's career. Properly funded, high quality education from nursery level throughout adulthood is an economic necessity if Britain is not to decline still further. And that means a willingness by the left to argue for the necessary funding, including by extra taxation. It is not enough to pretend that private/public sector partnerships can bridge the chasm in educational resourcing.

HOUSING AND COMMUNITY

From 1979 to 1993 the number of households annually accepted as homeless by local authorities increased from 55,530 to 134,190 - a rise of 142 per cent. This figure ignores the thousands of homeless people who sleep on the streets and in parks every night, destitute and sheltering in doorways or cardboard boxes. Whilst the housing boom created by Chancellor Lawson during the 1980s saw house prices rocket, so did the number of homeless. And when the boom turned to bust their numbers continued to soar as building societies and banks turfed out thousands of mortgage defaulters from their homes to protect shareholder dividends.

The virtual collapse of publicly funded housebuilding has contributed to this crisis. With council house sales, the amount of social housing available has fallen by 22 per cent, or nearly 1.5 million units, since 1980. The most desirable homes have been sold off and millions of poor families are trapped in sink estates. The application of market rents has meant that Housing Associations – assiduously promoted by the Tories as an alternative to council housing – are forcing their rents to prohibitively high levels.

Again a fundamental tenet of socialism needs re-asserting. The market has not, will not and intrinsically cannot, solve the housing crisis. It cannot provide housing for people who can only afford low rents. Whilst home ownership should remain as it always has been for socialists – a policy to be supported for those who want it – we may be near saturation point for this form of ownership, with nearly 70 per cent of homes owner-occupied. This leaves state provision, yet again, as the minority 'option' of the poor. Municipal housing needs to be reincarnated from the death prescribed by Thatcherism. Only local authorities have the critical mass and the resources to provide housing on the scale and with the flexibility to satisfy the needs of a variety of people, from single people to large families. An immediate start on housebuilding can be made by granting local councils the right to spend billions of pounds of their own housing capital receipts from the sale of council houses.

At the same time a new partnership is necessary to empower council tenants. They should be given rights to participate in the management of their estates and homes. Cooperatives should be encouraged. Too many large estates are now disfigured by the vandalism and lack of interest which comes from the absence of the kind of stake automatic in ownership. Tenants do not feel their block is 'theirs': it is 'the council's'. So if there is urine in the lift or rubbish on the stairs, people blame the council. But people do not have to be owners to be stakeholders. They should have much more control – and be delegated their own budgets – for managing and maintaining their own blocks and estates. With the right to council housing should come some of the responsibility for looking after it.

This may mean substituting 'professional' assistance from the town hall with cooperative effort. For example, caretakers have all but disappeared from council blocks. Why not give tenants the right to choose their own caretakers, funded by the Council? They would be part-timers, possibly a retired person or a single parent living nearby. They would have budgets to deal with some repairs or daily maintenance. And if – subject to council audit – they managed to accomplish such tasks by using their own skills, or access to informal expertise rather than relying upon external work, why not? This after all is how owner-occupiers behave. The modest financial investment in such new-style caretakers and locally controlled budgets would be more than repaid by cutting pressure on central council services to deal with vandalism and daily maintenance. This is the libertarian rather than the state socialist solution. It doesn't deny the necessity for a properly resourced public framework, but empowers the community rather than making it dependent upon the state.

EQUALITY FOR WOMEN

Equal opportunities have rightly been pushed up the political agenda, largely thanks to the efforts of the women's movement and years of struggle. Since the early 1970s the new wave of feminism has burst in from the cold and progressively forced its way into the political mainstream. The Labour Party in particular has responded with positive action policies, and drives to ensure the selection of more women to be Councillors and MPs. In the main, all this was achieved because women organised themselves and challenged the traditional paternalism not just of society but of the left as well. However today the situation facing women is very different from the 1970s and 1980s. Whilst a new generation of women take for granted the achievements of the past, they also face new problems and demand a new agenda.

Previous Labour governments did deliver a measure of justice for women, notably with the 1970 Equal Pay Act, the 1975 Sex Discrimination Act, the establishment of SERPS and of Child Benefit. But since 1979 there has been a disintegration of many of the rights and benefits which had previously been won. Monetarism and market forces have fractured women's rights and opportunities, forcing many into low-grade jobs. Whilst many more women have jobs, working-class women in particular have often found themselves in a reversal of roles as the only breadwinner – but on much lower wages than their male partners previously earned. This has all contributed to the creation of a core feeling of economic insecurity, and has buttressed further fears reaching into every aspect of women's lives – including fear of violence and crime, and fear of poor health provision.

One might imagine that women suffering as a result of Tory policies would turn naturally to Labour. But they didn't in 1992, when a gender gap of seven points had opened up amongst skilled working-class women voters, many of them over 55 years of age. That gap has yet to be bridged, and the results tested in a general election. If this is to happen Labour needs policies that match what women across Britain want.

The left could also blow away the chance to capture the 'seven million generation' identified by Helen Wilkinson in *No Turning Back: generations and the genderquake.* These are the seven million women aged between 18 and 34 who see feminism as irrelevant (ironically, because of the very 'feminist' successes of their mothers before them), who value autonomy, work and education more than family or parenting and who – because of these value gaps – believe that all political parties and institutions have failed them. Women are a diverse group. They do not all share the same aspirations. Some do not want paid work. Others do not wish to raise families. Some also endure other forms of discrimination – as members of ethnic minority communities, as lesbians, as people with disabilities, or as carers. The left's task is to celebrate that diversity and to adopt policies that reflect it. It also has a responsibility to create policies which offer genuine equality of opportunity. If Labour tries to be all things to all women it will fail – just as surely as it will fail if it tries to be all things to all men.

Nobody doubts the left's commitment to equality of opportunity or its passionate campaign against women's unfair treatment both at work and in society at large. Arguments for more flexible working time and child care facilities have rightly been pressed upon Labour by women. However, recent Labour policy has appeared to conflate this into the 'flexible labour market' agenda of the new right, which is almost being swallowed whole. This risks alienating a large chunk of Labour's own support – particularly in regions where part-time work is certainly not a pathway out of poverty but a snare into low-tech, low-paid repetitive work with no possible chance of advancement or training. Indeed, in 1994 672,000 women had more than one job (which naturally doesn't include the third job as unpaid principal home manager). And the evidence is largely that this is not out of choice but economic necessity.

The old-style, full-time, permanent, forty-nine years on-the-treadmill employment model was largely for men. But that is no basis for painting a rosy picture of the new supple, elastic, part-time tele-working world of work. For a start, this vision completely obscures the reality of most part-time work. One of the ambiguities of the reconstruction of the employment market is that whilst a few women have entered the professions and negotiated part-time hours around their family life, many more women are working in a deregulated, market with no contracted fixed hours. They have little or no pre-school or after-school support to accommodate the life-style available to the relatively few female professionals with sufficient resources to pay for childcare.

There are three times more women than men full-time workers in the poorest ten per cent of earners, but four times more men than women in the top ten per cent. Twenty-five years after the Equal Pay Act, women in manual full-time work still only earn 72 per cent of average men's pay and the hourly pay of women part-time workers is only 59 per cent of the hourly pay of male full-timers. Consequently, Britain has one of the largest 'gender pay gaps' in Europe.

What is needed is a recognition of the value of part-time work, so that it isn't perceived as low-grade, grubby and humiliating. The provision of a written guarantee offering full-time rights for part-time workers would end the cynical incentive for employers to replace full time jobs with low paid part-time jobs. It would, instead, allow people to work fewer hours without losing employment rights. This would encourage real flexibility at all levels in the marketplace; and those who genuinely choose to work part-time hours, whether because they have school-aged children, want to study part-time, or indeed do anything else, would be able to.

Central to equal opportunities for women is an innovative childcare policy which covers all areas of early learning in an integrated way. The current system is fragmented and insufficiently funded and the Tory voucher scheme for nursery education does not change this. Many women with children under school age who want to work don't do so because it costs them more in childcare than it would to stay at home on benefit. This is one of the major reasons why about 70 per cent of lone parents are forced against their will to live on benefit. A chasm has opened between those who can afford child care and those who cannot. As Lucy Daniels, Director of the Working Mothers' Association, graphically explained: 'It can cost nearly as much to put your child in a day nursery in London as to send your child to Eton.'

Britain is now almost unique in not having a national childcare policy; it has the highest number of working women in Europe but one of the least publicly funded childcare programmes. It is bottom of the league table of funded childcare for 3 to 5 year olds: in Britain just 35 per cent are covered compared with over 90 per cent in Belgium, France, Denmark and Greece. But, once more, a national childcare strategy is not desirable simply for reasons of equality. There are good economic reasons for harnessing the skills of women who wish to work. But there should be a range of choice – for instance, not every parent wants to drag their child across cities on congested public transport to a workplace nursery if there is suitable provision at home with flexible hours.

Over two and a quarter million women are also indirectly discriminated against because of government rules on Lower Earning Limits. Many earn less than the lower earnings limit (£58 per week as of April 1995) and as a result pay no National Insurance contributions, thereby shutting the door on benefit entitlements for unemployment benefit, retirement pension and statutory sick pay. Although employees earning less than the Lower Earnings Limit may not be able to afford to pay the full rate of the contribution, the rules ought to be reformed to enable the inclusion of low paid workers, or crediting of those earning below a certain level.

And a National Minimum Wage – linked to median male earnings – would level women's pay upwards not downwards. These policies are right, not only because they are fair and just, but because the introduction of equity in the workplace is central to improving the national economy. Current policy drives all wages downward as men and women compete for jobs in areas where traditional full-time jobs have disappeared and been replaced by low paid part-time jobs.

The combination of poverty pay and the gradual dismantling of the welfare state has led to another unhealthy phenomenon - the growing divide between work-rich families with two or more earners and work-poor families who remain trapped on benefit. In the race to win Middle England votes, the needs of the growing underclass must not be sacrificed. Many (but by no means all) women who are lone parents are ensnared in an insecure economic and physical poverty trap. They need policies that help them, not politicians who scapegoat them.

But it is not enough to prescribe from above what is best for women. Their near-invisibility in our major institutions needs forensic examination. Why have there only ever been 167 women MPs although 651 MPs are elected every five years? Why are 88 per cent of primary school teachers but only 50 per cent of headteachers? Why are they only 9.5 per cent of corporate managers and 2.8 per cent of managing directors? It can't just be because the average mother of two loses almost half her total working lifetime through rearing children, or that the UK has the lowest level of publicly funded childcare in Europe (compelling those these reasons are). There is a deep-seated institutional and cultural British gender gap, which must be tackled, among other ways, by the institution of a powerful Ministry for Women.

Amongst the policy priorities for women should be: a properly funded national childcare programme; an end to discrimination in tax, benefits and pensions schemes; improved law on equal pay and sex discrimination; improved laws on rape and domestic violence; gender awareness training for judges, police and the Crown Prosecution Service; better support for carers; better NHS services for women; and proper funding for women's organisations.

But it is equally important to avoid the compartmentalisation of 'women's policies' into a separate agenda. Otherwise they will continue to be downgraded and pursued only as and when other 'more important' priorities have been addressed and 'when resources permit'. Instead a women's agenda must from the outset be built into each policy area and the thinking of each Government department. For instance transport policy must address women's relative lack of mobility (since few have their own cars) and their need for safety. Employment policy must address equal rights for flexible or part-time workers. Child care must be addressed as an economic and not simply a 'caring' issue.

In order to achieve this, however, affirmative action will be needed to redistribute *power* from men to women. More women MPs and cabinet ministers are a prerequisite for more legislation reflecting women's views and concerns. More women in top positions in the media are needed to attack cultural sexism. More women at senior levels in the Treasury, the City and the major corporations are needed to protect women's economic interests – always remembering that feminism does not provide the answers to other forms of disadvantage, for example class. The advance of middle-class women into the structures of power is a big plus in the gender stakes, but it is naive to imagine that this will necessarily alter the plight of working-class women without a concerted commitment to policies that are both feminist and socialist.

RACIAL EQUALITY

Like other forms of inequality, racism can only be tackled by government intervention. However it requires much more than this. Because it is historically so deeply embedded in British culture, racism is institutionalised. Discrimination remains widespread, from the very top to the bottom of society. Despite the fact that black, Asian and ethnic minorities make up 4.7 per cent of the population (and nearly half were actually born in Britain), they have just 0.8 per cent of MPs (six out of a total of 651) and very few if any in senior positions in key state institutions, including the judiciary and the civil service. Senior black managers in the private sector are almost unknown.

Meanwhile grass roots racism has a long and unpleasant history. Fascist, racist or Nazi parties have periodically piled up votes, especially in local or national by-elections, usually concentrated amongst white working-class groups experiencing unemployment and hopelessness.

Support for such extremist parties reached a high point in the mid-1970s when the Labour government began adopting economic policies which hit working-class living standards; together with the French experience where working-class votes switched straight from the old Communist left to the new extremist right, this is a salutary lesson for future Labour Governments, which neglect their core vote at their peril.

For their part, far too many black people experience the daily grind of low pay, poverty and poor housing. More subtle discrimination is experienced in education, employment, training and promotion opportunities. The figures speak for themselves: the official unemployment rate for ethnic minority groups in Autumn 1994 was more than twice that for white people (19 per cent compared with 8 per cent). Among 16-24 year olds in each of the main ethnic minority groups, unemployment rates are significantly higher, rising to fully 51 per cent among young black men, compared with 18 per cent for young white men. (In some inner city areas black youth unemployment is higher still.) Average hourly earnings for whites were £7.44 in 1994 but across all ethnic minority groups £6.82, plummeting to £5.39 amongst Pakistani and Bangladeshi employees. All too frequently low pay is accompanied by some of the worst working conditions – long hours without a break, dangerous conditions and long and arduous shift work which disturbs family life. Free market policies of casualisation and deregulation have disproportionately hit black, asian and ethnic minority workers who are concentrated in the lower manual grades and ancillary services.

Eradicating racism is consequently dependent upon socialist policies. The growth in racist violence and the rise of fascist parties endemic across Europe requires vigorous campaigning against racism including a European directive to eliminate racial discrimination. Adopting the European Social Charter will help. So will new legislation to establish equal status for all employees regardless of race. The public sector should give a lead in positive action measures covering such matters as training, targeted advertising for posts and quality ethnic monitoring. The Commission for Racial Equality should have its investigative and enforcement powers strengthened. Racial harassment should be made a criminal offence, as should racial violence and group defamation.

It is perhaps insecurity which is the greatest problem facing blacks, asians and others from ethnic minorities – not just insecurity of employment but fear of racial violence and attack. During the last five years racially motivated attacks and incidents have doubled and racial killings have increased dramatically. The British Crime Survey estimated that there were 130,000 racial incidents of criminal victimisation against Asians and blacks in 1992; of these, 32,250 were assaults, 52,800 were threats and 26,000 were acts of vandalism. In 1993 the total increased to 175,000. But the official figures cover only those reported and are also restricted to the two major ethnic groupings. Racial harassment affects many other groups – not least the Jewish community; desecration of Jewish cemeteries has been rising.

Although the authorities need to take tough action to halt such outrages, they are not just an issue for government. Labour needs to work with local Racial Equality councils, pressure groups like the Anti-Nazi League and the Anti Racist Alliance, trade unions and local community organisations to confront racism locally. This is a good example of why it is necessary for Westminster and town hall to build links with grass roots initiatives so that people are involved in change at the base and not simply the top of society.

COMMUNITY

The rediscovery of 'community' in recent debate is welcome. It underlines the importance of collectivism rather than selfish individualism in binding society together and making it work efficiently. As has been shown, it also provides a springboard for libertarian socialism.

However 'community' can wear various ideological hats (in 1955 one sociologist identified ninety-four different definitions). More recently, 'communitarianism' has become voguish. Its prophet, Amitai Etzioni who wrote *Spirit of Community*, was feted by Labour modernisers and was said to have the ear of President Bill Clinton.

Communitarianism contains a welcome critique of the failings of free market individualism and especially its high social costs. Its emphasis upon individual duty and responsibility is also commendable.

There are obligations as well as rights involved in citizenship. And self-discipline is always desirable. These are indeed socialist attributes.

But there is also a disturbingly authoritarian streak to communitarianism. For example, it advocates fining parents whose children play truant. This does not address the reality that such families are very often deprived and stressed beyond endurance by low incomes and damaging social conditions. Other suggestions put forward by communitarians, such as threatening bad neighbours with eviction from their council houses, would simply increase homelessness. Both these examples also display a class bias: far fewer well-to-do families have truancy problems and owner-occupiers seem in the second example to escape the sanctions applied to council tenants. There *is* an issue here, but the solutions put forward by communitarians bear down oppressively and unequally upon those who may well be inadequate citizens, but who are also the most downtrodden victims of a rotten society. And there is something puritanically domineering about the communitarian insistence that divorce should be almost impossible until children are grown up, and that the traditional family should be enhanced by women returning to the home. Such proposals slip all too easily over into the agenda set by the reactionary right and more recently by the 'back to basics' campaign of John Major's Conservatives.

Communitarianism's attack on the welfare state is anti-egalitarian. Blaming the breakdown of family life and social disorder upon welfare benefits which support lone parent families or single youngsters is close to endorsing new-rightist scapegoating. It certainly does not reflect a socialist understanding of the reasons for social decay and fragmentation. It is whimsically nostalgic about the good old days of God-fearing, disciplined communities, as if these ever existed or could be recreated by preaching from Parliament. Etzioni blames divorce or absent parents for a great deal. In *The Parenting Deficit* he writes: 'gang warfare in the streets, massive drug abuse, *a poorly committed workforce* [my italics]… are, to a large extent, the product of poor parenting.' Does he have the faintest idea of what poor inner-city life is all about? Responsible parenting is vital and should not be treated dismissively by politicians when framing public policy. But responsible parenting does mean chaining women to the home. Such moralising about the underclass by communitarians is reactionary because it dumps virtually all the blame upon the individual, airily ignoring class divisions, inequality and the way that rampant market forces corrode responsible behaviour and social cohesion. It also ignores the maldistribution of power, both between men and women and between classes. As the socialist feminist Beatrix Campbell has argued, communitarians 'are reactionary rather than radical, because they sideline the problem of power.'

Their proposals blur into those from the new right. For example, Etzioni favours de-regulation, arguing that active communities do not need to rely so much upon governmental regulation, controls or sanctions. This overlap into extreme free marketism has been acknowledged and welcomed by writers from the new right Adam Smith Institute and Institute for Economic Affairs. Etzioni and the British communitarian Dick Atkinson advocate a minimalist state and even favour more 'self-governing' quangos as an alternative to what they see as an 'oppressive' local state, despite the fact that, unlike quangos, the local state is democratically elected.

These instant solutions seem faddish rather than serious: for instance Etzioni's call for a renewed obligation to home-based parenthood ignores new market pressures which force both parents to work simply in order to survive. As for his proposal that there should be 18 months unpaid maternity leave on top of six months paid, this is pure fantasy for couples whose two incomes are an absolute necessity. His communitarian world appears tailored for the lifestyles of the professional middle classes who can rest content that the poor are being knocked into shape.

The degrading individualism of the free market has unquestionably corrupted the social fabric. The creation of good society does of course depend upon having good citizens: individual irresponsibility, immorality and anti-social behaviour should not be excused. But communitarianism's focus on the micro level of personal behaviour sidesteps the inequalities of wealth and power which breed irresponsibility and corruption at the top of society and transmit a mirror image to the bottom. Property rights are equally as important as individual rights, and corporate irresponsibility is just as much of a problem as individual irresponsibility, if not more so. Yet communitarianism does not addresses either these macro level issues or the consequences of capitalism; instead it seems to blame the victims. Nor does it question the privatisation of caring for children, nor the burden placed on women by the traditional gender division of labour.

The libertarian socialist alternative shares with communitarianism concerns with responsible citizenship and accepts that they need addressing through public policies. It also acknowledges that the left has seriously neglected this agenda, turning a blind eye to the kind of social permissiveness which can slide over into condolence of anti-social individualism. But libertarian socialism insists that the collapse of society and the corrosion of social values can only be tackled by the principles of mutual aid and mutual cooperation, nurtured within a context which promotes economic democracy and social solidarity. Social and taxation policies which promote equality, curbs on destructive market forces, government interventionism to create full employment, popular ownership and control of industry and decentralised decision-making are all necessary to create a macro environment in which the micro behaviour which binds communities together becomes possible.

Communitarianism identifies a problem, but offers only retreat down a blind alley. It can be both intolerant and reactionary. A new popular egalitarianism offers the only solution to the increasing immorality, alienation and inequality which characterises modern society.

CHAPTER 4

Economic Renewal

If there was one area which epitomised the left's defensiveness and weakness throughout the 1980s, then it was economic policy. Perhaps the single most defining feature of a socialist approach to the economy is the importance and power of government intervention. But the grotesque inefficiencies and waste of Soviet-style centralised planning undermined socialist confidence, even though such command economics had nothing to do with democratic socialism. At the same time the experience of left governments throughout western Europe in the 1970s and 1980s hardly provided a robust antidote, and in Britain in particular, the bureaucratic sluggishness of the nationalised industries led to disaffection with state intervention, an attitude not shared by our European partners. The 1980s intellectual fashion for the free market saw the reincarnation of ideologues like Friedman and Hayek, who had previously been consigned to the eccentric fringe. The triumph of capitalism and the vanquishing of socialism was proclaimed. Even by the mid-1990s, the left was still suffering a hangover from this legacy.

Yet if the command economics of state socialism is obsolete, so too is free market capitalism. This was nowhere more evident than in Britain after the 1980s bubble burst. Although proclaimed by Thatcherites as an 'economic miracle' which delivered rising living standards for most people, the short-lived boom was the product of unique factors: about £150 billion of north sea oil and privatisation receipts, and the doubling of personal debt to help finance a credit explosion. All this was blown away in a consumption frenzy, bequeathing an economy geared to instant gratification rather than sustainable development, asset-holding rather than wealth creation, and speculation rather than production. It is worth noting that the conditions for this consumption-orientated economy were created by government – in reality Thatcherism intervened in the economy, albeit largely to organise its free enterprise ideology. Without a radical change of direction, the long-term future is bleak: a low investment, low income, sink economy. The left's challenge is to explain politically what people know instinctively: that the game is up for the fund-amentalist free market Britain of chronic short-termism and ugly me-firstism.

Unless there is a major transfer of resources away from consumption and into investment – in industry, skills and infrastructure – there is no prospect at all of reversing Britain's continuing economic decline. Reliance upon the free market alone has not worked in the past and will not work in the future. Only Government can switch investment into manufacturing, infrastructure and public services on the scale needed both to be competitive internationally and to sustain a decent quality of life for all.

BRITAIN'S LONG TERM ECONOMIC WEAKNESS

The left's task is to explain that Britain's trajectory of rampant free marketism cannot be allowed to continue, except at huge strategic and social cost. To win public understanding for this central reality requires winning the battle of ideas. In the 1980s and early 1990s the average citizen was captured for short termism: by the 'feel good' politics of income tax cuts, rising house values and privatised share give-aways, all timed to fit the electoral cycle. The booming share prices and buóyant consumption statistics of this period produced election victories for the right but they reflected a candyfloss economy. People need to be weaned from this addiction and persuaded to address the imperatives of long-term economics. With sluggish personal consumption and a stagnant housing market by the mid-1990s, there is an opportunity for the left to explain that the real economy is fundamentally and structurally weak. Indeed, Britain could be about to reverse modern history in which, by and large, each successive generation has been better off than its predecessor. Unless there is a radical change of direction, many of today's children could be worse off than their parents; already in the US, which has followed similar policies, the earnings of young men with high school qualifications or less are about 20 per cent lower in real terms than 25 years ago.

Living standards are almost always maintained at a constant level only by families having two earners. But one in four men are either officially on the dole or in enforced idleness. There has been a huge shift from well paid full-time jobs to part-time work. The much vaunted 'flexible labour market' is a recipe for structural insecurity bedevilling the whole economy. In the year of falling unemployment to autumn 1994, just 13 per cent of the net increase in employment was in permanent jobs: 46 per cent were temporary and 41 per cent self-employed. Official statistics confirm that more and more young people are working for lower real wages – something which also occurred in the US where real earnings have been falling for some years.

Although the money-for-nothing culture of Thatcherism savagely weakened the economy, it came on top of a century of relative decline. Since 1880, the rate of growth of Britain's national income has often been less than half that of its main competitors, and so has its growth rate in productivity. For a long time, people in Britain were cushioned from the reality of this decline by the country's large share of world trade, due to its empire, and its ability to expand as markets grew within that share. But this became increasingly difficult as Britain's share of world trade in manufactures fell from about 40 per cent in 1880 to under 7 per cent in the 1980s. The period since the Second World War can be divided in two: the boom between 1950 and 1973, and the recession which followed the oil crisis of 1973-74. Even during the boom years, Britain's performance was 40 per cent below the average growth rate for industrial countries, and this fell to 50 per cent below in 1973-79. According to the OECD, British manufacturing output rose by 21 per cent between 1970 and 1989, compared with 47 per cent in France, 60 per cent in Italy, 92 per cent in the US, 118 per cent in Japan and 202 per cent in Ireland. Of the ten leading industrial nations between 1950 and 1987, Britain had the lowest compound annual growth in GDP, productivity and net national investment. As a result, Britain slipped from number two in income per head in 1951 to number twenty in 1995.

Despite a welcome trend in export-led growth generated by the devaluation which followed exit from the ERM in September 1992, Britain's balance of payments deficit remains unsustainable. During the 1980s Thatcherites, led by Chancellor Nigel Lawson, argued that the trade gap could be financed by income from rapidly increasing British investment abroad. Few argue this now. As Will Hutton has pointed out, whilst British financial institutions have invested about £90 billion abroad, British banks have had to borrow much the same amount. Overseas assets may total 30 per cent of GDP, but so do short-term liabilities which are now the highest they have ever been in peacetime, and make Britain extremely vulnerable to the whims of foreign investors and foreign interest rates. This is no foundation for economic strength or stability.

Disproportionately high defence spending also continues to be a drag on the economy. Even after post cold war cuts, Britain will still be spending about 1 per cent more of its national income on defence than our European neighbours. This is a drag on the economy because resources are diverted into military rather than civilian production, distorting the priorities of technology, research and development towards modes of production that do not win mass markets. This again, is an example of state intervention to distort the economy. But market forces alone will not be able to solve the problem. About 40 per cent of Britain's skilled engineers are linked to the defence sector and about 300,000 people are employed in it. A government sponsored programme is vital to convert their skills and the capital of their companies into civilian production. Since it was the state which created the market for military production, it has a responsibility to create new markets.

By 1992, thirteen years of Thatcherite 'miracles' notwithstanding, a Government report showed that a huge competitive gap had opened up between British industry and its foreign competitors, with productivity lagging by at least 25 per cent. Comparing one peak for manufacturing output with another is perhaps the fairest basis for judging the Thatcherite record. Between the peaks of 1979 and 1989, manufacturing output rose by 13 per cent – an annual average of just over 1 per cent. German manufacturing output rose three times as fast over the same period, Japan's five times as fast. Today British investment per manufacturing worker is only half that of the USA and

Germany and just one-third that of Japan. Whereas manufacturing accounted for 27 per cent of UK Gross Domestic Product in 1979, this has now fallen to barely 20 per cent (compared with 30 per cent for Japan and Germany). Yet the pivotal role of manufacturing in Britain is shown by the fact that it generates two-thirds of all foreign earnings. A fall of one per cent in manufacturing exports needs to be compensated by a 2.5 per cent rise in exports of services, simply to maintain equilibrium. Britain neglects manufacturing at its peril.

Dramatically fewer strikes, more cost-conscious management, rising living standards for most and the skilful projection of Margaret Thatcher as a strong world leader, attached an international image of economic success to Britain in the 1980s. But this was an illusion. During the fourteen years from 1979 to 1993, Britain's economy grew by only 25 per cent, compared with 36 per cent in the previous, much derided, fourteen years of largely Labour rule. During the same fourteen year period after 1979 France's economy grew by 30 per cent, West Germany's by 33 per cent, the USA's by 35 per cent and Japan's by 63 per cent; Britain's record was actually the worst of any industrialised country since 1945. Some 'miracle'.

A MONEY FOR NOTHING ECONOMY

The basic problem is that Britain has for many years been consuming (as opposed to investing) far too great a proportion of its national income. The 1980s Thatcher boom was a consumption boom, with real living standards for the majority of people rising on the back of over £100 billion North Sea Oil revenues and an explosion of credit. During the 1980s, consumption increased by an average of 2.5 per cent per annum, whereas GDP increased by an average of 1.6 per cent each year. Between 1979 and 1992, consumer expenditure rose by 37.2 per cent and GDP by 22.3 per cent. This was a staggering gap of fully 15 percentage points.

It was bridged by increasing debt as the Government encouraged the nation to live on tick. Consumer credit more than doubled. At December 1994 prices, consumer credit was £450 per adult in 1979 and £1,240 per adult in December 1994. And this excludes the impact of negative equity affecting over one million home owners. Whereas in

1981 for every £100 of disposable income household debt was £57, by 1990 this had doubled to £114, dropping back to £106 in 1994. Corporate debt also rocketed and stood at an unprecedented high. Thus another consequence of the Thatcher 'miracle' was to bequeath a debt mountain blocking long term sustainable economic regeneration. As Will Hutton wrote: 'The economy was vandalised by the financial sector in the name of market freedoms.'

So long as investment continues to be sluggish and consumption high, the economy will remain out of kilter. At 65 per cent, British consumption as a proportion of GDP is already the highest in the industrialised world and is completely unsustainable. By 1994 the UK was consuming about £40 billion too much annually – consuming resources that should have been saved and invested. To build a strong real economy will require a shift in resources from consumption into industrial investment and skills training – by perhaps as much as seven per cent of GDP. This is the amount of investment (equivalent to £40 billion) which the National Institute of Economic and Social Research estimate would be needed every year for 10 years just to *halve* the skills gap between Britain and Germany.

How is this to be achieved? Free market economics is no answer, because it is too short-term and too geared to narrow private vested interests. It is vital to grasp this nettle of turning the whole priority, direction and motivation of society around. Otherwise, Britain's relative economic decline will continue. The blunt truth is that neither the short-termism of orthodox economics nor the top-downism of British government is capable of making these fundamental changes. Indeed, Britain is likely to become increasingly ungovernable unless radically different approaches are pursued. On the one hand, an increasingly embittered underclass will revolt as poverty deepens – even if by crime rather than political action. On the other, the policies needed for economic transformation cannot be delivered except with popular participation.

Only the left can seriously address the problem because only socialist policies of local control, public regulation and government intervention can create the necessary framework for economic revival. Only socialism's commitment to a fair distribution of wealth and income can create a workable consensus for the necessary changes;

otherwise many people will not be prepared to accept a short-term brake on rising living standards, to switch resources into investment and ensure long term security. And only the *libertarian* socialist emphasis upon local empowerment can create the structures to generate and sustain popular consensus.

THE NEED FOR COLLECTIVISM

The insatiable drive for innovation and higher quality which is the motor of modern industrial economies requires citizens to adapt and change. They won't or can't do so without the security that can be found only in cohesive, solidaristic societies which both protect all citizens and enable them to achieve their full potential. People need the security of such a society in order to cope with the pressures of change. That means collective provision – of training for example – and policies which enable communities and families to thrive, rather than to be fragmented and destabilised.

In an important report overseen by 25 leading businesspeople, the Royal Society of the Arts in 1994 found 'a strong correlation between the countries with the highest emphasis upon individualism and the poorest economic performance over the last 10 years'. It stressed how vital 'teamwork' is to economic success. Yet Britain is deficient in nearly all the ingredients of teamwork. Investors do not collaborate properly with managers and managers do not collaborate properly with workers. Bankers do not participate properly in industry and industry does not participate properly in the community. The RSA report is a devastating indictment of atomised free-marketism, pointing out that it simply does not work. The RSA contrasted British management's elitist and adversarial attitude to workers with the much more productive Japanese practice of building 'long term trust relationships'. The report also cited a speech by a leading Japanese industrialist made in 1979 which proved hauntingly prophetic. Konoke Matsushita told an American business audience: 'We are going to win and the industrialised West is going to lose out... For you the essence of management is getting the ideas out of the heads of the bosses and into the hands of labour... For us the core of management is the art of mobilising and putting together the intellectual resources of all employees in the service of the firm.' (However, this is not to say that the Japanese model should simply be reproduced. It is a strongly paternalistic and hierarchical society.)

Free markets destroy the very institutions and social values upon which the success of modern economies depends. The new right culture of 'me-first' individualism in which the employer has no loyalty to the employee, and the associated world of short-term contracts and casualisation, means that the worker has no commitment to the firm. The supremacy of unfettered capital, the worship of profit and the promotion of executive self-interest means the worker has no stake in the firm either. Yet successful enterprises now depend more than ever upon employee loyalty and willingness to adapt. The very complexity of high technology means that the Managing Director understands less and less and depends more and more upon the employee, particularly the highly skilled one. Yet the fashion for labour market 'flexibility' is probably hindering economic growth because employers are less willing to train workers they might soon lose. Although such flexibility may drive costs down, and thereby satisfy the demands of bankers and monetarists, it is self defeating in the long-term.

Similarly, the war of the capitalist jungle destroys the cooperation – on technology transfer for instance – that makes industrial sectors successful. Research and development is increasingly a team effort. It is fantasy to suggest that research and development fits the atomised model where the discoveries of lone individual scientists are seized upon by lone individual entrepreneurs. R&D is a collaborative venture, depending upon both public funding for scientific excellence and private cooperation. The new right ignores the fact that Britain's historic success in scientific innovation was nurtured by public funding, including (that term of abuse) 'subsidy'. How else did Britain achieve world leads in for example radar, synthetic rubber, computers, fibre optics and the jet engine? Huge cuts in funding for research and development are an appropriate monument to the failure of free market mania.

The desperate short-termism of an economy obsessed only with the quickest and highest return blocks the long term investment needed to create stable, successful enterprise. In other words free market mania fails on its own terms: modern capitalism must be transformed for economic success.

The new right's agenda of cuts in public services and public investment – apart from undermining the quality of life – are counter-productive because they undermine growth and weaken the real economy. For example, carefully targeted subsidies to industry do work, as has been shown by the independent Business Strategy Ltd. Its study of regional selective assistance (which provides grants to encourage companies to locate in deprived areas) showed that manufacturing output was significantly higher than it would have been without assistance: 15.4 per cent higher in 1991 for the North of England and 28.1 per cent for Wales. Whereas during the 1980s industrial aid as a proportion of GDP was cut in Britain, it was maintained or even increased in competitor countries like Japan, Germany and France whose economies gained consequent competitive advantage.

Other evidence exposes the shortcomings of new right nostrums. Deregulated labour markets, wage cutting and attacks on employee rights do not, as has been claimed, generate jobs. The abandonment of Wages Councils, the refusal to implement the European Social Chapter, the attacks on trade unionism and other assaults on workers' protection by the Conservatives –all this has been done in the name of creating a new tier of lower paid jobs. But it has not done so. A survey by the Low Pay Unit published in August 1994 showed that pay had dropped significantly for the 2.5 million workers previously covered by Wages Councils since their abolition. But there was no sign that lower wages had priced more people into jobs in these sectors. Free market dogma that low wages correspond to high employment and vice versa does not stand up. David Blanchflower and Andrew Oswald found exactly the reverse in their 1994 study of twelve countries: the higher the wages, the lower local unemployment; and the lower the wages, the higher local unemployment. As another economist, Robert Solow, has put it, the labour market is a social as much as an economic institution, and the way in which employers and employees interact with each other is not the same as in a fish market: free market theory seeking to interpret and then organise labour markets as if they involved the supply of and demand for dead fish is irrational.

Furthermore, notions of fairness and working relationships which promote high morale are actually more important to high productivity than the raw pressures of performance-related pay, individual contracts and wage cutting which are favoured by new right ideologues. As the Institute of Manpower Studies reported in 1994, managements which build relationships of trust, mutual respect and employee participation are more successful than those which adopt the frontier spirit of hire and fire, where the worker is treated as a chattel rather than a human being.

LOW COST VERSUS HIGH QUALITY

The Tories' exclusive reliance, at least in rhetoric, upon unfettered market forces is contradictory in other ways. The deliberate strategy of casualising Britain's workforce and promoting low pay is seen as encouraging foreign investors. In fact, as an OECD survey published in July 1994 showed, foreign companies pay wages more than 15 per cent higher on average than British companies; they employ fewer part-timers and invest more in their workforces, and collective bargaining with trade unions is more of a feature in their management strategy. Furthermore foreign investors are equally, if not significantly more, concerned with high standards of infrastructure and skills which Britain does not have. Indeed during the 1980s frenzy for low labour costs combined with cuts in investment in skills and technology, the share of foreign-owned companies in UK manufacturing employment actually fell.

The case for the 'low cost' approach is also based upon the assumption that it will enable British companies to produce goods and services cheaper than competitors. But even if this might buy some competitive space against 'high cost' countries like Germany, all the evidence is that high skill, high investment economies are more successful. As Michael Porter showed in his monumental study, *The Competitive Advantage of Nations*, low labour costs are easily beaten by competitors through better design, higher skills, more flexibility or more modern production techniques. Policies based on low labour costs can in any case be undermined by relocating to still lower labour cost areas. A race to the bottom is unwinnable. It is pure fantasy to imagine that Britain could succeed in a 'low cost' contest with countries such as those in Eastern Europe and the Pacific Basin. These have much lower social costs, with Chinese wages a fraction of Britain's. The only option for Britain is the 'high quality' one: an economy producing high value-added products, at the leading edge of innovation, with high technology which establishes a competitive edge through quality, and through agenda setting for products and services.

As Robert Reich, the US Labor Secretary and Harvard economist has persuasively shown, the link between skills and growth is now much more important. In his book, *Work of Nations*, he showed how economic globalisation was increasingly ensuring that the skills base of a nation becomes the critical issue distinguishing it from others. With modern technology, cheaper transport and free movement of capital, companies are able increasingly to locate production away from their home economy or even their main markets. They can choose to locate in a country or a region where it suits them best. At the same time, a country's finance can be raised in the international money or capital markets, and need not be generated internally via savings. So a country's domestic capital resources are not necessarily decisive for its economic success: foreign capital inflows can finance investment. According to Reich, therefore, a country's competitiveness and its wealth will more and more depend upon the richness of its skills. This will determine companies' location decisions.

If this conclusion is accepted, how can the high quality option be feasibly pursued? Certainly not by exclusive reliance upon market forces and competition. Britain's skills base has contracted alarmingly, both in real and relative terms, under the impact of de-regulation, cuts in public spending, privatisation and the rampant play of market forces. If this continues, Britain will turn into a skivvy economy even for areas of the world like East Asia which traditionally lagged behind but are now racing ahead with massive investment in education and infrastructure. The requirement for a high-skill workforce and a high-grade infrastructure means investment in education, lifetime re-skilling, research and development, communications and technology transfer. The market economy has not delivered in these critical areas and is incapable of doing so: there is no alternative to socialist policies of public intervention, investment and spending.

The right's low cost option, by contrast, is turning Britain into a low skill, low wage, sink economy which will cease to be competitive in the future. It also deepens the budget deficit because low earnings mean lost revenue to the Government from tax and national insurance contributions. The combined impact of this lost revenue was estimated in 1993 at £5 billion a year.

Add to this the £12.5 billion burden of increased social security payments to compensate for the growth of the low pay economy since 1979, and you get a major structural factor in Britain's current fiscal plight. And this ignores perhaps another £7.5 billion estimated to be the total of corporate and private tax avoidance. About half the 1993-94 Budget deficit of £50 billion could be accounted for in this way: another consequence of unbridled market forces and do-nothing government.

REFORMING THE CITY

The City's financial institutions must be democratised and decentralised in order to ensure that they operate in the public interest, and are forced off their chronic addiction to short-termism. Nearly 90 per cent of loans to business have to be repaid in under five years. Whereas in the 1960s the average period for pension funds to hold shares was fifteen years, by the 1990s this had fallen to between three and five years.

The financial institutions now own three-quarters of all equity but their relationship with the rest of industry is problematic because these institutions regard themselves as dealers in company shares rather than as a long-term owners. Consequently they have no real stake in industry. There is too much emphasis on take-overs and stealing a march for financial gain. The share price becomes an all-decisive measure, shifting company resources into dividend payments rather than research and development, for example. As Will Hutton argues: 'Pension funds and insurance companies have become classic absentee landlords, exerting power without responsibility and making exacting demands upon companies without recognising their reciprocal obligation as owners.' This has horribly skewed the priorities of the UK economy: for example, between 1979 and 1992 the real value of shares increased twenty times more than the real increase in manufacturing investment. The huge surge in share prices was exacerbated by the Tories lifting controls upon dividends which were imposed by Labour in the 1970s.

Investment in research and development has lagged seriously. Britain now invests less of its GDP in manufacturing than all bar two of the 24 OECD nations. During the last twenty years, whilst spending on industrial investment in R&D remained static in Britain, it doubled in Germany, Japan and France and increased by a third in the USA.

The diversion of resources away from wealth creators to asset-holders is shown by a dramatic increase in the percentage of after-tax profits taken in dividends. In 1979, this was a modest 17 per cent which compared favourably with Japan at 24 per cent and France with 39 per cent. The only country in Europe where the proportion was lower was Germany, with 9 per cent. But by 1991 the percentage in Britain had jumped to a staggering 60, compared with Japan at 28, Germany at 13, France at 42 (the latter countries only marginally edging upward). Not surprisingly the proportion of national income going to shareholders nearly doubled between 1984 and 1993 – from 2.6 to 4.9 per cent. This is extremely significant because most industrial investment comes from profits ploughed back, not from the issue of new shares. As a result the pattern of UK firms, distributing a much larger share of their profits in dividends, means fewer resources for investment.

Britain's financial institutions need radical reform to mobilise finance for investment, develop new technology to modernise the economy and to raise skill levels. New structures of corporate governance are needed and the City must be properly regulated.

The City of London has been self-destructing, with its culture of opulence and elitism, its predilection for fraud and insider dealing, and with television images of frantic young men with red braces arrogantly making money at the expense of every one else epitomising all that is worst about the 'square mile'. It is run by a small elite – almost always privately educated, exclusively housed and socially isolated – which has no loyalty to the wider public interest, whether this is expressed nationally, by company or by local community. Young City traders may now come from Epping and Uxbridge, but those in control still come from Eton and Oxbridge.

Yet the financial services sector plays a critical role. It is responsible for nearly a fifth of GDP (about the same as manufacturing), employs an estimated 2.6 million people, and grew by 30 per cent from 1983 to 1993. It earns £15.6 billion from the world, making an important contribution to Britain's balance of payments.

The heart of all the problems with the City is the insistence that it can and should be self-regulated. Yet the deregulated 1980s saw sleaze and fraud on a grand scale: Barlow Clowes, Polly Peck, Blue Arrow, Guinness, Maxwell, BCCI, Lloyds and Barings being only the most notorious cases. Self-regulation has equalled self interest. Proper, democratic regulation of the City is crucial to creating a successful economy in Britain.

It is claimed that statutory regulation will reduce competitiveness by adding to costs, that it is expensive and time consuming and that it goes against the grain of European regulation. But the US Securities and Exchange Commission is self-financing and in 1991 raised 132 per cent of its operational budget in fees. European legislation sets minimum rather than maximum standards and provides no bar to strong regulatory control in the UK. Statutory regulation is no more time-consuming or expensive than self-regulation. However, regulation is more effective if it is be independent and transparent. Ultimately it is not just more democratic, but more efficient.

There should be a strong statutory regulatory body which oversees enforcement of regulations for banking, building societies, insurance, corporate governance, accountancy, Lloyds, and pension funds. In tandem there should be an overhaul of insolvency laws preventing cowboy businesspeople from rising phoenix-like from the dead to start anew without paying off previous debts.

The new statutory regulatory body for the City should be independent, non-partisan, and quasi-judicial. It should report annually to Parliament on its administration of financial and company law. The Serious Fraud Office would become the enforcement agency, taking over all the fraud work and the regulatory function which is currently within the DTI. But it is important that the SFO's remit is re-written to look after the small investor as well as the financial institutions. Its newly acquired responsibility for investigations (previously within the cumbersome DTI) would help speed up this vital area of enforcement.

The Bank of England would remain responsible for supervising the Banking Acts. It would still carry out monetary policy, but it would be answerable to Parliament, through the Chancellor and a new Monetary Policy Board – whose membership would comprise regional represent-atives, alongside trade unionists and industrialists. Again, the Monetary Policy Board would be transparent, producing regular public reports. The supervision and regulation of consumer protection (for deposit-holders or business clients) would pass from the Bank of England to the Statutory Regulatory Body, thus linking it with the regulation of building societies and the insurance sector.

One of the central imperatives to future economic success is a reformed banking system. British banks are also driven by the all-pervasive footloose and greedy shareholder demands for the quickest, highest return. And they do not compare very well internationally. The cost of capital provided by UK banks is just about the highest in the world: over the last thirty years, the cost of bank capital in Britain averaged 10 per cent, compared with 7 per cent in Germany, 5 per cent in Switzerland and 3 per cent in Japan. To force the national clearing banks off this crippling short-termism, they must be radically reformed. Japanese banking provides a persuasive model. It is geared towards developing productive industry through the provision of long-term loans which tie the fortunes of finance and industrial capital together intimately. Investment is secured against long term profitability, not fixed asset values as tends to be the norm in Britain. For firms in difficulty, injecting additional finance for new research, development and investment is as likely a response as foreclosing. Additionally, the huge, government-established Industrial Bank of Japan is required by its charter to provide long term cheap finance for industry. The Japanese banking system is consequently a central government tool for industrial growth and export-led expansion. Germany, Sweden, France, Belgium and Holland have similar banking institutions closely linked to Government.

British banks should be reformed along these lines and at the same time decentralised so that they are brought closely into touch with local or regional needs, rather than acting according to the whims of their City-based directors. As experience in more successful competitor countries has shown, such devolution of banking is vital for industrial restructuring and manufacturing competitiveness, because it brings the sources of capital finance closer to industry and it eases the pressure on companies to distribute as dividends the profits that they make, leaving more to be ploughed back into the business. There should also be regional public banks with 'governors' chosen by regional parliaments, to ensure democratic regional accountability. These regional governors would sit on the central Bank's Board, replacing the Bank of England's Court and so helping to break the gentlemanly clique which has run British finance so badly for so long.

Similarly, democratic reform of pension and insurance institutions is necessary, bringing in trade union and consumer directors and decentralising their organisations. In particular, pensions represent deferred pay to achieve security in old age and should be controlled by employees and retired employees, not by a managerial elite. There should be wider controls on the pattern of investment by pension funds and insurance companies, which between them own some two-thirds of the shares in British industry. This principle has already been established, since both Labour and Conservative Governments have in the past used controls on investment and lending by banks. Such democratisation would create the necessary mechanisms and ethos for governments to exert pressure for long-termism.

Credit controls of the kind widely adopted in more successful competitor countries are essential to directing resources away from consumption and into production. It is essential to introduce controls over the banks to block off liquidity leakages which merely increase both indebtedness and private consumption. This could be achieved by imposing reserve asset ratios – i.e. limits on bank lending relative to the assets of individuals and the banks themselves – so closing the classic British loophole where house mortgages with tax relief are used to finance holidays or new cars.

MOBILISING CAPITAL

New public banks should also be established with the specific remit of mobilising private, and not simply public, resources. There should be a National Investment Bank, a Small Business Bank and a Housing and Construction Bank. Their capital base would be funded by the

Government and – as important – by the financial institutions, including Building Societies, whose huge resources must be mobilised for production.

The new banks would each issue multi-billion pound bonds which the pension funds, insurance companies and building societies would buy, if necessary directed by legislation in the absence of voluntary cooperation. No doubt pension fund trustees will cry 'foul' and whip up propaganda in the Tory media about 'government interference'. But the public needs to understand that, unless the massive resources these funds command are directed into our productive base, there can be no economic security for either pensioners or younger citizens.

The National Investment Bank would not simply provide cheap, long-term loans; it would also take equity stakes and force the commercial banks to do the same, thus altering the whole relationship between loan finance and industry. This needs restructuring along the lines to be found in Germany and Japan, for example, where banks become positive actors in the industrial economy. They should be backing business, instead of being preoccupied with lending for consumer spending or property development and speculation. Socialist themes of partnership, democratisation and decentralisation are not simply politically desirable, they are economically necessary; the left should seize the high ground by promoting the only agenda which can achieve economic prosperity and success.

The Small Business Bank would provide cheap, long-term loans. Government could subsidise bank loans to small businesses and extend Personal Equity Plans to provide tax breaks to individuals who provide equity finance. Another option would be to provide a tax incentive to banks to take an equity stake in client companies. This would create a partnership relationship where, as in other countries (e.g. Germany), banks are encouraged to promote the long-term interests of industry rather than, as now, to seek a quick return.

The Housing and Construction Bank would pioneer cheap mortgages to those on low incomes, financed by progressively phasing out mortgage tax relief which distorts the housing market and encourages disproportionate resources to be invested in homes at the expense of industry. Society needs to be weaned from the concept that the property owning democracy is more important than the industrial owning democracy. Extending the example of TESSAs, building Societies should be able to create their own industrial bonds, on sale to the public at competitive interest rates plus tax incentives for the purchaser on the interest received if the bond is held for, say, 5 years. These bonds could also be issued through the Post Office and major clearing banks.

Through all these reforms, the objective is a clear industrial strategy to develop a prosperous manufacturing sector: maximising indigenous technology and concentrating on high value products, coupled with increasing the status of industry as a fulfilling and rewarding career, and building respect for industry's central role in Britain's economic future.

OWNERSHIP AND CONTROL

But although this recognises the important role of the private sector, the question of ownership remains. So long as ownership is concentrated in the hands of a small elite, the economy will continue to be run in the interests of a self-serving few. It will also remain incapable of reaching its full potential because the majority of the population have no stake in its success beyond the desire for a decent income, which is a necessary, but insufficient, motivation. This is the essence of the socialist critique of capitalism: not merely that it is unjust and immoral, but that it is ultimately inefficient.

Whatever may be claimed on behalf of the Labour Party's new Clause IV, socialisation of the economy must still be an important objective if socialism is to mean anything. Popular ownership, to transform capitalism, should be promoted by tax incentives, local, regional or national government stakes, and encouragement for cooperatives and employee share ownership schemes, underpinned by industrial democracy.

Public ownership – and in particular renationalisation of the privatised utilities – also needs a fresh perspective. Opinion polls continue to demonstrate that most people are at one with the Labour Party's opposition to privatisation. Shareholder greed, personal aggrandisement by senior executives, short termism, social dumping of the poor – all are fertile electoral ground for the left. There is also a very strong case for utilities which are monopolies, or near monopolies, to be publicly owned.

But before addressing the feasibility of renationalisation, democratic socialists must answer the question: what would be its *purpose?* How would the utilities be run differently? What would be the practical consequences for the economy and the citizen? In the past, socialists have treated nationalisation almost as an end in itself, a holy grail, rather than a means which might or might not be appropriate in modern times.

After all, the utilities – telecommunications, gas, electricity and water – hardly fared much better under public ownership. Then there was direct government intervention and day to day self-regulation (expressed in the interpretation, civil service style, of each industry's own legislation). This had the advantage of requiring the nationalised industries to follow broad public policies – for a balanced energy supply for example. But successive Tory and Labour governments never had a clear philosophy for managing nationalised industries properly, to secure industry-specific objectives. Instead they were used as tools of short-term economic management. For example the 1970-74 Heath Government imposed price controls on them which did not apply to the private sector. The 1974-79 Wilson/Callaghan governments reversed this policy when they decided the industries were becoming too much of a drain on public sector borrowing. As a result, their investment programmes were the victims of stop-go macro-economics. Water suffered particularly badly. Together with Gas and Electricity, Water had negative net investment in real terms for every year from 1972 to 1980 (in other words the stock of buildings, infrastructure, plant and equipment was wearing out faster than it was being replaced). There was no strategy for the industries themselves; they were simply used as convenient tools in the broader economy.

So a new approach to public ownership is essential. Alongside the private sector there should be a new model of the public sector that is dynamic and aggressively enterprising. Management should be given key quality of service obligations and other appropriate targets. Public corporations and services should be able to enter the market and compete with the private sector, to participate in joint ventures and to involve private capital where this is appropriate. Local authorities should be encouraged to initiate joint ventures and municipal enterprises, as should regional authorities.

The Post Office is an example. Since the late 1980s it has been profitable, debt free and indeed a massive net contributor to the Treasury (bringing in over £1.5 billion at current prices during this period). There is no reason why as a trading enterprise it should not have full commercial freedom to operate effectively in an increasingly competitive communications market, both at home and especially in Europe. Only the dogma of Treasury rules, which absurdly categorise it in exactly the same way as a government spending department, prohibits this. Thus investment in a new sorting office self-financed by postal customers is treated as a burden on public borrowing, in the same way as a new school funded by taxpayers.

The rules should be changed in line with many other countries which do not erect such rigid barriers, and where the boundaries between public and private sector are much more blurred, to mutual advantage. In 1993 the International Monetary Fund, the OECD, the European Commission, the United Nations and the World Bank set out an internationally agreed practice – the system of national accounts (SNA). This excludes from the general definition of government borrowing the borrowing of public trading enterprises like the Post Office, with the Government removing its guarantee and instead monitoring activities like any shareholder.

Such a modest change would enable the Post Office both to remain a publicly owned and accountable corporation and to operate in an enterprising and competitive manner. It would be free to raise funds on the open market where appropriate and to establish collaborative ventures with private and public operators in Europe, to rival the single carrier networks offered by foreign-owned multinationals such as United Parcels Service, DHL and TNT. Units within the Post Office (such as TV licensing, catering, information technology, security and transport) should also be able to trade externally and tender for contracts. There should be managerial autonomy within stringent performance and quality of service targets, freeing managers from suffocating Whitehall control. This is quite distinct from old style nationalisation. It marries public accountability with commercial freedom: the real alternative to privatisation.

The Labour Party has stated that on financial grounds it would be unable to re-nationalise the privatised companies, the stock market valuation of which stood at over £72 billion in April 1995. Avoiding this huge cost through traditional left-wing demands for 're-nationalisation without compensation' (or even diluted calls on the basis of no speculative gain from the original sale price, as in the 1987 Labour manifesto) is not serious politics. This is primarily because the dominant shareholders of the privatised utilities are overwhelmingly the funds which hold pensions and insurance policies of ordinary citizens; there are also some 10 million individual shareholdings.

Exchanging shares for bonds – another traditional route – is in principle much more feasible since it is in current spending terms cost-free. The Government could issue interest-bearing bonds equivalent to the value of shares and exchange them. As a result the national debt would increase, but so also would national assets; the net liabilities of the Government would be unchanged. Although future government interest payments would rise these would be balanced by 'dividends' from highly profitable industries. As Professor Malcolm Sawyer of Leeds University has pointed out: 'There is no economic reason why the acquisition of an asset (say the water industry) through borrowing (issue of bonds) which has no net effect on the balance between assets and liabilities or between income and expenditure should have a negative effect on recurring expenditure on health, education or anything else.' But even if it does not effect current spending, it would impose an alternative claim on public *borrowing* and thereby thwart if not completely undermine giving a *priority* to borrowing for investment in infrastructure, skills and industry so vital to a socialist economic recovery programme.

Renationalisation has been made complicated by de-regulation, the existence of rival operators in competition with the privatised utilities, technological diversification (notably in telecommunications) and ownership globalisation. Furthermore, nobody is really suggesting a wholesale return to models of Morrisonian nationalisation, which were highly centralised and bureaucratic, discouraging investment, managerial initiative, worker participation and consumer responsiveness. Thus a new approach is called for.

DEMOCRATIC REGULATION

On the other hand, the socialist principle that there should be universal access to key services through collective provision remains just as valid as ever. So the question becomes: how can this commitment be realistically advanced today? There is a radical alternative to the present regime which does not involve full scale renationalisation. (See my *Regulating for the Common Good.*) It focuses upon reforming the regulatory system, which is a fundamentally flawed but nevertheless powerful mechanism for determining alternative policies for gas, electricity, water and telecommunications.

Regulation was conceded by the pro-privatisation lobby in the face of mounting criticism that the public would lose out if nationalised monopolies were merely succeeded by private ones. OFTEL, OFGAS, OFWAT and OFFER which in 1994 together employed 600 staff on a total budget of £32 million were largely afterthoughts: bait to catch the privatisation fish. Over the last ten years regulation has evolved in an ad hoc fashion, becoming complex, over-technical, rambling and undemocratic.

Regulators are independent and all-powerful. They have extensive discretion which has often been exercised in a highly personalised fashion – the prime example being Gas, where the eccentricity and egotism of Sir James McKinnon's regulation was legendary. Each regulator has enormous discretion to determine competition policy as they see fit for their own industry, without regard to the knock-on effect. In 1993 the Electricity Regulator, Professor Stephen Littlechild, insisted that forcing the electricity generators to maintain existing coal volumes would infringe competition rules. His intervention amounted to a veto on an alternative energy policy, by an unelected public appointee. In 1995 he announced he was reopening his decision the previous year on electricity prices, right in the middle of the sale of further power shares, triggering losses of over £4 billion and throwing into chaos a takeover bid of Northern Electric.

So who has benefited from this system? Shareholders have been delighted with soaring dividends – up by 85 per cent to 1992 in the case of Water and a massive 63 per cent for the first year of electricity privatisation. Profits have soared and were running at more than £21 million daily in April 1995. Industry chiefs have enjoyed a pay and shares bonanza. In the year 1994-95, board members, including chief executives, were given £21 million in share options on top of £35 million salaries: a total of £56 million in annual remuneration, a rise of 700 per cent over the £7 million before privatisation. By contrast, job losses in the privatised utilities will by the mid-1990s have totalled a staggering 200,000. And as the National Consumers Council has confirmed, they have at best a mixed record on prices. Cost related charging has produced anomalies such as a charge of £9000 for a four foot water connection to residential homes. On the whole, business customers have had relatively lower prices whilst residential ones have not. The balance sheet for the public purse is hardly clear-cut. Fifteen years of receipts from privatisation amounted to over £70 billion. But against this must be set over £6 billion in net debt right-offs, £5 billion losses through knock-down share sales, and £1 billion in fees to advisers, consultants and brokers; additionally, billions have been lost in annual income to the Treasury and the public sector has been stripped of important assets.

Furthermore, the benefits of privatisation measured by conventional commercial yardsticks are very far from those claimed so extravagantly by its advocates. A report in 1994 by the right of centre consultancy, London Economics, showed that, whether measured by profit (before interest and tax) or return on capital employed, privatised companies had not in fact shown any substantial improvement. The main spur for improvement came from increased competition rather than privatisation. Indeed the report showed that nationalised corporations compared very favourably with privatised companies on efficiency. Between 1989 and 1994, for example, the Post Office's record on increased productivity was much better than any privatised company apart from British Telecom, and despite the fact that it is much more labour intensive, giving less scope for the leaps in productivity that come from technological advance in an area like telecommunications. It is also worth noting that British Airways, often paraded as a flagship for privatisation, had a productivity record nearly three times better in the ten years before privatisation than in the ten years afterwards.

The Thatcherite assumption that the individual *shareholder* interest necessarily equates to the *public* interest has to be challenged. Individual shareholder or consumer interests, compartmentalised off from each other, do not inevitably aggregate into the general public interest. Indeed, selfishly pursued, and often with the support of the Regulator, they act to thwart policies serving of the general interest, in such matters as the ability of strategic national companies to compete in world markets, environmental protection and the preservation of precious natural resources.

One result of this compartmentalisation of policy-making is that Britain has no sensible energy policy. The Regulator's encouragement of the 'dash for gas', for electricity power station baseload is depleting North Sea reserves by perhaps 15 years usage, and is a most inefficient use of the fuel. Coal was sentenced to death while coal imports soared and nuclear power had a £1 billion plus subsidy.

The driving objective of the Regulators to promote competition almost at all costs invited foreign companies to enter the UK market on very advantageous terms, whilst British companies were barred from reciprocal rights abroad. This is most striking in Gas, and in telecommunications where American-owned cable TV companies are capturing important markets. British Telecom has not been able to enter the US market on equivalent terms and is further penalised by being barred from offering broadcast services over its lines like Cable TV. Britain's industrial interests are being undermined as BT is forced to concentrate upon competition in its backyard at the expense of international competition.

Competition dogma is also tending to force the privatised utilities to concentrate upon the most lucrative, fast growing markets where competition from new entrants is fiercest, at the expense of protecting the interests of low income communities. This so-called 'cherry-picking' means the most profitable users get the cheapest and most sophisticated services, such as telecommunications in the City of London.

By contrast, there is 'social dumping' of rural areas and poor inner city areas where competition is limited or non-existent. For example, installation charges for telephones are very high and well beyond the reach of many people on low incomes. Privatised British Gas is in many instances refusing to extend the mains an extra few miles to supply villagers. The new competition regime will also put up gas charges for the poor (they already pay 5 per cent more by not having the facilities to pay by direct debit) and reduce charges for the rich.

Competition is not a value-free concept. Nor is regulation some value-free, 'non-political' exercise carried out in an objective, technical fashion. We need to put democratic politics back in charge of the utilities, bringing to an end the emergence of policy by default.

An incoming Labour Government – or, in the case of regionally based utilities, regional government – should retain or take an ownership stake in the utilities, appoint a Director and exert influence directly at Board level. Properly managed in consultation with the large financial institutions which own nearly 90 per cent of shares in the utilities, such a change need not be disruptive, especially since the utilities are seen as safe havens in the stock market.

Whilst this is no substitute for public ownership – the rights of shareholders under company law would still be supreme – it could still afford considerable influence by a Government determined to exercise it. But there should be no misunderstanding about the aim: to ensure that the utilities serve public rather than private interests. If such a reform is resisted or fails, further socialising measures will need to be considered.

The very existence of Regulator discretion means even the existing system could be deployed in favour of alternative policies where competition was not at the expense of social, economic or industrial objectives. On coming into office, a Labour Government should immediately appoint new Regulators with a different ideological remit and thereby begin to change the direction of the utilities. Their objectives should be amended to ensure that policies to advance strategic national and social interests always take precedence over promoting domestic competition or shareholders' profits.

The utilities already have a series of non-commercial obligations. Furthermore, Regulators have been promoting competition which in practice transfers shareholder value from the existing utility to new market entrants. So shareholders' rights under company law to get the best return on their equity are already circumscribed under the current regime. But in spite of this small room for manoeuvre, the objectives of the Regulators may still need to be redefined by

Parliament to assert the primacy of strategic national or social interests over those of shareholders.

However, in order to avoid day-to-day Whitehall interference, which can so suffocate enterprise, Regulators should be required to submit rolling plans of action which Ministers would approve. The regulatory regime could then be assessed against performance targets such as: universal tariffs, protection of supplies to the elderly and disabled, research and development, levels of investment and international competition.

Accountability could be improved by establishing a Parliamentary Select Committee to scrutinise the utilities. They could be compelled to report once or twice yearly alongside an annual debate on the floor of the House. But MPs are not the best people to perform the kind of continuous and detailed scrutiny needed. A Utilities Commission should be established to bring the existing Regulators under one roof. This would promote policy consistency between the different Regulators housed within it. Whilst being democratically answerable to Government and Parliament above, the Commission would act as a channel for organised consumer representation and individual grievances from below.

It would be a quasi-judicial body akin to the Monopolies and Mergers Commission, but with Select Committee-type powers of scrutiny and subpoena. It could be governed by a Board of representatives from all sectors – consumers, senior managers, trade unions, shareholders and academics – appointed by the Secretary of State. Enabling the different Regulators to share common resources would bring economies. Each Regulator would still be pro-active and have considerable operational autonomy, but each would be supervised by the Commission's Board. The Board would have an advisory role for government on policy and strategy, acting as a transparent forum, carrying out inquiries, conducting public hearings and arbitrating in disputes between Regulators and industries or consumers where there appears to be a matter of public concern. Other procedural changes are needed, beginning with an end to the Regulators' 'right to silence'. They should be required to explain the reasons for their decisions either publicly or privately to the industries concerned. To overcome the problems of compartmentalisation and to enable the system to take proper account of strategic interests, the Regulators should also be re-grouped and merged into one for Energy, Transport, Communications (telecommunications and broadcasting) and Water.

Such a programme of fundamental reform to regulate for the common good combined with an ownership stake could protect the ordinary citizen and advance the country's strategic interests.

TAXATION

Radical tax reforms are needed to end the Thatcherite free ride for some. Britain is now a grotesquely unequal society as the rich benefit from lavish tax handouts and the poor slump deeper into poverty. Taking all direct and indirect taxation, Government figures for 1993 show that whereas the top ten per cent of the population paid a modest 34 per cent of gross income in taxes, the bottom 10 per cent paid a massive 46 per cent. The Thatcherite litany that tax cuts act as an incentive for harder work and greater enterprise has been disproved by successive studies, from one conducted by the Treasury itself in 1986 to a survey by the Policy Studies Institute in 1994. The only qualification appears to be that tax cuts for the low paid *do* make it more worthwhile for those on benefits to seek work – but then of course that does not fit with new right dogma.

Taxes for the great majority of people should not be increased. There should be reductions for the low paid to eradicate the poverty trap and give an incentive to work. But the rich have had tax give-aways of over £8 billion annually since the late 1980s. Including National Insurance, someone on £2,000 weekly is taxed at a marginal rate of just 40p, whereas a £200 a week earner is taxed at 35p. This tiny gap is indefensible and will remain indefensible even if the basic rate of income tax is reduced a little. It is also inefficient: redistribution would inject extra demand into the domestic economy, because the low paid tend to spend on home-produced goods and services what the rich spend on property and luxury imports. Taxes should be increased for those earning over about £50-60,000, which could raise at least £4 billion – equivalent to over 2p on the basic rate of income tax. VAT should be applied to private health and private education, raising a further one billion. Together with the phasing out of tax relief on mortgages and pensions, these measures could make a significant contribution to re-distributing income and re-directing resources into investment and production.

The tax dilemma for Labour needs to be faced squarely. Re-positioning to rebut charges of being a 'high tax' Party is sensible and was adroitly accomplished after Labour's tax debacle in the 1992 general election. Because the Conservatives imposed the biggest tax hike in peacetime (equivalent to 7p on the basic rate) in the mid-1990s, their credibility as tax-cutters was damaged. But the left cannot win a low tax auction against the right without jettisoning commitments on public investment and spending which would make it impossible to achieve high quality public services and a high quality economy. Whilst being prudent about pre-election commitments, Labour needs to mount an ideological offensive to persuade voters of the necessity for adequate tax levels to finance decent public provision for education, health, employment and so on. Otherwise – especially in the short term – there will not be the fiscal resources to put clear water between Labour and Tories in office.

GREEN ECONOMICS

Environmentally responsible fiscal measures and investment are also needed. The threat to the environment – whether the greenhouse effect, ozone layer or pollution – cannot be overcome by reliance upon the market, which favours short-term profit rather than long-term protection. The hole in the ozone layer will not be plugged by putting the task out to competitive tender. Government action and controls over industry are essential. Reductions in carbon dioxide emissions from lower vehicle use will only be successful if accompanied by investment in public transport. Taxation to make polluters pay and subsidies to promote conservation, recycling and ecologically friendly goods and modes of production are vital. Otherwise responsible companies will be undercut by environmental free-riders. Once again, this is an agenda which can only be delivered by a socialist approach to society. At the heart of modern socialist economics must be a commitment to growth which is *sustainable* rather than growth for its own sake which continues to be ecologically destructive.

There should be a new focus upon 'environmental productivity': that is to say maximising output from given levels of resources and minimising waste and pollution. Whereas huge increases in labour productivity characterised the twentieth century, rises in environmental productivity will be a feature of the next century. Economic success will therefore depend in part upon being a world leader in new techniques which boost environmental productivity. For example the global market in pollution abatement technology was worth £130 billion in 1990 and could be three times that amount by the end of the century; yet the UK share is minimal. Building a sustainable economy is not just about altruism. Neither is it a soft option. It will be critical to future prosperity. Government investment in green industrial methods is needed, including financing research and development.

The impact upon employment could also be positive. Energy efficiency programmes could create tens of thousands of jobs. In many cases it is currently cheaper to adopt capital intensive, high pollutant production processes than to use greener processes which are also labour intensive. But the costs (in terms of health and despoilation) are dumped onto society. Changing the way the tax regime works to favour 'goods' rather than 'bads' would reduce social costs and also boost jobs. Higher environmental standards and a green industrial strategy will lead to higher GDP and higher employment, as is confirmed by a number of studies not just in Britain, but in the US and Europe. For example Cambridge Econometrics estimated that over 680,000 jobs could be created in Britain by adopting higher standards and other interventionist green measures.

FULL EMPLOYMENT

The Government's zealotry for price stability is an industrial killer because it requires squeezing out demand and interest rates which are very high in relation to inflation. Instead, full employment should be the main objective of economic policy. The Tories' monetarist obsession with satisfying bankers rather than industrialists must be challenged. This does not mean being reckless with inflation. On the contrary, low inflation is desirable. It is important to distinguish between *low* inflation and *near-zero* inflation, and the monetarist framework necessary to secure it.

The Tories target of keeping prices down to the bottom of their chosen 1-4 per cent target range is industrially counter-productive, even if it wins plaudits in the City. It can only be sustained by deflationary monetarist policies at the expense of jobs and services.

Full employment won't happen by reliance upon market forces alone. Because of the capital intensive nature of new technology, even industrial investment will not generate sufficient jobs. Indeed the vogue for downsizing and out-sourcing coupled with the micro-chip and fibre optic threatens a jobs haemorrhage even with growth. William Bridges suggests in his book *Jobshift* that, on present trends, half the population could be working 60 hours weekly in the future while the other half are unemployed. To achieve full employment requires supplementing industrial investment with public spending and public investment, switching borrowing to invest in jobs and growth rather than to finance dole queues.

To promote full employment and transform a sluggish recovery into sustainable growth, a massive programme of public expenditure driven investment in infrastructure, training and skills is essential. This will need to be of the order of £20 billion annually to create a million jobs and turn the economy around. As is explained in chapter seven, such a programme could easily be financed by a combination of modest extra borrowing, specified tax reforms, a training tax on companies and by mobilising wasted or idle resources such as the several billions in council housing capital receipts and the estimated nearly £25 billion cost of unemployment.

This is essential to boost demand in the UK economy and bring down unemployment. We have to be prepared to spend to recover, as Keynes pointed out. The choice is between borrowing to finance unemployment or borrowing to invest. The alternative is to slash public expenditure on a scale the Tories are having to consider but which, presumably, Labour could never tolerate. Such cuts would in any case be counter-productive, since they would reduce demand in the economy and deplete an already inadequate infrastructure.

Is public borrowing for investment really the ogre we are asked to accept by the new right and those on the left who have caved into their agenda? They allege that public borrowing is 'bad', whilst private borrowing naturally is 'good'. Apart from a blinkered preoccupation with reducing the public sector, the argument is that public borrowing would increase interest rates. Actually, this is not the case – at least for Britain. Because capital markets are increasingly global, the impact on interest rates of sensible increased public borrowing in a small economy like Britain's is negligible. In the late 1980s, for example, long-term rates were higher despite the fact that there was a public sector surplus. Another argument is that increases in public borrowing require interest payments which increase the burden of public debt. But public sector debt in the UK currently, as a percentage of GDP, is low both historically and by international comparison.

An alternative way of financing increased borrowing is through government-created credit. Although it could be inflationary - the standard 'printing money' charge of the right – this is unlikely in circumstances of very low inflation. And even if inflation did edge up slightly as a result, this would be a small price to pay to revive an economy which will otherwise be trapped into steady decline. It is a question of balancing the benefits of investment with those of low inflation.

However, increased public borrowing must not be geared towards boosting consumption since that could be both destabilising and inflationary. It must be directed at investment – in skills, infrastructure and manufacturing – with the overriding aim of promoting industrial growth through Government intervention and expansionary macro-economic policies.

INCOMES POLICY?

To help overcome short-termism, we need labour market reforms which strengthen the real economy and therefore boost the real living standards of workers and protect jobs against a background of rising unemployment. Instead of force-feeding the consumption diet by a bargaining culture which chases the next pay increase, we need to reform workplace practices to achieve full employment, higher productivity, investment and justice and thereby sustainably higher earnings. This should include statutory access for workers to information and consultation – perhaps through the German works council model - recognition rights for unions and positive employment rights. Otherwise workers and their unions will remain locked into seeking gains which are here today and gone tomorrow: shop floor short-termism. We need a policy that is seen to be in the interests of ordinary workers, but not solely through the means of real wage increases in the short-term. This, clearly, implies some kind of policy for incomes.

Given the unhappy experiences of the 1960s and 1970s, there is an understandable reluctance by Labour and trade union leaders to discuss openly the basis for a coherent policy on bargaining and incomes, lest it be interpreted as a stalking horse for the centralised control of pay which proved so disastrous. What may have begun as a genuine attempt to curb hyper-inflation in 1975 ended in tears, with the 'Winter of Discontent' of 1978-79 that helped eject Labour from office.

Additionally, the 1980s phenomena of decentralisation of bargaining, contracting out, privatisation and competitive pressures to increase job flexibility, make it unlikely that government imposed wage restraint would be as effective as it was in the short term during the mid-1970s. The fact that the proportion of workers covered by collective bargaining agreements fell from three-quarters in 1979 to half in 1993, and that a majority of companies now link pay to profits, are other reasons why centralised controls would be hard to enforce.

Nobody can credibly promote a return to statutory pay restraint or old style centralised incomes policies. But remaining silent about the relationship of independent collective bargaining to public policy leaves a vacuum which could provoke a crisis in the next Labour Government and, at worst, a replay of the 1970s. It is far better honestly and openly to clarify the issues and, ideally, reach an understanding beforehand, rather than slide into a possible conflict in Government born out of lack of preparation and lack of discussion at rank and file level.

With one in five workers still in the public sector, the Government cannot in any case avoid having a view on public sector pay and - given its linkage to pay movements and levels in the private sector – a general view of private pay levels as well. Indeed despite their anti-interventionist rhetoric, the Conservatives did impose a public pay restraint policy from 1979 whilst leaving the private sector alone.

There are several other important factors to be looked at when considering incomes policy. First, a statutory minimum wage which is so essential to tackle the curse of low pay would undoubtedly have an impact upon differentials. To avoid simply moving the pay ladder upward, there would need to be a wider pay policy. Second, huge constraints on government policy result from the greater coordination and management of European exchange rates: the ability to pass on the extra costs of pay increases through the traditional route of devaluation is steadily reducing (and, in the case of a single currency, would disappear entirely). Third, to modernise the UK economy, collective bargaining must go well beyond the annual pay round and encompass a series of key issues – training, equal opportunities and work re-organisation.

These issues cannot safely be left to the whims of 'free collective bargaining' if Britain is to prosper in a single European market and if workers are to achieve justice. Letting events take their course in a free-for-all is not a serious option, least of all for socialists. A new approach is needed: one which preserves the autonomy of unions and their ability to bargain effectively with employers, but within an overall policy context based, where possible, upon agreement between government, unions and employers about national economic objectives.

This is hardly revolutionary. Every negotiator marshals arguments about the going rate, whether expressed in terms of external settlement levels, average earnings rises, growth prospects or the rate of inflation. The difference will be that, by setting an overall economic strategy, Government, unions and employers will be seeking to influence these factors rather than simply to 'follow' them.

But there should be be no sanctions against collective agreements which breach what may be deemed as the 'going rate'. In the *private sector*, bargaining will be relatively more autonomous, as indeed it should be if workers are to achieve rewards in line with company performance and profitability. Nevertheless, a Labour Secretary of State for Employment could actively campaign for policies on training and equal opportunities. Government procurement policy should be backed up with powers to require 'contract compliance' with such policies. In the *trading public sector*, workers are again entitled to ensure that their rewards reflect their industry's performance, though there is also in these industries a clear Government interest. In the *non-trading public sector* (civil service, local authorities, health service etc), the Government is ultimately the paymaster. Independent mechanisms for determining comparability and where necessary arbitration are needed, though there should still be space for collective bargaining.

Independent bargaining within the context of a nationally coordinated framework already occurs in successful economies, notably Japan, Germany and Sweden. In Britain, a public discussion could be launched by the Government with the TUC and CBI before the annual Budget and economic statement. Following the Cabinet's public expenditure settlement in the summer, there could be Government consultations with employers and unions prior to the November Budget. The Government could then suggest a range for pay settlements in line with national needs.

Informed by, rather than rigidly bound by, this range, major pay negotiations could then be synchronised to avoid the well-established pattern of leapfrogging. If earnings went above the recommended range, interest rates could be altered at any time and, the following year, the Chancellor could adjust fiscal and monetary policy to keep the economy in balance. Adjustments to taxation, the social wage and the new national minimum wage could also be made in line with the outcome of the 'pay season'. Sceptics have pointed to the difficulties of achieving such 'synchronisation'. But most of the key pay deals already occur in January and April. It would not be asking a lot to shift settlement dates backward or forward by several months, especially if the Government led by synchronising dates within the public sector.

A key part of this new agenda is to insist that pay is not the be-all and end-all of bargaining. To compete effectively in the 1990s and beyond, and to secure the social justice to which workers are entitled, priority must be given to issues of equity, fairness, work reorganisation and efficiency, which Britain has traditionally neglected. Whilst such coordination will necessarily be at a national level, it can only be delivered by decentralising power to achieve the consent of local workforces. Industrial democracy is essential to mobilise a common purpose between worker and manager.

GOVERNMENT'S RESPONSIBILITY

But the state still has an important function to perform: not by rolling back its frontiers as the new right demands, nor by managing every nook and cranny of economic life as the old left demanded. But by planned and strategic intervention. 'Planning' has become another term of abuse in UK political circles. Certainly centralised, bureaucratic Soviet-style planning discredited itself. But planning in the sense of having long-term objectives and a strategy for implementing them is vital and can only be achieved through mobilising the power and resources of government.

In their different ways Sweden and Japan illustrate this. The Swedes managed huge processes of change – in steel and shipbuilding for instance – because their state intervened to ensure diversification and restructuring. As well as a widely admired welfare system, Sweden has also had an impressive record on full employment, precisely because of government intervention, not least in 'solidaristic' bargaining achieved jointly with the trade unions. Japan's lesson adds an extra dimension. A combination of central direction through powerful economic ministries and a banking system organised for long term investment, meant the Japanese had the institutional means to turn a largely rural and war shattered economy into the world's most powerful industrial force. Today, Japan's success continues to flow from what can be called 'guided competition'. The Ministry of International Trade (MITI) has over the years worked closely with firms and financiers to guide investment into potential growth sectors. Taking a long term view, it has ensured strong research and development, leading to heavy capital investment for mass production which has been successful internationally.

Much the same approach has been adopted in the fast-growing 'tiger' economies of the Pacific Basin which, whilst hardly an advertise-ment for socialism, provide a potent antidote to do-nothing government. South Korea, for example, has grown explosively with its private companies guided by a government Five Year Plan and its state-owned steel company is the most efficient and profitable in the world. Areas of Europe such as Baden Württemburg and North-Rhine Westphalia in Germany, Rhône-Alps in France and Lombardy in Italy which have accomplished a transformation from old smoke stack industry to a modern economy, confirm that state intervention – whether national, regional or local – is indispensable. This is not a matter of 'subsidising' the private sector. It is rather a question of providing the necessary framework for economic prosperity, in terms of strategic investment, training, research and development, technology transfer, transportation, communications, services, adequate housing and a decent environment, in which a modern high value, quality economy can flourish.

Without institutional reform – backed by the constitutional reform proposed in chapter two – it will not be possible to halt the decline of the British economy, which is bound to produce falling living standards and permanent high unemployment. There must be investment in people as well as investment in plant and machinery, and lifetime learning as well as new product development.

Having had little serious to say on economic policy during the 1980s, the left must now set a new economic agenda. There would be a role for the market economy as for public ownership, for individual entrepreneurs as for government intervention, for public spending as for private enterprise. There would be a commitment to regulation rather than deregulation, popular ownership and industrial democracy rather than ownership and control by a small minority. The precise mix of these is a matter not for abstract or theological dispute, but should be left to emerge as a practical outcome, guided by the principle that a framework of democratic collectivism rather than selfish individualism is both more efficient and more desirable.

Britain faces some tough choices. Between low taxation and public investment. Between personal consumption and industrial production. Between continued industrial decline and regulating finance capital. Now that the new right nostrums of monetarist economics have failed, the left has a great opportunity to present a winning alternative. But grasping that opportunity requires boldness and radicalism.

CHAPTER 5

A People's Europe

There is an urgent need to change the terms of the British debate on Europe. It has been falsely polarised between Little Englanders and Europhiles. As a result the real issues have been obscured behind caricatures of 'Eurosceptic' or 'pro-Europe', which reflect positions taken a quarter of a century ago on initial membership of the Common Market. A serious stance from the left should be pro-European but anti-Euro-monetarism.

Today Europe is imperilled, not by the issues which excite chauvinist fantasies in the British right, but by its self-imposed monetarist straitjacket and its preoccupation with free market competition. Instead of full employment, growth, investment and redistribution being the overriding goals of European economic policy, price, currency and interest rate stability are being pursued to an obsessive degree, together with tight restrictions on public spending, public borrowing and public debt. These policies are directly at the expense of an industrial strategy capable of meeting global challenges, not least from the Pacific Basin countries. In today's Europe bankers and the money markets rule the roost. According to the Merchant Bankers S.G. Warburg, for example, the drive by EU Member States to convince the foreign exchange markets of their financial rectitude forced public spending cuts which alone led to an average 1.25 per cent drop in GDP during 1993.

As a result the numbers of those officially described as living in poverty across the EU has shot up – from 38 million in 1975 to 53 million. Total EU unemployment has been driven up to nearly 19 million or 11 per cent and, according to the OECD, is likely to continue increasing, with all the social disintegration that implies.

About 5 million young people have no recognised, marketable qualifications in a technological age. The toehold on power established by fascists in Italy and France, and serious outbreaks of racism and Nazism across the EU are disturbing enough without being boosted still further by even greater poverty and unemployment. The EU is also being buffeted by the pressures for enlargement, by obsolete political structures and by the increasing problems over foreign and defence policy.

To survive and succeed Europe needs to break from its current monetarist trajectory and give a priority to full employment and industrial investment and to high quality welfare and social conditions. It must also be democratised and decentralised. In turn, Britain's future depends to a great extent upon this because its trade and its economy is now so closely intertwined with EU countries.

TWO AGENDAS

There are two broad agendas for the future of the EU. The right has consistently argued for a wider *free market*, with individual enterprise to the fore and social and government action sidelined. The left has been more concerned to achieve *social cohesion* and collective solutions to collective problems. The right's objective is a single market suitable for business. The left insists on a framework of democratic control which protects citizens' rights. Put another way, the right favours capital and self-interest, while the left wishes to defend the interests of labour and the common interest. However, although analysis and debate over the EU is helped by this framework, the various protagonists do not always fit neatly into it. Thus for example some in the European right are fully supportive of social protection. The British new right is strongly in favour of a single market, but not a single currency: they see monetary union as producing a loss of sovereignty in a way that the single market does not. They put nationalism before capitalism over the pound but not over trade.

The left's position is complicated by the fact that most European socialist parties have accepted the framework of monetarism – which is actually anti-socialist. And the imperatives of being good 'pro-Europeans' have led some on the British left to go along with this –

including in the early 1990s a Labour leadership desperate to give reassurance that the Party's previous 'anti-Europe' stance had been buried once and for all.

Nevertheless the contrast between left and right agendas helps to explain developments such as the Maastricht Treaty signed in 1991, the complexities of which often obscure the real ideological issues at stake. There is a continuing conflict between these two agendas over what some may see as arcane issues. Thus, for example, for economic matters (until Maastricht) majority voting (as opposed to unanimous consent) in the Council of Ministers was in place, and this favoured the right. It meant that it was impossible for any one country to exercise a veto against the interests of capital and that market forces therefore triumphed. By contrast, a veto could be exercised on social and environmental matters. And this was no accident. The absence of qualified majority voting (QMV) in these latter areas meant – and to a large extent still means – that a country (such as Britain) could block measures protecting workers or consumers where it was unable to veto measures to open up the European market. (QMV weights each country's vote roughly according to size and the approval of at least 71 per cent of votes is needed for a decision.)

Consequently economic harmonisation has received much greater priority than social harmonisation. Specifically, convergence over monetary policy (with tight targets for inflation, interest rates and exchange rates) has been put before social convergence (with respect to living standards, minimum wages, welfare benefits and social infrastructure). This enabled John Major to win acceptance for sidelining social policy from the Maastricht agreement negotiated in 1991, whereas a Labour Prime Minister would never have got away with sidelining a central issue of competition policy.

As the original Common Market evolved through the European Community to the European Union, the left across Europe has been increasingly cornered by an agenda which is not its own. The goal of European unity has always been a noble one for socialists. There could be few more desirable ambitions than overcoming the divisions which plunged the world into two devastating wars. But the central problem for the left is that this political goal has in practice always been secondary. European unification has progressed by putting economics before politics and markets before democracy. Economic integration has occurred ahead of the democratic mechanisms to hold it accountable. This has presented socialists with a dilemma, and especially British socialists who became isolated from their continental counterparts as part of the wider British isolation. On the one hand the socialist instinct is internationalist. Furthermore, a Marxian interpretation would stress that if capital extends its terrain across frontiers then so too must labour. On the other hand, the driving thrust of European integration was a capitalist one. Everything else – democratic structures and social policies – was subordinated to the Treaty of Rome's insistence on a free market for capital.

Perhaps this could not have been otherwise. Perhaps under capitalism, economics always has been the motor of political and social change. Perhaps therefore the European left felt it had to go along with an alien economic agenda to gain the greater prize of political integration and social protection, which had wider support on the European Christian Democrat right, if not amongst British Conservatives. Certainly, socialists carved out important social rights and social action programmes along the way, and democracy has gradually been extended. But the price exacted has been high: a dominant monetarism which if not abandoned threatens to destroy both democracy and social cohesion.

SOVEREIGNTY

In formulating alternative policies, however, it is necessary to be clear about the issue of 'sovereignty'. Most criticism of European integration in general, and Maastricht in particular, insists that Britain is losing control of its own destiny. We hear that increased power to the European Parliament will be at Westminster's expense. But to pose the choice as one between London and Brussels is to misrepresent or to misunderstand the distribution of power in modern Europe. The right's antipathy to the EU tends to be nationalistic and reactionary. But some of the analysis from the traditional left over 'loss of sovereignty' is also distinctly un-socialist. The fact is that 'sovereignty' has already been ceded to the Euro level, not just politically but, more important, economically. In a nutshell, capital has gone Euro, but labour has not. Attempts to establish European wide trade union bargaining are still in their infancy. Business and finance now operate at a European, if not a global, level. Yet there are no powerful democratic mechanisms to exert a countervailing influence.

To their credit, continental socialists have long understood this even if some in the British labour movement have not. They look in wonderment at the obtuse British debate, which suggests that Bonn, Madrid and Paris might for some odd reason be more desperate than London to cede power to Brussels. Unlike British romantics who pine after 'loss of sovereignty', they at least understand that the real issue is one of *reclaiming* some sovereignty via the only feasible institution appropriate: the European Parliament. The real question is not one of surrendering power from the British people to European institutions. Substantial power was surrendered long ago. In reality, the issue is whether power should be discharged by free-wheeling Commission technocrats and the Council of Ministers or by directly elected representatives: an issue which will be addressed later.

Furthermore it is simply not possible for the UK to set its exchange rate and interest rate independently of the actions of other economies. This is due to the marked increase in the international mobility of capital in recent years. If speculators believe that the pound may be devalued, interest rates must be raised *relative* to the rates prevailing in other countries to compensate for this risk. Although, in addition, foreign exchange reserves can be used to purchase pounds, even with massive support from other central banks, the resources that can be mobilised for such intervention are tiny in comparison with the $1,000 billion that may now be placed in the foreign exchange markets *each day*. While it is obvious that the British government has significant (and sometimes understated) influence over domestic economic events, it is equally clear that there is no such thing as an unconstrained economic policy.

This is true inside or outside the Exchange Rate Mechanism – or indeed the European Union. One year before Britain joined the ERM, in October 1989, the Bundesbank raised its base rate. The then Chancellor Nigel Lawson spent £2 billion from the Reserves in a futile attempt to prevent a UK interest rate rise on the eve of the Conservative Party Conference. Forty minutes after the Bundesbank's announcement, UK rates went up too. So much for British 'autonomy'. Much the same is true for countries which at the time were not members of the EU, let alone the ERM. The Swedes, for example, were forced to hike up interest rates by 8 per cent to 24 per cent in September 1992 (with overnight rates rising to a staggering 500 per cent). They had to act because of high German interest rates and the high level of the Deutschmark to which the Swedish economy was effectively tied. Another country outside the EU, Switzerland, has effectively shadowed EU interest rates for many years.

Part of the left's case for establishing Parliamentary democracy – a case prosecuted in Britain by the Levellers in the seventeenth century, the Chartists in the nineteenth and the Suffragettes in the twentieth – was to establish national control over a capitalism which had gone national. So the objective must now be to establish European mechanisms for democratic control over a capitalism which has gone Euro. It is equally clear that European cooperation makes it much easier to achieve economic goals such as full employment. Britain, of all the European economies, is perhaps the most dependent upon international trade and therefore the most vulnerable to international, and certainly European, pressures. The abolition of exchange controls; the de-regulation of international finance; the tremendous leverage speculators have over newer financial instruments ('futures', 'derivatives', 'off-balance sheets') and the resolve of the multi-nationals to ignore state frontiers as they switch capital and cash within their operations – all of these factors mean that it is not possible to 'go it alone'. History shows that it was always difficult to build 'socialism in one country'. Now it is impossible.

The aim must therefore be to construct a new Europe to impose democratic accountability and leverage on Euro-capitalism. This means democratising European institutions by subjecting them to popular accountability. It means building a pan-European Socialist Movement to supersede the present Party of European Socialists which is essentially a confederation of leaders and therefore vulnerable to capture by Euro elites. It means building a strong European trade union movement through which workers can exert collective power against European bosses.

A UNITED EUROPE?

A genuinely united and democratic Europe is also an important prize. The British left has long argued for a united Europe, east and west, primarily for political reasons, including uniting the working classes of its different nations. One of the reasons for Labour's traditional suspicion of the EU is that the Treaty of Rome effectively specified a capitalist club, excluding other European countries. In the post-Gorbachev era, it might appear that enlarging the EU eastward is common ground. But it is hardly conceivable that John Major would have announced that he favoured an EU stretching from the Atlantic to the Urals if the former Soviet satellites had not lurched so enthusiastically towards the free market. The British right are now keen supporters of extension, but there is a hidden agenda in this support. Like other areas of European policy, extension is a complex issue, in which the interests of a United Europe have to be weighted against other considerations, in particular the effect extension would have on current policy debates – and these effects, of course, are the prize which the right are pursuing.

Cyprus and Malta are set to join. Hungary, Poland, the Czech Republic, Slovakia, Bulgaria and Romania already have associated status within the EU. The Baltic countries could join in the future. At the turn of the century there is the prospect of 25 or 30 member states. But, although it is politically desirable, enlargement throws into sharp relief the political economy of the EU. At present British taxpayers, along with the majority of member states which are net contributors to the EU budget, are subsidising the citizens of Ireland, Greece, Portugal and Spain which are the main recipient countries. The new members – Sweden, Finland and Austria – are together net contributors, so their admission has posed no difficulty in financial terms; indeed the EU's GDP per head rose by one per cent with their accession. But if – as is envisaged – enlargement includes the eastern and central European countries where GDP per head is one third of the EU average, they will be net recipients on a massive scale. There are three potential fiscal problems with their admission: their economies are far more agricultural, so the Common Agricultural funds would have to be even higher; they are poor; and they have large populations.

All of this means they would be heavily dependent on EU budgets. So their admission is incompatible with current EU budget contributions, let alone monetary union.

Extending the EU would also threaten political paralysis without a change which extended qualified majority voting (QMV) in the Council of Ministers. Yet the British right has made macho noises about retaining the British veto whilst simultaneously encouraging the admission of more countries. Unanimity, in fact, has been doubled-edged. Paraded as a means of protecting national interest, it can actually allow member states to be held hostage by the vetoes of other countries and can lead to lowest common denominator decision-making. For instance the scandal ridden Common Agricultural Policy will not be reformed without subjecting it to QMV. It is necessary to extend QMV to prevent states with small populations from imposing their will on the majority (whilst they must still retain the right of veto on such matters as Treaty changes, foreign policy, defence or the EU budget).

EU enlargement would improve both political stability in Europe and the prospects for world peace. But the British right is promoting it as as a spoiling tactic to block political and social integration and strengthen the free market: a wider EU stands in tension with a deeper EU. To put it another way, enlargement is a means by which the economic interests of capital will continue their dominance over the social interests of labour. There is a real risk that rapid enlargement to include much poorer countries in eastern and central Europe could dilute the social dimension which remains the EU's most attractive feature. Because these poorer states have lower social and employment costs and standards, it is economically impractical for them to undertake early implementation of the Social Chapter. In turn this could undermine the social dimension in the wealthier countries. Production and capital is already tending to shift eastward because of lower costs and this could accelerate within a single market, thereby undermining social protection and employment in the west. Enlargement must not be an excuse for postponing policies for social cohesion in existing EU countries.

Monetary union is even more problematic with extension. If most existing member states find it difficult to achieve the economic convergence necessary to make a single currency work, new ones to the east will find it impossible for the foreseeable future. It may be that there is a choice to be made between the rapid economic and monetary integration of the EU states – the 'fast lane' decided at Maastricht – and enlargement of the Community to include all the west European states and Eastern and Central Europe. If member states accelerate integration of their economies, this may effectively prevent enlargement because the entry conditions for other European countries could well be prohibitive. On the other hand, if economic integration is not systematically pursued throughout the Community then the leading EU countries – Germany, Holland, Belgium, France – may adopt their own 'fast lane' to economic and monetary union resulting in a two-speed Europe. The 1994 elimination of border controls within the so-called 'Shengen' area of nine out of the fifteen member states could be a foretaste.

For all these reasons premature enlargement of the eastern and central countries is impractical. Instead, ways should be found of building closer links, and supporting their development to help upgrade their social and employment standards, without a laissez faire dilution of standards in EU countries.

MONETARY UNION – AT WHAT PRICE ?

Monetary union would bring undoubted efficiency gains from eliminating the costs of exchanging currencies (about £12 billion across the EU); American Express estimated that a traveller beginning with £1000 in London and changing into the local currency on entering each member state would be left with just £605 on returning home without spending a penny. Also eliminated would be risk due to exchange rate uncertainty, thus preventing currency speculation. These benefits can be significant for an open economy like the UK. One third of our GDP is exported and a similar proportion of domestic expenditure is spent on imports. Moreover over 60 per cent of UK trade is with the EU. For a Labour Government, often in the past prey to the vagaries of currency speculation, there are undoubted advantages in avoiding these through fixing exchange rates. Another argument is that if the UK were to opt out of monetary union at a time when other member states were determined to proceed with it, this would make the UK significantly less attractive to international capital with damaging effects on its already weak economy.

On the other hand a single currency would impose major restrictions upon the use of macroeconomic policy instruments which, without offsetting policies, would give rise to growing unemployment in less competitive regions. With monetary union, each country ceases to be able to change the price of its currency and has less control over its monetary policy. The removal, or limitation in the use, of these policy instruments should cause no problem for the right. Free marketeers argue that adjustment to changing levels of competitiveness will come from labour mobility between countries and/or changes in relative prices (the nationalistic right, of course, preferring the second course).

However, in reality labour mobility in the EU will remain small, since labour is not a commodity like others. As already argued, people cannot be treated as if they were on sale in a fish market. It is ridiculous to think that people will continually up sticks and run round Europe in search of jobs. Excessive labour mobility is also inefficient since housing and other infrastructure is even less mobile. Moreover, experience suggests that prices are not as flexible as free marketeers like to assume. In practice, therefore, adjustment to changing levels of competitiveness most commonly takes the form of changing levels of unemployment. With monetary union, a worsening of a country's competitive position inexorably gives rise to growing unemployment unless there are offsetting interventionist policies. Even the ERM's limited degree of monetary union contributed to the high unemployment, high interest rates and low growth of the UK economy over its two years of membership; in 1991, national income fell by 2.4 per cent. Following Britain's exit from the ERM, the beneficial impact of devaluation and lower interest rates helped spark a recovery.

Within existing 'nation state' monetary unions (i.e, within national boundaries which have historically accepted a common currency as part of nationhood) there is substantial government intervention, such as active regional and industrial programmes and redistributive budgets. Such intervention helps to offset the impact on weaker regions of their inability to price themselves back into competitiveness by devaluing 'their currency', since they do not have one of their own. Intervention may be passive through benefit payments from the centre offsetting lost income, or positive through regional aid provision. Effectively what happens through this process is a redistribution of income from more to less prosperous regions.

Nation state governments typically appropriate and spend around 40 per cent of national income, which enables this redistribution of income to poorer citizens and regions. The EU budget is *just over 1* per cent of EU countries' national incomes (1.27 per cent of community GNP by 1999 agreed at the Edinburgh summit) and equivalent to less than 4 per cent of their average central government expenditures. This means that it is not of sufficient size to make the kind of regional redistributive allocations that would be needed to offset the negative effects of monetary union. Of course the remaining national state budgets mean that a literal comparison of the 40:1 ratio of national to European budgets is not valid. But even taking account of this, the authoritative MacDougall study in 1977 recommended a budget of 5-7 per cent. As Sir Donald MacDougall wrote: 'I fear that an attempt to introduce monetary union without a much larger Community budget than at present would run the risk of setting back, rather than promoting, progress towards closer integration in Europe.' The Governor of the Bank of England, Eddie George, in his speech in Luxembourg in February 1995, pointed out that fiscal transfers from West to East Germany amounted to 4 per cent of all-German GDP after the monetary union which followed reunification. This is equivalent to a budget three times the present European one.

The implications are clear. Monetary union should *only* be supported if there is a much larger centralised European budget – perhaps three or four times its present size – and automatic redistributive mechanisms, as well as highly interventionist regional and industrial policies.

But it is not desirable to shift member state's resources to the central European Union level without its thorough democratisation. This means much greater power for the European Parliament over the Commission and the Council of Ministers, and also, crucially, over the European Central Bank. The policy, legally enshrined in the Maastricht Treaty, of a European Bank independent of democratic control and dedicated almost exclusively to price stability must be reversed. It is economically disastrous and politically dangerous.

Although Conservative supporters of monetary union like Kenneth Clarke maintain that it has no constitutional implications, this argument is specious. As Dr Hans Tietmeyer, President of the Bundesbank, said in March 1995: 'It is more than a union of central banks – a system which decides monetary policy. Every politician, and I think every voter in the country, should be aware that monetary union is more. It has a political dimension.'

Premature deadlines for EMU should be abandoned. Putting monetary integration first is putting the cart before the horse. For managed exchange rates and ultimately monetary union to be feasible, let alone desirable, requires convergence in the 'real economies' of member states. Convergence in the rate of inflation and interest rates alone is unsatisfactory and unacceptable. As was apparent during 1991, some convergence in inflation rates between the UK and Germany was possible, but only in circumstances during which the Germany economy was growing by 3.5 per cent annually and the British economy shrinking by 2.5 per cent. This right wing, monetarist policy of convergence by recession – by squeezing out demand – should be totally rejected. It buys only a temporary reduction in inflation at a very high cost to the productive economy.

Monetary union can only proceed on the basis of real convergence in growth, balance of trade and employment levels. There need to be comparable skill levels, the same proportion of people in higher education, similar childcare provision and common minimum standards of social protection and employment rights. If it be counter-argued that these criteria are utopian, they are no less so than monetary union pursued without them. But above all, without a much larger EU budget monetary union must be resisted. That may well mean not having it at all. The prospect of raising member state contributions by around four times their present level may not be practical politics, especially for Britain which is one of the largest net contributors.

History provides ominous lessons for fixed exchange rates. When Churchill took Britain onto the Gold Standard in the 1920s, the consequences were disastrous and one result was the General Strike of

1926. The ERM caused mass unemployment, high interest rates, cuts in welfare and economic stagnation in Europe in the 1980s – especially once it had lost its flexibility by being tied to a Deutschmark set too high in order to curb inflationary pressures resulting from an unrealistic currency exchange in German reunification. A policy obsession with a high currency level has been similarly negative. The sharp Thatcher recession of 1979-81 was made much worse by adherence to a grossly overvalued pound. By contrast, the UK economy started to grow after the Gold Standard was abandoned in 1931. A post-1981 devaluation of about 30 per cent sparked off surging growth and the post ERM devaluation of nearly 20 per cent also led to growth from 1993 (although this is not to suggest that devaluation is without inflationary implications).

MAASTRICHT

To ensure a full employment, high quality Europe the Maastricht Treaty must be renegotiated and a different programme agreed at future Inter Governmental Conferences. The timetable and framework for monetary union set in the Treaty is impractical and its imposition of monetarism is both deflationary and reactionary.

Maastricht specifies rigid economic constraints, most notably that public sector deficits must not exceed 3 per cent of GDP and total public debt must not exceed 60 per cent of GDP. In the third and final stages of transition to monetary union, the avoidance of 'excessive budget deficits' becomes mandatory and subject to penalties: a kind of European 'state-capping'. These criteria are set out in Article 3A and more precisely specified in Article 109a-m. Effectively, they swamp aspirations for greater social cohesion and improved citizens' rights contained in Article A and Article B. They would prohibit policies for full employment and undermine the expansionist strategy necessary for economic regeneration. Rigidly maintaining the UK budget deficit at three per cent could severely restrict the use of public expenditure to drive economic growth (in Britain at the time Parliament endorsed the Treaty, in 1993, huge cuts or tax increases of over £30 billion would have been needed; even excluding public investment from this three per cent limit, cuts of over £20 billion would still have been needed).

In an important paper, the European economist, Stuart Holland, estimated in 1995 that meeting the Maastricht convergence criteria could reduce employment across Europe by more than ten million.

The central driving force behind Maastricht is the competitive, single market. Price, currency and interest rate stability predominate, together with tight restrictions on public borrowing and debt, almost regardless of the consequences for employment, growth and redistribution. While there are strict criteria for monetary stability there are no comparable targets for growth, full employment or resource redistribution. Indeed, so strict are the monetary targets that they would impose deflation on member economies (with devastating effects on the weaker ones). This process has been foreshadowed in the operation of the Exchange Rate Mechanism (ERM) which is a precursor to monetary union. For example in the early 1990s there were savage public spending cuts in Italy and Spain as they strove to meet the Treaty's convergence conditions. An additional threat comes from the commitment to the free movement of capital. All restrictions are to be prohibited, entrenching power in speculators and international financiers.

Maastricht did establish an industrial policy for the first time under Article 130. And the Delors White Paper on *Growth, Competitiveness and Employment* in 1993 proposed a raft of Keynesian interventionist measures to secure economic growth and create 15 billion new jobs over 5 years. A second Commission White paper on European Social Policy in 1994 stressed that even more jobs would not overcome social exclusion and poverty, and put forward a comprehensive programme of action. These initiatives were an acknowledgement that the free market is insufficient.

Nevertheless if the monetarist regime of Maastricht were to be implemented in line with the Treaty's legal obligations, democracy would be consigned to the scrapheap. For not only would control of monetary policy be handed over to unelected bankers, control over fiscal policy would be subject to the strict limits prescribed in the Treaty and control over currency levels would be relinquished. What scope would remain for national governments to shape policy in line with their electoral mandates? Virtually none.

Instead there should be agreement amongst the European Socialist parties on a programme that fully implements the White papers, that facilitates, rather than blocks, policies for reflation and incorporates specific measures to counter regional imbalances. This programme should include a much larger EU budget and the redistribution of wasteful farming subsidies towards investment in industry, infrastructure and training. Regional policies take up just 15 per cent of the central budget whereas the Common Agricultural Policy absorbed 53 per cent in 1993. The regional dimension is a key one. There is a real danger of EU growth and wealth being concentrated at its 'hub': Western Germany, France, the Benelux countries and perhaps Northern Italy and the South-east of England. Meanwhile its 'periphery' will decline. Unless there are strong EU regional investment policies, vast areas of the EU will become poorer and, following capital to the hub, political power will indeed be increasingly centralised.

But changing the direction of Europe means changing Britain's traditional stance of acting like a death's head at the feast. The miserable Conservative stance of grudging mean-mindedness towards Europe means Britain cannot influence the debate. To influence it we must be part of the European family, and our partners must feel us to be part of it. That is the only way to shift European policy.

Otherwise monetary union will happen – if only for some countries – and it will happen on the wrong terms, at the wrong time and for the wrong reasons. Britain, as has happened consistently on Europe, will be left outside until the multinationals, the unelected bankers and the deregulated financiers progressively corner us into joining a monetary union on *their* terms, rather then terms which might favour our voters.

THE EXCHANGE RATE MECHANISM

Meanwhile the left should adopt a clear stance toward the ERM, which is a precursor to monetary union. Maastricht specifies that the ERM should be transformed into a system of locked exchange rates. It also requires as another convergence condition that participating currencies should have been within a *narrow* ERM band (sterling was in a broad band) for at least two years without severe tensions. Following successive currency turmoils since the Treaty was signed –

notably the September 1992 debacle – and the shift to very wide 15 per cent fluctuation bands in August 1993, it is doubtful whether this aspect of the Treaty is feasible. Nevertheless, the basis for any re-entry to the ERM will be an important question for Britain.

The principle of exchange rate stability promised by the ERM is one that ought to commend itself: a mechanism that limits the power of currency speculators in favour of the real economy would particularly benefit governments of the left. But, as the dramatic events in September 1992 proved, the ERM does nothing of the kind. The absence of exchange controls (hastily re-introduced by Spain, Portugal and Ireland), financial deregulation and the lop-sided operation of the ERM which has forced weaker economies to deflate, means that it has become an impediment to European unity.

As a first pre-condition for any British re-entry, there must be new controls over the foreign exchange markets. These should thwart the short-term capital flows which now account for all but 5 per cent of currency dealings: 19 out of 20 deals done on the foreign exchange markets represent a speculative gamble and perform no useful purpose. The most effective method, as the economist Ruth Kelly has shown, could well be to tax short-term flows to make currency speculation less profitable. It is also necessary to control the leverage that the new financial instruments provide for speculators. It would be desirable to implement such measures, not just on an EU but on a global basis, presumably through the International Monetary Fund and the World Bank. Secondly, the ERM must be radically reformed to allow flexibility and to prevent stronger economies deflating the others; this can best be achieved by exchange rates that are fixed at any one point but adjustable over time. Thirdly, the pound must be at a level commensurate with the real strength of the UK economy (not the ludicrously high DM2.95 level of its previous membership). Interest rates should also be low. Fourthly, convergence of 'real' economies – through common employment, growth and investment targets – should be promoted in place of the monetarist ones in Maastricht. Fifthly, a planned increase in the central European budget must be put in place.

EUROPEAN ECONOMIC EXPANSION

Complementing such reforms, there should be a coordinated EU programme for expansion and full employment. As the Delors White Paper argued, a European-wide industrial strategy of supply-side measures is necessary. This should include increased public investment and spending on training, research and development, technology transfer and infrastructure. But the White Paper's recommendation for a £15 billion annual expansion to create 15 million new jobs is woefully inadequate: it is equivalent to just £1000 per year for each targeted job. Similarly the 1994 Social Policy White Paper's proposal for extra annual EU expenditure on training of £100 million rising to £130 million by 1999 does not even begin to confront the training mountain that much of Europe must climb to be competitive in world markets. Much more ambitious programmes are needed, especially since not even the modest proposals of the two White Papers have been implemented by member states, as Jacques Delors complained when he spoke of a 'wall of indifference' in September 1994.

Other interventionist measures should include:

- extending credit facilities to the economies of central and eastern Europe, enabling them to import more from the EU and to export more as well
- increasing the European Investment Bank's borrowing powers from the private sector and supporting it with the injection of considerable public capital, possibly by issuing 'European Recovery Bonds', as well as giving it new interventionist powers to boost industrial investment
- a coordinated reduction of interest rates
- a reduction of VAT rates to stimulate growth
- the construction of a high speed trans-Europe rail network and a fibre optic telecommunications 'superhighway' to put Europe in the forefront of information technology across the world
- the prioritising of investment in environmental protection, energy conservation and the development of modes of production which ensure environmentally sustainable growth strategies
- a coordinated reduction in working hours.

There will be no reduction in unemployment without increased public expenditure and the left throughout Europe should press for such a reflationary strategy. A strategy for high quality, high skill, high wage economies concentrating upon value-added manufacturing production is necessary if the EU is not to lose out to Japan, the low labour cost, fast-growing Tiger economies and the low cost sleeping giant of eastern and central Europe.

DEMOCRATICALLY ACCOUNTABLE CENTRAL BANKS

The European Central Bank (ECB) is another vital issue. Under Maastricht, the central bank would be an independent institution, single-mindedly dedicated to low inflation. The idea of making the Bank independent was hatched during the high tide of monetarism in the late 1980s. It was to drive Europe uncompromisingly towards monetary union by enforcing price, currency and interest rate stability. The consequences for employment, growth and redistribution would be entirely secondary to the all-powerful Bank. But the monetarist economics of Maastricht were out of date even before the ink on the Treaty had dried. The pressures which resulted from German reunification, rising EU unemployment and the ERM's implosion underline this.

Under Article 3a of Maastricht, the primary objective of economic policy is 'to maintain price stability and without prejudice to this objective, to support the general economic policies in the Community in accordance with the principle of an open market economy with free competition... these... shall entail compliance with the following guiding principles: stable prices, sound public finances and monetary conditions and a sustainable balance of payments.' So, other economic goals (for example full employment) can only be pursued 'without prejudice' to this 'primary objective' of near zero inflation.

Furthermore, it is specified that national central banks will be subordinate to the unaccountable ECB and not to their elected governments. Indeed the Treaty specified that the Bank of England would have to be privatised by 1999 in line with other countries. The independence of the ECB is uncompromisingly spelled out in Chapter III: 'When exercising the powers and carrying out the tasks and duties conferred upon them by this Treaty... neither the ECB nor a national central bank, nor any members of their decision making bodies shall seek or take instructions from community institutions or bodies, from any government of a member state or from any other body. The community institutions and bodies and the governments of the member states undertake to respect this principle and not to seek to influence the members of the decision-making bodies of the ECB or of the national central banks in the performance of their tasks.' This is about as uncompromising as it could be in shielding the bankers from democratic accountability. For socialists, such a transfer of power to unelected bankers is completely unacceptable.

The argument for political independence is that freeing the Bank from the vagaries of the political cycle could lead to a stable monetary policy and low inflation. Some enthusiasts even go so far as to predict higher rates of economic growth. But a respected 1990 Harvard University study of 17 OECD countries over a 35 year period by Alesina and Summers concluded that, while independent central banks seem to deliver low and stable inflation, they do not lead to more dynamic or stable economies: more fundamental structural matters were crucial. Other studies, including one published in the *Bank of England Quarterly* in May 1995, have shown that there is no correlation between low or zero inflation and growth. On the contrary, tight monetary policy run by bankers tends to jeopardise growth. It can certainly threaten employment. A pre-occupation with price stability tends to squeeze demand and deflate economies, thereby undermining jobs. Whilst no serious politician wants to risk a return to the high inflation of the 1970s and early 1980s, an obsession with maintaining inflation at under 2 per cent can only be at the cost of jobs.

The German Bundesbank is frequently cited as a model for all. It is claimed that the Bank's independence has been the key to German success. Of course Germany has had low inflation – averaging 4 per cent between 1960 and 1988 compared to Britain's 8 per cent and Italy's 10 per cent. Moreover, although the Deutschmark has appreciated in value against almost every other currency since the end of fixed exchange rates in 1972, because of low inflation this has not made German exports less competitive. But there are other reasons for post-war German economic success: the strength of its political system, its tradition of high skills, long-term corporate financing through its banks, effective partnership with trades unions, and most of all because of its trading structures which export high value goods and import lower added-value goods. In short, Germany in the last 20 years has achieved monetary stability by its economic leadership of Europe, not through its unelected central bank. Frustratingly, the Bundesbank has subsequently acquired a kind of mystical infallibility while the elected fiscal authorities have born the brunt of public unease by rejection through the ballot box. There is an ominous portent here: if democracy surrenders power over economic policy, voters could become completely alienated from parliamentary politics.

Bank independence can mean bankers making judgements that determine spending levels on welfare and infrastructure which are highly political and should be democratically accountable. Indeed, in the 1920s, the Governor of the Bank of England, Montagu Norman, insisted that he should have the right to set policies free of 'interference from politicians'. It is worth remembering that although prices were indeed stable in Britain between 1923 and 1925, there was no economic recovery. During the crisis which finally led up to the abandonment of the Gold Standard in September 1931, there was plenty of evidence that the then independent Bank of England extended its remit well beyond 'operational' matters to ones of policy. Its responses over the summer of 1931 were not democratically accountable. Its insistence on maintaining the Gold Standard was disastrous. And when that was eventually abandoned – having conveniently destroyed a Labour Government in the meantime – such was the grip of the prevailing orthodoxy that Sidney Webb was reported as saying: 'Nobody told us we could do this.'

Operational Bank independence is not the issue. But the fully fledged independence to which the EU is now legally committed amounts to the privatisation of monetary policy. Why should monetary policy be taken out of democratic politics and left to bankers? If there is a balance to be struck between low inflation and high unemployment, why should that be handed over to the bankers to decide? As Jeremy Leaman of Loughborough University has shown, the political power wielded by these independent bankers can be pernicious. He cites evidence that the Bundesbank helped to get rid of the Keynesian finance minister Karl Schiller in 1972, that it contributed to the resignation of the Schmidt Government during the recession of 1981-82, and that it recently exploited the asymmetries of the European and world currency markets to the sole benefit of the Deutschmark.

There is a hidden agenda behind the pressure for bank independence whether at a UK or a European level. And it is not forward-looking at all. On the contrary it goes back to the politics behind the Gold Standard which, in the late 1920s and early 1930s, became a mechanism for ensuring that market forces undermined social protection. Fixing interest rates independently of democratic accountability (which was the consequence of currencies being tied to the Gold Standard) meant that the financial institutions determined the money level of wages. As Brian Burkitt and Mark Baimbridge point out in their pamphlet from the Full Employment Forum:

> Independent central banks, national or continental, are currently being advocated as the vehicle to implement this sea-change in the class struggle. Socialists, on the other hand, must continue to assert the primacy of democratically accountable control over the money supply, in order that the goals of full employment, rising living standards and distributive justice can be pursued. Otherwise the business and moneyed interests, which control credit flows and determine financial confidence, will exert a silent veto.

Significantly, the former Tory Chancellor, Nigel Lawson, argued in his memoirs that independence would have the virtue of being a bulwark against an incoming Labour Government pursuing expansionist policies: monetarism would remain in power even if not technically in office.

To have the Bank floating free, with an exclusive commitment to low inflation and currency stability, is to concede the rightist concept of an EU driven by monetarism. On the contrary, the objectives of the Bank must include the maintenance of full employment and it must be made answerable, not merely to ECOFIN (the European Council of Finance Ministers), but to a rejuvenated European Parliament.

DEMOCRATISING THE EUROPEAN COMMUNITY

Since European capital and the world's financial markets have already stripped Westminster of significant autonomy, there is a need for maximum possible democratic control over the economic forces that are dominating the EU. The obvious mechanism is the European Parliament. Sweeping democratic reforms are needed.

Although there is an obligation on the European Commission (the EU's Executive) to consult the Parliament, MEPs cannot initiate legislation, nor can they control the Commission. The Commissioners and their officials wield considerable power, only marginally circumscribed by Maastricht. Nevertheless, diatribes against Brussels bureaucrats miss the main point. To be sure, they are not democratically accountable. But then neither is the Council of Ministers which is the all-powerful body in the EU. Although it has some claim to democratic legitimacy, since it consists of representatives of member-states, it acts as a secret cabal. Its decisions are not open to scrutiny, and because it operates by brokerage and wheeler-dealing, it is very difficult to influence from the outside.

More fundamentally, the whole point of a European Parliament is to express the general interest of the EU citizens as a whole. To deny it that power in favour of an indirectly appointed body is equivalent to saying that representatives of an association of local authorities rather than elected MPs should determine the policy of the UK Government.

Again it is instructive to look at the different agendas of left and right. British Conservatives oppose strengthening the European Parliament. They favour something called 'inter-governmental cooperation'. This amounts to operating through the Council of Ministers and thereby perpetuating the secretive, undemocratic mechanism described above. Of course it is no accident that the right favours such a course, because it will allow business to operate relatively unfettered. The left agenda should reject this and insist on full democratisation.

Furthermore, it is important to be clear about the term 'subsidiarity'. This has been commandeered by British Conservatives to favour Westminster over Brussels. In fact, as specified in the EU, it means decentralisation of power to the appropriate level, whether

European, national, regional or local, on the basis that decisions should be made as close to the relevant political unit as possible. For a Conservative Party which opposes devolution to Scotland or Wales and which has supported the emasculation of local government in Britain, an enthusiasm for subsidiarity is ironic to say the least. The left is in favour of genuine subsidiarity in the European sense.

FEDERALISM

Another matter which other European socialists find difficult to comprehend is the aversion in Britain, including on Labour's left, to the word 'federalism'. Many critics in the UK seem ignorant of the meaning of 'federalism'. It does not mean greater centralisation, 'fortress Europe', 'stripping Westminster of its authority', etc. On the contrary, a federalist structure is one where the powers residing at each *level* of government are clearly defined. Each level is given 'sovereignty' over appropriate decisions and duties specified as its own responsibility. Crucially, at each level, appropriate decisions are not delegated by some higher authority, they are taken as of right. It was Harold Laski who stated 'all power is federal', by which he meant that, in a genuine democracy, power is dispersed on a pluralistic basis.

The Labour Party has inched towards a federalist structure in Britain, notably by advocating devolution, whether in the form of a Scottish Parliament, a Welsh Assembly or elected Regional Authorities in England. A European Parliament worthy of the name would be the logical next step above the national tier at Westminster.

In a European context, federalism is a means of harnessing power to democratically elected institutions – power that will otherwise remain centralised in unaccountable Euro elites. It is significant that the most economically successful EU nation, Germany, has a federal structure with considerable autonomy delegated to the Länder. The case for such decentralisation is thus as much a democratic as an economic one.

Federalism also becomes a logical structure given the importance in the modern EU conception of the regions, as evidenced in the Committee of the Regions established under Maastricht. The whole thrust of EU evolution focuses on both the centre and the region, with the national level receding in influence. Links between Brussels and, for example, Catalonia or Wales can override links with Madrid or London. The EU's structural funds are geared towards re-distribution or compensation at the regional level.

The British left should therefore insist upon an active regional policy for the EU and the democratic mechanisms to facilitate this, including devolution to Scotland and Wales and the English regions, and strengthening the role of the Committee of the Regions. These are vital means of ensuring that the regional dimension is not just a one-way conduit for aid from the centre, but an active channel for empowering outlying areas and nations.

POLITICAL REFORMS

The powers of the European Parliament must be enhanced, not over national parliaments but over the structures of the EU. It is unacceptable that the European Commission should retain the sole right to initiate legislation. The Commission comprises 20 politicians appointed by their own governments, whose allegiance is to the Commission. They are not directly accountable to the European Parliament and they oversee a large and powerful bureaucracy. Why should this unelected Commission have these sole legislative rights, whilst elected European and national MPs remain relatively impotent?

Doubtless this was an understandable arrangement when the EU was still a fledgling body. But economic integration has given the Commission massive powers. Although it may be argued that the Council of Ministers reflects national parliamentary views, none of the Ministers from member states has been elected with a European mandate. Whilst MEPs who have such a mandate are shut out, Council meetings take crucial decisions guided by Brussels bureaucrats and their own civil servants whose expertise in EU complexities gives them disproportionate executive power. Such complexity also promotes a mystique which is anti-democratic: few British MPs, let alone voters, can get to grips with the range of decision-making processes in the EU.

Although the 626 member European Parliament has consultative rights, in practice European legislation which may have been rejected by voters when they elected their MEPs, can still come into force. The

Council and the Commission are all powerful, as is the European Court of Justice. The Parliament should be given the right to initiate legislation and control over EU monetary and fiscal policy. This is fundamental. However, it is also right that national governments should retain an important say. The way in which both these rights can be accommodated is by ensuring that EU legislation could only be adopted by 'co-decision' of both the European Parliament and the Council of Ministers. This would obviously require a culture of negotiation and brokerage alien to Britain but which exists already in Germany and many other democratic nations. In the European context it would have the great merit of being out in the open, whereas today the process of compromise is secretive, open neither to democratic scrutiny or challenge.

The Labour Party now favours co-decision in principle. The Party also favours a body to act as a 'regional voice' within the EU. The left should go further. The objective should be to create a 'bi-cameral' European Parliament with the second chamber consisting of members elected from both national parliaments and regional assemblies who would not be national government appointees and who could consequently represent their own domestic electorates. This second chamber should have consultative rights and be able to scrutinise legislation from the European Parliament and suggest amendments before it was finally agreed through the process of co-decision with the Council.

The advantage of such a second chamber would be to build in a checking mechanism of elected members from the nations and regions of Europe. This is perhaps more important for the regions in order to help exert a countervailing force to the centralising imperatives within the EU. It is also important to increase Westminster's scrutiny over the increasing flood of European legislation, perhaps through the creation of a European Grand Committee.

Additionally, the European Parliament should be given the right to elect the President of the Commission after each European election, ending the system whereby the Council of Ministers makes the appointment. The Parliament should also be given much greater powers over the Commission. In theory, it already has the ability to fire the whole Commission, but in practice this would be such a wholesale overthrow of an established structure as effectively to rule it out as a possibility.

A far better proposal would be to grant Parliament the ability which it does not now enjoy to dismiss individual Commissioners (perhaps on a two-thirds majority). This could be coupled with much greater rights of scrutiny over Commission business and the ability to question individual Eurocrats (whether Commissioners or senior officials) in a House of Commons Select Committee-type setting. There must also be a right to question the rotating President of each Council of Ministers, since each Presidency has considerable power and the ability to re-shape EU policy.

A final part of the democratic jigsaw would be electoral reform. Whether or not proportional representation is accepted for the House of Commons, there is a strong case for applying it to British MEPs so that they are in line with their European colleagues. The case for having a body of MEPs who genuinely reflect all opinion in Britain is strong, perhaps elected by a regional list system or a single transferable vote in multi-member constituencies.

In all these proposals, the guiding framework is that authentically democratic European institutions are needed to protect the ordinary citizen, and to counter the growing power of both Euro-bureaucracy and Euro-capital. An expansionary economic programme, positive rights for workers and citizens and democratic reform are components of a vision capable of mobilising a popular enthusiasm for Europe patently absent at present.

Without such a vision, the danger is that it will increasingly be seen as an elitist outfit, remote from the concerns of its citizens who face the problems of unemployment and public expenditure cuts and are perhaps even seduced by the simplicities of racism or nationalism. And so long as Europe is dogged by the monetarist orthodoxy of the 1920s, history suggests that democracy could face a threat as it did in the 1930s, institutional 'integration' notwithstanding.

The choice ought not to be between Euro-fanatics on the one hand and Euro-phobes on the other. Instead a socialist agenda should shape a people's Europe.

CHAPTER 6

The Global Economy

A remarkable orthodoxy has gripped discussion about international policy. Triumphalism about history's onward convergence to a capitalist ideal of free markets has even appeared to cow the left which has hardly offered a serious or consistent critique of the 'new international order'. Perhaps put off by the impenetrable complexities of GATT negotiations, conducted as if on another planet without connecting into popular debate, the left, with very few exceptions has allowed the right to capture the agenda. Mainstream left politicians have marched along with the 'inevitability' of free trade, pausing only to plead for grafting on a bit of regulation, improved worker protection and more overseas aid. There has been a resigned acceptance of the new 'global economy' in terms which suggest there is no alternative but to obey its dictates. So, deregulation, labour market 'flexibility', slashing public spending, adherence to rigidly low inflation and 'dynamic market forces' become the watchwords. Instead of cooperation, the imperative is exploitation.

Although nobody can dispute the ideological dominance of this new international order, it has brought a sharpening divide between rich and poor, and despair to developing nations crushed by debt and punitive trade relations. It presides over horrifying world poverty, rising ethnic nationalism, extremist religious fundamentalism, regional conflict, social instability and a deteriorating environment. It is run by an elite who control the transnational companies or play the international financial and currency markets. To the many hundreds of millions starving, warring, scrambling for jobs, or suffering ecological fallout, the ruthless application of free market forces is oppressive, not optimal.

The contradictions in this new international order are not anomalies, the exception to the rule. They are systemic. Thus strong rich countries rig trade and world markets against the poor. The European Union produces food in vast excess and dumps surpluses on world markets whilst African agriculture is destroyed and millions starve. Productive capacity in rich Northern countries is wiped out at huge social cost whilst the indigenous economic potential of poor Southern nations is strangled. The old Soviet bloc may have been liberated from bureaucratic tyranny and economic failure, but is its soaring crime, endemic mafia-style corruption, raging inflation, massive unemployment and disappearing welfare really any better?

There are now three main trading blocks: the European Union, the North American Free Trade Area and the Pacific Rim countries. On present trends they look likely to drive each other down in a vicious spiral of competitive deflation rather than cooperative reflation. The result has been a rise of beggar my neighbour regionalism driven by a harsh new right ideology, as in America, and increased racism as in Europe. Protectionism of the powerful is also emerging as the rich countries look after themselves whilst forcing free trade on the rest. How can anyone seriously suggest that this new world order is desirable, faced with its inability to achieve even the most obvious matching of resources to need?

The international Keynesianism which produced the 'golden age' of 1950 to 1973 has been abandoned in favour of tight-fisted – and to date far less successful – monetarism. During the golden age economic growth per capita in the four leading OECD countries, at an annual average of 3.8 per cent, was over double the rate achieved before this century; and it halved to 1.9 per cent during 1973-87. The main reason for the success of the golden age was the commitment of OECD countries to full employment through the mobilisation of government resources and demand management in a way that had not been implemented before and which has been abandoned since. During this period, for example, the International Monetary Fund had as its objective the promotion of full employment – something jettisoned in favour of price stability and low public spending as a condition for its financial blessing.

THE GLOBAL ECONOMY

What then are the salient features of this 'global economy'. Capital has globalised and finance even more so. Companies now cross frontiers to locate and invest almost at will. Integrated international production is becoming the norm. In the absence of any strategic intervention or proper regulation by governments, the transnational companies' insatiable drive for profits leaves in its wake huge social dislocation. A combination of international *laissez faire* and modern information technology has blown away controls on international finance, which is now footloose in search of quick returns regardless of long term consequences. About 95 per cent of international currency movements are now purely speculative, whereas before deregulation this same proportion accounted for real trade. Daily turnover in the foreign exchange markets is now about $1,000 billion. This system is inherently unstable, and the supremacy of finance has ominous implications for the world economy. As J.K.Galbraith observed: 'The sense of responsibility in the financial community for the community as a whole is not small. It is nearly nil. Perhaps this is inherent. In a community where the primary concern is making money, one of the necessary rules is to live and let live. To speak out against madness would be to ruin those who have succumbed to it. So the wise...are nearly always silent. The foolish thus have the field to themselves. None rebukes them. There is always the fear, moreover, that even needful self-criticism may be an excuse for government intervention. That is the ultimate horror.'

In *The Spectre of Capitalism*, William Keegan has demonstrated the interdependence of the world's economies. For example, from the mid-1960s to the early 1990s there was a sharp growth from one eighth to one fifth of the proportion of international output that is now traded across frontiers. Two thirds of this is in manufactures, overwhelmingly from the industrial countries which have thereby increased their hold over the developing nations. The concentration of economic power is striking. Huge sectors of the world economy are dominated by very few companies or countries. For example, six countries account for 90 per cent of all arms trade. A handful of companies dominate grain trade and America is responsible for over half world exports of grain.

A third of world trade is actually 'intra-firm' trade – across nations but within transnational companies – and is increasing: it is up from a fifth in the early 1970s. This, as Keegan points out, means that the old protectionism which might have favoured the self-interest of nationally-based companies or small businesses – and which was often fanned by right-wing populism – has become obsolete: it does not serve the interests of an increasingly dominant international, as opposed to national, capitalism. The transnationals treat the world not simply as a marketplace, but as a production base and want to be free of barriers and restrictions.

Demands for 'free trade' may be seductive. Who wants trade to be 'unfree'? Who wants to be associated with 'self-interested' and 'reactionary' protectionism? But here language has been appropriated for quite a different purpose. 'Free trade' today means free reign for transnational companies, international financiers and currency speculators. It prescribes a world run by a rich elite in the interests of a rich elite.

As Noam Chomsky has shown, in his *World Orders, Old and New*, 'With capital highly mobile and labor immobile, the globalization of the economy provides employers with the means to play one national labor force against the other. The device can be used to diminish living standards, security, opportunities, and expectations for the great mass of the population, while profits soar and privileged sectors live in great luxury.'

The 'new internationalism' is consequently something very different from the old notions, dear to the left, of world working-class solidarity and international brother- and sister-hood. Internationalism has been hijacked by capitalism. This does not mean that the rest of us can therefore escape back into the nation state or even further into the local community. On the contrary it means that we must engage with this new terrain, finding new mechanisms, institutions and movements to intervene and shape a radically different world based upon a true spirit of internationalism.

Presiding over this new international order is an ideology of 'global monetarism'. Exchange rates are prey to planned speculation by international currency traders. Organisations such as the Organisation for Economic Cooperation and Development (OECD), the International Monetary Fund and the World Bank preach, and where possible rigidly enforce, a doctrine of cutting public expenditure, deregulation, and near-zero inflation. The consequences are frequently catastrophic for the ordinary workers and citizens on the receiving end. The left meanwhile has been transfixed by the apparent triumph of capitalism. In fact the demise of the Soviet bloc should have liberated the left from any identification with a perverted and oppressive brand of statist 'socialism'. But, in the absence of a coherent ideological alternative, many have been seduced by the seeming invincibility of the free market, seeking merely to ameliorate its destructive consequences, when the world is crying out for a radically different agenda of international intervention and regulation for the common good.

The truth is that whilst state socialism has failed, capitalism has *not* succeeded for the majority of people: a fifth of the world is hungry and a third unemployed or seriously underemployed and over one billion live on less than one dollar a day. Capitalism has imposed a new imperialism – a new order governed by the IMF, the World Bank, the G-7 countries, GATT and other mechanisms which serve the interests of the transnational companies and international finance bodies. As the South Commission chaired by Julius Nyerere reported in 1990, 'the most powerful countries in the North have become a *de facto* board of management for the world economy, protecting their interests and imposing their will on the South' whose governments 'are then left to face the wrath, even the violence, of their own people, whose standards of living are being depressed for the sake of preserving the present patterns of operation of the world economy'. These institutions, Chomsky notes, have 'immunity from popular influence, even awareness. They operate in secret, creating a world subordinated to the needs of investors, with the public "put in its place", the threat of democracy reduced.' Economic globalisation is reversing the expansion of democracy over the centuries. International capitalism was of course never much interested in democracy in the first place. This was brutally confirmed by the influential American adviser and diplomatic historian, George Kennan. He wrote in a US State Department policy review in 1948: 'we should cease to talk about vague and...unreal objectives such as human rights, the raising of living standards and democratization'; we must 'deal in straight power concepts', not 'hampered by idealistic slogans' about 'altruism and world-benefaction' in order that the US maintained its 'position of disparity' over the rest of the world. Forty years later this doctrine was unchanged and perhaps even blunter. In Latin America, a senior CIA historian, Gerald Haines, wrote in 1989, that Washington's goal was 'to eliminate all foreign competition' so as 'to maintain the area as an important market for US surplus industrial production and private investments'. Such evidence reveals how subordinate is the *real politic* of international policy to the imperatives of the global economy and in particular to its dominant powers.

A DIVIDED WORLD

Despite centuries of technological progress and capital investment, the division between rich and poor is now as sharp, if not sharper, than ever before. The end of the Cold War has drawn aside a curtain which, for some, hid the reality that the West – often in the name of 'anti-communism' – was perpetuating and in some respects deepening this divide.

United Nations figures show that global inequality widened dramatically between 1960 and 1990: the gap between rich and poor nations actually doubled. Whereas in 1960 the richest 20 per cent of the world's people absorbed 70 per cent of global income, thirty years later this had climbed to 83 per cent. Meanwhile the poorest 20 per cent saw their share in of global income drop from a tiny 2.3 per cent to an even tinier 1.4 per cent. Measured by nation, the richest fifth of the world's population today earn over 60 times more than the poorest fifth. Between 1980 and 1988 the developing nations' share of global wealth fell from 22 per cent to 18 per cent. The plight of sub-Saharan Africa has become progressively more desperate, with its income from primary commodities declining in real terms by 50 per cent over this period. During the deregulated 1980s, per capita incomes in sub-Saharan Africa fell by 25 per cent and in Latin America (after a sustained rise since the war) by 10 per cent.

This gulf of inequality is not merely morally obscene and socially unjust; it damages and distorts the whole world economy by promoting overconsumption at the top and gross deprivation at the bottom. The developed countries of the North have only a quarter of the world's population but consume 70 per cent of world energy, 75 per cent of metals and 60 per cent of food. The average citizen in the industrial countries has 23 times the income, consumes 18 times as many chemicals, ten times as much energy and three times as much grain as an average citizen of a developing country. And, as the Worldwatch Institute points out, 'People at either end of the income spectrum are far more likely than those in the middle to damage the earth's ecological health – the rich because of their high consumption of energy, raw materials and manufactured goods, and the poor because they must often cut trees, grow crops or graze cattle in ways harmful to the earth simply in order to survive.'

Workers' rights are under consistent attack throughout the world. In 1995 membership of a trade union could still cost you your life. For example, in Colombia the national trade union centre reported the killing of 1,020 of its members between 1986 and 1994, with a correspondingly high number of massacres, disappearances and death threats. A survey by the International Confederation of Free Trade Unions documented how often men and women are still murdered, tortured, forced into exile, imprisoned, harassed or dismissed simply for defending legitimate and internationally recognised workers' rights. The ICFTU shows that these attacks have been fuelled by the wave of crude free-marketism, deregulation and labour flexibility. Anti-union repression has gone hand in hand with globalisation. Significantly, none of the countries that practise it can boast an improvement in their economic performance. On the contrary, most are locked into poverty and underdevelopment.

Child labour is a world phenomenon increasing everywhere. At the Dhaka International Conference against Child Labour held in January 1995 it was reported: 'The rampant increase of child labour in Mexico is the direct result of the imposition of the Structural Adjustment Plans by the IMF and the World Bank. These plans are responsible for the dramatic decline in real wages and in the overall standard of living of Mexican working people, making it necessary for more family members to seek jobs to supplement the family's income.'

FOOD AND FAMINE

The world's population is growing explosively and is expected to more than double from its present level of 5.5 billion within the next fifty years. Stagnating grain production, a decline in world fishing catches because of factory fishing, and the erosion of agricultural land by population growth in the South means that a quarter of humankind is now under threat from famine.

But, as Nigel Harris shows in *Of Bread and Guns*, food and famine are not the product of natural shortages. They are the product of economic and political forces. Free trade and the free market do not deliver equilibrium: they actively promote shortage amidst abundance and deprive the developing countries of the ability they might otherwise possess, if not to prosper, then at least to feed themselves. The world system has removed from millions of people the ability to grow grain and from their governments the resources to buy food imports. Before the war only Western Europe was a net food-grain importer. Fifty years later, the developing world imports over half its wheat and experiences chronic food shortages. Quite against the trend of its inherent natural resources, Western Europe has become the largest exporter of dairy products and sugar and, with the USA, controls three-quarters of the world grain trade.

The world food system is structured specifically to ensure that the rich have more than enough to eat. In particular far too much (around a third) grain is now grown to feed livestock to produce meat. This is an extremely inefficient use of land, as it takes 16 kg of grain to produce 1 kg of beef. Grain production is also largely controlled by the transnational companies involved in agri-business, and is subordinate to their search for profit. Over-production is not conducive to high profits, but scarcity is. Hence, food surpluses are deliberately wasted rather than placed on the market for consumption. Furthermore, scarcity assists these transnationals to corner the market: for example, a third of the grain growing areas of the four major cereal producing nations were taken out of cultivation in just two years between 1968-70. The US government had a specific policy in the 1960s of taking out of grain production one hectare in every five to keep up prices.

At the same time the agricultural output of developing nations has been curbed and distorted by the need to produce what are called 'cash crops'. These are sold to the rich world, at low rates fixed by international deals outside their control, thereby earning precious foreign exchange (which however then ends up being partly spent on the very food imports necessitated by imposed cuts in domestic food production). It is a vicious spiral of decline. Free trade's steadily more punitive terms makes it necessary to step up cash crop production to keep standing still. For instance in 1963 Tanzania had to produce five tons of sisal to buy a tractor; seven years later it took ten tons to buy one. And to make matters worse the cultivation of sisal, like other cash crops, depends increasingly upon fertilisers and pesticides produced by...northern-based transnationals again.

We can put people on the moon, and engage in foetal surgery, but we cannot feed the world equitably. And this is no accident: it is the direct result of the operation of a punitive and discriminatory system of trade which has failed to deliver anything like acceptable living standards for the great majority of people. The world food market is dominated by the rich North and organised for its benefit. Whereas the poor South is forced to dismantle trade barriers and tariffs and liberalise its agriculture, the rich North is protected by heavy subsidies: in the OECD countries these totalled about £330 billion a year. This plunges poor countries into even greater debt as they come to depend upon importing food surpluses from the North. As Nigel Harris demonstrates, 'Protection of "market incentives" takes priority over the survival of the poor.' In parallel food has become a means of asserting power and enforcing dominance. America now supplies nearly half the world's wheat – and food, as the former US Agriculture Secretary, Earl Butz, candidly argued 'is a tool in the kit of American diplomacy'.

The consequences are all too stark. One billion people – nearly a fifth of the world – live on less than a dollar a day. In 1980 every ninth person suffered chronic hunger, one in seventy-three died from malnutrition and many more died from diseases caused by poor diet. Twelve million children died because of protein deficiency and a quarter of a million were blinded because of Vitamin A deficiency.

While 40,000 children die *every day* from easily preventable diseases, the governments of developing countries devote half of their total spending to armaments and debt servicing. UNICEF estimates that at least five million children could be saved for the amount spent by the world's military in just one day. In Britain arms-related spending is about ten times the overseas aid budget.

AID AND DEBT

Under the free market, aid itself is not really about philanthropy. Instead it secures the interest of rich northern countries. The post-war American 'Marshall Aid' to help reconstruct war-torn Europe was given less out of generosity than from a prudent conviction that US companies needed a strong, stable European market for their goods. In a dress-rehearsal for later Western aid to developing nations, 77 per cent of Marshall Aid bought US-produced goods and services. As the former US Secretary of State, Dean Acheson, frankly admitted, Marshall Aid was seen by Congress as a mechanism to 'block the extension of Soviet power and the acceptance (by Europe) of Communist economic and political organisation and alignment.' This does not mean such aid should be spurned; rather that its ideological context should be acknowledged.

The 1950s US Food for Peace programme was no simple humanitarian gesture either. It publicly subsidised US agribusiness and advanced US political interests by encouraging people to 'become dependent upon us for food', as Senator Hubert Humphrey put it. But there is even more to it than this bluntly stated purpose. Noam Chomsky unravels the trail: 'undermining food production for domestic needs and thus helping to convert Third World countries to agroexport, with accompanying benefits for the powerful US transnational food industry and producers of fertilizers and chemicals; contributing to counterinsurgency operations through the military use of local currency counterpart funds; and financing the creation of a global military network to prop up Western and Third World capitalist governments by requiring that counterpart funds be used for rearmament, thus also providing an indirect subsidy to US military producers.'

The US is not alone. It has been estimated that in 1991 three-quarters of bilateral British aid was tied to British goods and services and that each pound of aid channelled through multilateral agencies generated 1.4 pounds of the spending on British products. About half of all world aid is tied in this way to donor economies and it has two other notable features. First, it gets channelled into the hands of the richer rather than poorer sections of developing country populations; and second, much goes to countries with high military rather than health and education budgets. In her book *Lent and Lost* Cheryl Payer exposes a series of myths about trade, aid and debt. She shows how aid and capital inflow from the North has substantially worsened the plight of the poor South, leading 'directly to the extraction of wealth from these countries' and forcing them into debt.

In 1990 just *one third* of the $1,200 billion debt owed by the Third World to First World Banks was the original debt: two thirds was in the form of cumulative interest and capital liabilities. This has provided a ready lever for Northern countries. As the South Commission observed: 'the North has used the plight of developing countries to strengthen its dominance and...to reshape their economic policies to make them more compatible with the North's design.' Between 1980 and 1990 the debt burden increased by 61 per cent and in 1991 debtor countries actually paid $24 billion more on interest payments then they were 'given' in new loans and aid. Because of this the developing nations were by the early 1990s net contributors to the IMF and the World Bank.

The resulting instability is counter-productive even for the smooth functioning of the global economy. When combined with 'hot capital' flows, major crises can occur. For example a peasant uprising in the southern Mexican state of Chiapas triggered reverberations through the international financial system. The small number of poorly armed Zapatista guerrillas who set up roadblocks and fired a few gunshots in December 1994 precipitated a panic amongst investors and contributed to a collapse of the Mexican stock exchange and a major devaluation. The US was faced with demands for $40 billion in guarantees without which American businesses involved in exports to Mexico would have faced a catastrophic crisis. As Mexico's delegate to UNESCO explained: 'the cause of this problem is not the Mexican people, who are paying the social cost, but the international financial centres, which are creating a currency crisis by withdrawing resources and which want to profit greatly but not take risks at strategic times.

The loans that Mexico has asked for are not to pay for its social problems but to go to meet large interest payments or pay rich investors who are out to make fast, easy money... we are witnessing the war of the markets and no country is immune to that.'

The Mexican experience is instructive. It had been a model of servility to the IMF and the World Bank – their 'darling' as the *Financial Times* reported in March 1992. As a result Northern investors poured in hot money – but only on the basis of returns well above the norm. Amongst other things the peso was kept artificially inflated so as to allow foreign investors to get favourable conversion back into dollars. But if northern financiers and the rich Mexican elites were kept happy by this regime, the real economy, along with the Mexican people, suffered – hence popular discontent, manifested in the uprising by Zapatista guerrillas. The response to the rebellion was also instructive. The Chase Bank of New York, with billions at stake, called upon the Mexican government to 'eliminate the Zapatistas'. Along with others on Wall Street, it favoured virtual dictatorship in Mexico.

It is important to note that the plight of the South has become much worse as the fashion for free markets and free trade increased in the 1980s. A UNICEF report in 1992 showed that during this period the structural readjustment programmes – always based on tightening monetary and fiscal policy, leading to cuts in public expenditure – forced upon the South saw a sharp reversal of progress in infant mortality, nutrition and education, as well as a rise in child labour and child prostitution. In Latin America, Cuba proved the exception to this trend, but its success was quickly killed in the 1990s by the withdrawal of economic support by the former USSR, and economic warfare from the US and its allies. The only other exception was Nicaragua until it too was strangled into submission by Washington and the IMF. Cuba and Nicaragua could not be tolerated because Castro and the Sandinistas offered an ideological challenge to international capital. Sandinista health, nutrition, literacy and agrarian programmes which had transformed the conditions of the poor were all scrapped. Thereafter, no doubt new right free traders took comfort in the fact that whilst four million Nicaraguans faced starvation, with their country the most indebted in the world, inflation was the lowest in the Western hemisphere.

ENVIRONMENTAL DESTRUCTION

Environmental protection has been undermined as well. Chronic debt is forcing poor nations to asset-strip their natural resources. Guyana, for example, is clearing its forests to finance heavy debt repayments. The 1994 General Agreement on Tariffs and Trade (GATT) will make this worse. It liberalised trade in natural resource-based products (for instance furniture) which means international competition will overcome conservation. The new GATT also makes it difficult for countries to implement stringent environmental standards. This is because it prevents the imposition of tariffs against environmentally unfriendly production. Free trade also undermines a policy of encouraging domestic producers to improve environmental standards because they could face competition from imports not constrained by such restrictions. Public subsidies or incentives for green production could also fall foul of GATT rules against 'restraint of trade'. As Tim Lang and Colin Hines show (in their book *New Protectionism*), 'Overall the main beneficiaries of GATT reforms will be the TNCs [transnational companies] and the main losers the environment and the world's poor.' The new GATT drives a coach and horses through green policies.

Lang and Hines also show how rising global trade flows mean rising transport costs and therefore increased energy use and pollution. One eighth of world oil consumption goes on transport for international trade. In 1991 the four billion tonnes of freight transported on ships used the same energy as Brazil and Turkey combined. On top of this is the energy used in plane, rail and road transport. Free trade will enormously increase the waste of energy and pollution in this transportation. Why keep two factories going when output can be increased from one and goods trucked far afield? In the European Union, the lifting of trade barriers under the single market is estimated to result in an increase of up to 50 per cent in cross-border lorry traffic. Lang and Hines challenge the consequences of free trade, which mean that, for example, citrus fruits are brought 10,000 miles from Latin America while Mediterranean countries dump fruit. This only makes financial 'sense' if the full environmental costs of transportation are ignored – such as air pollution, acid rain, and global warming as well as non-renewable resource pollution. Yet free trade ignores such costs and indeed makes it hard if not impossible to make them sufficiently transparent for enforcement.

Population pressures and the timber trade voraciously eat up forests and increase local flooding and the greenhouse effect. By promoting freer trade GATT in effect prevents localised conservation. For example, Canada was barred from imposing restrictions on exports of unprocessed herring and salmon from the West Coast, a move designed to protect the local fishing industry and conserve stocks. In another infamous case GATT was used to over-rule US restrictions on the number of dolphin that could be killed when fishing for tuna. Environmental protectionism was now to be equated with trade protectionism. If a 'green world' is the objective, there is no alternative but to challenge the direction of global capitalism.

CONCENTRATED POWER

Transnational Companies (TNCs) now dominate the new international order. The investment and jobs they bring to lower wage countries is of course welcome. But, accounting for a third of global output, they are increasingly a law unto themselves, outside the control of national governments. Indeed the output and assets of many TNCs exceed the Gross National Product of many countries. In 1986 World Bank figures showed that 167 top TNCs in each of the mining, manufacturing, banking, securities and insurance sectors had annual sales in excess of 64 countries' Gross Domestic Product. The dwarfing power of TNCs is evident even in an industrially advanced country like Britain where, in 1991, total international manufacturing production of TNCs based in the UK amounted to £78 billion, or a quarter of gross output, and accounted for the employment of three-quarters of a million people (a fifth of all those employed in manufacturing). Their powerful position is revealed by the fact that the top 350 TNCs control about 40 per cent of world trade, and the top 500 about two-thirds of world trade. During the free trade era, from 1980, as the top TNCs massively boosted their profits and output, they also shed millions of jobs. Between 1982 and 1992, the top 200 TNCs doubled their combined turnover to $6 trillion, whilst the top 500 got rid of over 4 million workers.

The growth of Transnational Banks (TNBs) has been even more dramatic. Between 1965 and 1974 US Banks saw the value of their foreign assets jump from $9 billion to $125 billion. As the Cambridge economist, Mica Panic, points out, 'Given the resources at their disposal, it was sufficient for these transnationals to switch a relatively small proportion of their assets from one currency to another to cause a major exchange rate crisis.'

A United Nations report confirmed that the 1994 GATT agreement increased the ability of TNCs to operate and accelerated the pace of global economic integration. Attempts to develop a code of conduct for TNCs broke down in July 1992. Significantly, free trade to boost their power and dominance was given the go-ahead whilst action to regulate their activities was restricted. The global economy is being managed in the interests of the TNCs and the international financial institutions. It is also a system in which power is increasingly concentrated. In their *Beyond Capitalism: Towards a New World Economic Order*, Keith Cowling and Roger Sugden identify a strong 'centripetalism' as a systematic feature of the global economy: 'Thus amongst transnationals strategic decision-making is concentrated in a handful of major cities of the world. At one and the same time the major corporations are internationalising production and drawing the control of the use of an ever-increasing share of the world's economic resources into the ambit of the key cities of the world – like New York, Tokyo, London, Paris.' Decision-making is concentrated in these 'command cities' along with income, wealth and power at the expense of local, regional and national autonomy. The idea that 'national sovereignty' seriously exists is a nonsense. The old slogans are redundant, whether 'Little Englanderism' from the old right or 'socialism in one country' from the old left.

WAR AND ECONOMICS

Globalisation has increased world military spending. It quadrupled in real terms between 1945 and 1980 when it reached 500 billion dollars. The pace of spending accelerated in the late 1970s as the free market caused increasing instability, conflict and chaos. Whereas cumulative arms spending totalled 3,325 billion US dollars between 1960 and

1976, cumulative aid totalled just 162 billion dollars. In 1993 global spending on arms amounted to £550 billion – equivalent to about a million pounds a minute.

Such massive resources have had a consistently negative impact. During the height of the Cold War, for example, the US and the Soviet Union undertook some 80 per cent of all the research and development spending in the world on military purposes alone. Britain has had a military budget disproportionately large compared with its role and importance as a world power – and has suffered the consequences. Military activity distorts economies and diverts production away from civilian needs and the competitive requirements of civilian industries.

The world arms race also encouraged poorer countries to join in or to defend themselves against what they perceived to be external threats. Often, of course, this suited the interests of the dictators of military juntas which tended to govern these countries. As their internal stability deteriorated, partly under the impact of punitive trade terms, their governments armed themselves more and more to crush dissent. The result, as Nigel Harris demonstrated, has been a further twist to the world divide: 'The richer the power, in general, the less the share of its national product it needs to devote to arms in order to achieve the most deadly effect... those who... are poor will be obliged to spend the largest shares of current income on arms.' Which means arms imports are paid for out of desperately scarce resources that should be devoted to feeding local people or invested in economic self sufficiency.

Throughout modern history, this system of global militarism has been sustained in order to advance and protect the economic interests of the world's major powers. In the post-war period the US has been the dominant power. The Cold War was not just a matter of security and but also one of who would win the economic struggle. As Nigel Harris pointedly wrote: 'Moscow [was] the pretext for the maintenance of the power of Washington over a majority of the States of the world. If Russia did not exist, the United States would perforce have had to invent it.' At the end of the Cold War several objectives had been accomplished. Authoritarian state socialism was imposed in the Soviet bloc, and partly sustained by invoking the 'threat' of the West. Meanwhile the US was able to deploy the Soviet 'threat' to cow the unions and the left internally, whilst externally, in the South through a combination of economic manipulation, aggression, subversion and sometimes outright terror, it enforced its own interests in the name of anti-communism, all along 'laying the basis for a world system dominated by transnational corporations and finance', as Noam Chomsky has demonstrated.

The strategic consequences were not only military but also economic. In the early 1950s the Korean War gave a powerful boost to US, European and Japanese economies. In the late 1950s and through the 1960s, the Vietnam War was a factor in the march of Japan toward economic power status, whilst assisting the long European boom and giving a lift-off to the newly industrialising East Asian economies. Vietnam was a classic case. Prosecuted without any moral, political or legal justification – or even any logical military necessity – it was only when the resistance to the US invasion triumphed at the Tet offensive in January 1968 that American business (which had previously benefited) decided the war was proving too costly. This, coinciding with the rise of the anti-war movement, proved decisive in the subsequent American retreat and ultimate withdrawal. In 1949, the *Magazine of Wall Street* had argued that military spending was a way of injecting 'new strength into the entire economy'. By the early 1950s it was finding it 'obvious that foreign economies as well as our own are now mainly dependent on the scope of continued arms spending in this country' – what Chomsky wryly calls 'international military Keynesianism'.

Another example of military Keynesianism was President Reagan's Star Wars project, which never had any serious military prospects. But it was partly sold as a means of supporting private capital through spin-offs into leading edge civilian technology. The Gulf War in 1990-91 followed the strategic threat to US and western world interests posed by the threat of Iraqi control of Kuwaiti and Saudi oil, but it was also a convenient boost to the US arms industry after the end of the Cold War, and was followed by a relentless arms sales drive by the US. By the mid-1990s 'dovish' President Clinton was spending more in real terms on defence than 'hawkish' Richard Nixon two decades before. In the military sphere, US capitalism has not relied upon the free market it insists must be inflicted upon the rest of its workforce and indeed the world. The US arms industry has always been significantly pump primed and heavily subsidised by the state and has supported US dominance of the global economy. In the large civil aircraft market, fo instance, American dominance was subsidised by large military order which effectively funded development costs of their airlines, and wa only challenged when the European Airbus consortium used nationa subsidies to finance its development costs (subsidies which the US ther complained contravened 'free trade').

'FREE TRADE'

Against this background of structural inequality, endemic poverty power centralised to an historically unprecedented degree, and economically driven militarism, trade policy must be reconsidered 'Free trade' is not a neutral force automatically enlarging prosperity for the benefit of humankind, with competition creating some optima equilibrium. It is an ideological force which advances certain dominant world interests at the expense of the rest. This is fundamentally, because free trade always favours those who are in the strongest position.

The Second World War marked the high water mark of planning and state intervention in the economy. These Keynesian policie rescued world capitalism from slump and created the foundations fo the 'golden age' of the 'long boom' which continued through to the early 1970s. The Keynesian influence, as William Keegan shows, wa not confined to domestic economic policy: 'The preponderant theme of the international discussions that led up to the Bretton Wood conference of 1944, and the subsequent formation of such international institutions as the International Monetary Fund, the World Bank, the Organisation for Economic Co-operation and Development and the General Agreement on Tariffs and Trade wa the belief that enlightened co-operation *between* capitalist countries wa also necessary.' Although the IMF and the World Bank were instruments of American foreign policy – situated in Washington, with most top officials US citizens – this regime ushered in nearly thirty years of what Nigel Harris calls 'global social democracy'. There was a managed dismantling of trade barriers through GATT, managed exchange rates through the the Bretton Woods system overseen by the IMF, and co-ordinated international loans through the World Bank.

GATT was signed by 23 countries in 1948. This rose to 108 countries by 1993 by which time it covered over 90 per cent of world trade. GATT rests upon several key principles promoting free trade: 'non discrimination' under which import duties imposed on one country must be applied equally to all, 'reciprocity' whereby a tariff reduction by one country should be matched by its trading partner, and 'transparency' of non-tariff barriers such as quotas on imports. Under its progressively liberalised regime, world trade increased fourfold. But although the 1994 GATT agreement promised to maintain and even accelerate such a rate of increase, this claim is very doubtful.

The early 1970s marked a turning point. The Bretton Woods system had never operated as originally envisaged. Instead of being managed by international institutions, the world economy was dominated by the US and the dollar became a world currency. And when the post-war dominance of the US started to erode, so did the system. Managed exchange rates collapsed in 1972 after the US drew back from spending abroad and floated the dollar. This encouraged huge currency speculation and surging capital movements. The international financial system was thrown into chaos and the foreign exchanges closed for more than two weeks before they reopened in a new world of floating currencies in March 1972. The next year oil prices quadrupled, sending further shock waves through the international economy. The following years of sharply rising inflation further undermined the post-war Keynesian consensus. As workers responded with catch-up pay militancy, inflation became the pre-occupation of governments and policy-makers. Fighting it took precedence over employment creation and demand management, and so monetarism eclipsed Keynesianism.

In parallel, worldwide deregulation of finance occurred. Exchange controls started to be abolished. Financial institutions were progressively given access to markets other than those to which they had been confined (for example in the UK building societies moved into banking). Credit controls were abandoned and a global market in monetary instruments established.

The 'golden age' had not been without its structural problems, of course. North-South inequality increased and the terms of trade for developing countries worsened. Poverty remained stubbornly widespread. Global 'social democracy' was an inadequate mechanism for creating a just and economically prosperous world. But it was far superior to the naked monetarism which followed it. Growth, employment, investment, infrastructure and welfare achieved new heights in the North, and all because government intervention and international co-operation rather than the unbridled free market were the watchwords.

By the time global monetarism was in its stride in 1980, the North-South Commission under Willi Brandt reported 'an unprecedented mixture of starvation, inflation, escalating unemployment, international monetary disorder, protectionism, major tensions, advancing deserts, over-fishing, pollution of air and water, and the arms race.' However, its call for a 'collective effort' to overcome these problems was largely ignored as the blizzards of competition blew aside its sensible proposals. Tight money policies promoted financial stability (especially in prices) over employment. High interest rates reduced investment and slowed trade. Overseas aid from the rich North was not increased but cut whilst the reverse was true for arms spending. The IMF was prevented from promoting employment and growth. The World Bank's funding was cut, in the process virtually bankrupting its soft-loan agency. In a world of increasingly mobile capital, financial deregulation and subservience to market forces, the Brandt Commission's brave attempt to revive a measure of global social democracy was doomed to failure.

It was certainly killed off by the outcome of the latest GATT round. The new General Agreement on Tariffs and Trade, known as the Uruguay Round, took seven years to negotiate and was signed by 116 countries in April 1994. It established a new World Trade Organisation from 1 January 1995 to police much freer trade in manufactures, services, textiles and agriculture.

Its effect will be to further penalise the non-industrialised South and within the North to widen existing inequalities of income and employment. GATT is now forcing the developing nations to liberalise and open up their economies to foreign trade and competition. Their agriculture will become increasingly open as well, which is likely to cripple food self-sufficiency and make them still more dependent upon the US and Europe for food. (The latter's agriculture is still protected by the CAP against competition from developing countries.) As the UN Food and Agriculture Organisation reported in 1995, low income developing nations which import food will be significantly worse off. The new GATT is a charter for the rich and the transnationals. They will be able to penetrate at will the economies of the developing nations and to increase their stranglehold over new technology and intellectual property rights.

The much trumpeted claim that the new GATT will create $270 billion of world-wide growth must be put into perspective: it is equivalent to just 40 dollars per person and will only reach that level by about 2004. Not only will GATT continue to penalise the developing nations, it will also hit the nations of the North by encouraging the newly industrialised economies of East Asia in particular.

Tim Lang and Colin Hines have offered one of the few cogent critiques of GATT and its notion of free trade. They paint a convincing and devastatingly bleak future for countries like Britain. As tariff barriers crash down, they ask, how can Europe's workers compete with low-wage economies, especially those in eastern Europe and east Asia which have high skills? For example, they observe that in 1993, West Germany's manufacturing labour costs were $24.90 per hour, Japan's $16.90, the US's $16.40, France's $16.30; and Britain's $12.40. These compared with hourly rates for manufacturing labour of $4.90 in South Korea, $1.80 in Hungary – and with China out of sight at $0.50. On these rates, there is no possibility of countries like Britain out-competing in a free market where labour costs determine investment and production location. No wonder one commentator quoted by Lang and Hines observes that some transnationals have 'found a way of coping with a fundamental problem of European manufacturing... trying not to have any.'

Labour costs are not everything, especially in advanced manufact-uring where they form a decreasing share of overall company expenditure. Some suggest that the labour element in *direct* costs (i.e. those which vary directly with each unit of output, such as material costs) may be less than 10 per cent and for standard products such as motor seats it could be just 5 per cent. If so, competitive advantages from cheap labour could easily be outweighed by transport charges or small tariffs. Japanese just-in-time production methods encourage suppliers to locate near to factories and, in any case, the European Union's economy is 93 per cent self-sufficient. So labour costs are not necessarily the principal determinant. A report from Andersen Consulting in 1994 contained a warning: 'Global investors beware: betting on taking advantage of only one positive aspect of a location [labour rates, for example] is a false hope. Only those companies who set ambitious performance goals and consciously balance process discipline, supply chain integration and local advantages will lead worldwide competition.'

But figures from the 1991 Census of Production show that labour costs for all manufacturing in Britain are 25 per cent of total costs (including indirect costs such as rent of buildings and purchase of machinery) – clearly a much more significant proportion, though one that has since continued to reduce. On this basis, competitive advantage of relocation to low wage countries could be much greater. So although that wholesale relocation of manufacturing from Europe to the Pacific Rim is not inevitable, it is nevertheless a real threat and, in the case of new investment rather than relocation, a difficult one to thwart, especially given the high skills and infrastructure standards which have been achieved in the East Asia 'tiger' economies. The latter now put a much higher proportion of their young people through college and university than the UK and US and this gives them a significant comparative advantage in international trade.

So at best GATT is a negative force for maintenance of indigenous production and at worst a positive enemy which actively encourages production to locate in cheaper labour markets, provided of course they have the necessary skills.

The expansion of trade over the past few decades has undeniably linked the labour markets of the North more closely to the South. The benefits may seem benign: living standards have risen in the North and there has been development in the South, particularly the Pacific Rim. But the North's unskilled workers have been badly hit as they have suffered from widening inequality and rising unemployment. (Conditions for workers in the South are, unsurprisingly, even worse – it is partly their cheap labour that has made them attractive to foreign capital.) Trade patterns have changed as exports from South to North have risen from a negligible amount in the 1950s to $250 billion by 1990 – an average growth of 15 per cent annually. The South – especially the East Asian bloc – has ceased to be merely an exporter of primary goods. As Adrian Wood shows in his exhaustive 1990 study, *North South Trade, Employment and Inequality*: 'The old pattern of trade, in which manufactured goods from the North were exchanged for primary products from the South, has largely been replaced by a new pattern, in which the North and South each specialise in different sorts of manufactured goods.'

As a result demand in the North for production of skill-intensive goods has increased, whilst demand for labour-intensive goods has sharply reduced. Labour intensive production has shifted to the South. This has produced a devastating reduction in unskilled labour in the North. The rise in demand for skilled labour was not correspondingly large and Wood estimates that the cumulative impact of North-South trade up until 1990 upon manufacturing jobs in the North was the loss of about 9 million person years of work. This represents the loss of about 8 million jobs from the US and Europe, half a million of these from Britain. The position of unskilled workers deteriorated more in Northern countries with higher Southern import penetration.

Employment patterns altered dramatically. British companies either withdrew from areas such as textiles, shoes, toys and consumer electronics, or relocated production to the South. Those that remained switched to value-added, upmarket production. From 1979 to the early 1990s, the percentage of manufacturing workers with no educational qualifications dropped by a third in Britain. In tandem relative wages of skilled to unskilled workers shot up over this period.

Wood shows that the reduction in trade barriers was the main cause of this change in the pattern of North-South trade and concludes that further reductions will increase the trend. Yet this 'free trade' is precisely what the latest GATT agreement promotes. In a context of better transport and communications, increasing digitalisation and information technology, there will be a further loss of secure jobs across all categories in the North and a further shift in intermediate and unskilled jobs to the South and, increasingly to Eastern Europe. Such an outcome can only be avoided by breaking with the contemporary ideology of 'free trade'. This is not to say that the left should oppose the development of the newly industrialising countries, or call for a reinstatement of the old patterns of trade. Rather, a framework needs to be created in which indigenous development in all countries is achieved by means other than the exploitation of cheap labour, and that the standard of living within one country is not raised at the expense of the standard of living of those in other countries.

Within this overall picture, there are individual differences, with important implications for policy. The widening gap in skill and pay differentials was greater in free-market countries, notably the US and UK, and weaker and less consistent in other European countries with more interventionist governments and better infrastructure. (The suggestion that the spread of new technology in the North based upon imported micro-processors was the main cause of widening skills differentials is not borne out by the experience of Japan and Sweden, which had more industrial robots yet smaller widening skill gaps than other Northern countries; they also had more interventionist regimes.)

To point out the negative consequences of free trade does not imply an argument for beggar my neighbour protectionism, which would plunge the world into recession. But the 'free trade' we are invited to endorse is actually a very different animal from the international co-operation that in the post-war period provided an alternative model to the protectionism between the World Wars. The current model is really about deregulation; about liberalisation of financial services so that power is ceded to international bankers and currency speculators; and it is also about enhancing the dominance of the transnationals. As Noam Chomsky states so succinctly: 'it is not "free", it is not about "trade", and it is surely not based on an "agreement" among the irrelevant public. The "free trade agreements" impose a mixture of liberalization and protection, going far beyond trade, designed to keep wealth and power firmly in the hands of the masters of the new imperial age.'

INTERNATIONAL MONETARISM

Authentic free trade may be desirable. In theory free trade should allow countries to produce what they are good at, resulting in what economists call the principle of 'comparative advantage', through which competition and efficiency thrive and global demand and prosperity is raised. Like most free market theory, however, it founders on the reality, which is that there is never truly free competition. The armies of capital group together to create world conditions in which the odds are stacked in their favour. And as long as capital is free to pursue absolute profitability wherever it likes and regardless of the consequences, comparative advantage theory is a pipedream. Instead of a trade regime geared to maximising the economic interaction of countries and regions to mutual benefit, we have one which, whatever its rhetoric, is distinctly 'unfree' in its impact upon the poor and the powerless. It is also counter-productive in that it destroys the ability of its many victims to purchase the goods and services on offer.

This free market regime has had a negative impact upon employment in each of the G7 leading industrial nations. Over ten years in the deregulated era of 1983-92 unemployment shot up in comparison with the Bretton Woods period of 1964-73: it was eight times greater in Western Germany, over four times greater in France, over three times greater in Britain and over twice as high in Japan. The post-Bretton Woods imperatives of floating exchange rates, global market deregulation and massive short-term capital flows have been hugely deflationary.

A study of World Bank data on 76 nations in the poor South and in eastern Europe showed that the structural adjustment programmes forced upon them by the institutions of international monetarism during the 1980s also had an overwhelmingly negative impact. Whether measured in terms of investment, growth or employment, these countries were much worse off than in the bad old days of regulation and government intervention.

Eastern Europe provides a classic evidence of this. The shock therapy of instant market forces imposed by the West may have suited the transnationals in their quest for larger markets which had been denied them by the Iron Curtain. But it was devastating for the people. In Russia, for example, hyperinflation went on the rampage, with prices going up hourly or at best daily. Life-long savings were virtually wiped out. Real earnings collapsed. Poverty on scales unknown for generations became endemic. Industrial production fell by at least half. Previously strong health, welfare and education services collapsed or disappeared. Capital took flight, leaving behind a twilight world of money laundering, rampant corruption and the emergence of a rich elite amidst mass near-starvation and spreading diptheria, tuberculosis and other forgotten diseases. Life expectancy for men in Russia fell from 65 years in 1987 to 59 years in 1993. Civil society and its ethos of solidarity and community was destroyed as everyone turned to selfish self-preservation. In just one year (1991) the average gross domestic product of the old Soviet bloc declined by 15 per cent. As the countries of eastern and central Europe were opened up to free market capitalism between 1989 and the end of 1992 output fell by between 16 per cent and 42 per cent. Nothing like this had been experienced since the inter-war years of the Great Depression. This is not to defend the earlier system, but it indicates that unregulated capitalism was not the answer to these countries' problems.

A Marshall Aid type programme of investment and support from the West could have accomplished the transition that was necessary. Instead the free market was left in charge. Aid workers were quickly replaced by privatisation consultants from the West: some reports in the US put the proportion of American 'aid' going on US consultants at between 50 and 80 per cent by 1993. Chomsky summarises the picture: 'From 1989, the economies of eastern Europe went into free fall under the World Bank-IMF regimen, with industrial output and real wages deteriorating radically while the new rich enjoyed great prosperity and foreign investors gained new opportunities for enrichment, on the familiar Third World model of an "active part in the global economy"'.

In Third World economies, the free market 1980s saw the development process stagnate. Whereas in 1965-73, GNP per capita grew by 4.3 per cent annually, this slowed to 2.7 per cent in 1973-80 and dropped to 1.2 per cent in the 1980s. Keith Cowling and Roger Sugden show how the restrictionist monetarist policies adopted by the industrialised North in the late 1970s led to higher interest rates and worsening terms of trade for the poor South: the terms of trade deteriorated by 35 per cent between 1978-80 and 1986-88. This remarkable fall was greater and more intense than during the Great Depression. And we are asked to support even more of this 'free trade'

As Cowling and Sugden argue, this trend hardly gives 'a reason for exposing these countries to even more market shocks, but perhaps a strong argument for establishing greater governmental, or joint governmental, control over such markets.' After all, these markets are controlled by a small number of buyers based in the rich North. 'Free trade' has led to a position where between three and six transnationals control 90 per cent of coffee exports, 80 per cent of tea exports, 85 per cent of cocoa exports and 85-90 per cent of jute exports. Unless these giant transnationals are subject to international and national regulation, it will not be possible to restructure trade relations in a way that benefits the South and thereby boosts the world demand which also favours the North. Another necessary step is reform of Europe's agriculture policy, including scrapping the common external tariff on food imports, to allow EU consumers to pay lower prices for food from the South.

For the gap between rich and poor has widened in the West too, most sharply in the strongest deregulators, Britain and America. In the latter, for instance, one of the most significant measures, inequality of mortality rates, more than doubled between 1960 and 1986. Income inequality in the US had been reducing until 1968, but then rose to levels which now surpass those of the Great Depression. During the 1980s and into the 1990s real incomes fell for the great majority of US citizens, excepting of course the very well-off. In most of the countries of the rich North, income inequalities widened during the free market 1980s according to the OECD, which also showed that the most extreme cases were Thatcherite Britain and Reaganite America with their deregulated, cut-price labour markets. By 1994, the International Labour Organisation estimated that 30 per cent of the world's workers were unemployed or seriously underemployed. There is little or no prospect of reversing these trends within the regime of international monetarism.

Meanwhile, the world's financial system has been spinning out of control. Its inherent instability was graphically exposed by the sensational collapse of the venerable British merchant bank, Barings, in February 1995. The derivatives market – which amounts to an institutionalised mechanism for betting against future currency movements – has grown exponentially from $500 billion in 1986 to

$4,449 billion in 1991: an increase of 790 per cent. By 1994 the total volume of these derivatives had reached a staggering $12,000 billion According to the economist Ruth Kelly, the entire world financial system is now exposed to 'systemic risk'.

Cross border lending has mushroomed, now exceeding one quarter of the Gross Domestic Product of the industrialised countries Between 1972 and 1992 international banking grew at twice the rate of world trade and world output. International bank assets are now more than double the volume of world trade; thirty years ago they formed just 10 per cent. Capital roaming free across frontiers has no matched the investment of the golden age since it has been competing for the quickest, highest return. 'The real enemy,' Will Hutton argues 'is global deregulation and volatile capital flows. Post-war stability has been replaced by a new instability – good for the brokers and traders bad for employment and investment.'

As Cowling and Sugden argue: 'It is important to emphasise tha what we observe is a crisis of the world, capitalist economy. It is not jus a British crisis, or a Russian or a United States crisis, or a Third World crisis, but a crisis of the capitalist system as a whole... markets are controlled and manipulated by a powerful subset of the population – the few who control the transnationals. These elites influence situations and events for their own benefit... not for society as a whole As a consequence a free market economy is a socially *inefficien* economy.' The international world economy is infected with 'systemic short-termism' where the drive for quick profits subsumes long term strategic objectives. But, as Cowling and Sugden state – in a crucia pointer for an alternative – 'This is not a problem of markets *per se* rather a problem with the way markets are used by the powerful to further their own interests.'

POLICY LESSONS

Markets will continue to have an important role in the international economy; otherwise we must opt for failed command economics. As Aldous Huxley wrote in 1938, 'Capitalism tends to produce a multiplicity of petty dictators, each in command of his own little business kingdom. State socialism tends to produce a single centralised, totalitarian dictatorship, wielding absolute authority over all its subjects through a hierarchy of bureaucratic agents.' In the global economy, the issue facing us is how to regulate and control markets for the common good rather than the private benefit of the few.

There are important lessons to guide this task. First of all, the most successful economies of the world have extensive government intervention, regulation and, dare one say it, planning. Much notice has been taken of the phenomenal growth rates and success of the east Asian 'Tiger' economies. We must not ignore the oppressive labour relations which tend to operate in these countries and the short shrift often given to human rights. But they are not the free market capitalist utopias sometimes pretended.

South Korea, Taiwan, Singapore – and now Malaysia and Vietnam – have followed Japan down a road which specifically rejects the ideology of the unbridled free market and free trade. They did not open their economies to foreign investment and foreign trade. Nor did their governments stand back and await the invisible hand of competition to produce the industrial development necessary. In the first instance, their governments adopted a clear strategy of nurturing and fostering manufacturing industries in sectors which it was considered would enable domestic production to substitute for imports: computers, motor cars, for example. Then they moved on to promote exports, which extended to shipbuilding and aerospace.

A variety of measures were deployed by their governments. Tax incentives and subsidies were used in a consciously strategic fashion. For example, subsidies were removed if industries were unable to compete abroad. The private sector was not simply told to get on with it. The whole of their societies were driven by macro and micro economic policies to produce high skills and high investment, with no ideological hang-up about public intervention and public investment and spending. In 1991 even the World Bank – rather churlishly contradicting its own monetarist ethos – admitted: 'Selective state intervention has figured prominently in two of the most impressive success stories of development: Japan and the Republic of Korea. Both countries employed taxes and subsidies, directed credit, restrictions on firm entry and exit, and trade protection to encourage domestic industry.' The latter admission about trade protection is significant. If

Japan and the Tigers had relied upon 'free trade' they would still be lagging far behind economically. They did not. Their governments actively 'managed' their trade relations, just as they managed their economies.

In Japan, the government employed the kind of protectionist measures which free market theory would denounce as leading inevitably to 'inefficiency'. But the distinction is that, instead of creating a siege economy using negative protectionism, Japan adopted positive protectionism within a planned industrial strategy. Fledgling industries were protected from foreign competition, but there was no feather-bedding. Domestic competition was encouraged and industrial strategy consciously promoted innovation and new technology. The banking system, government spending (for example to subsidise a modern transport system), taxation and indeed the welfare state were all subordinated to the needs of industry. In the past this made for a rather spartan lifestyle by comparison with Europe. But its focus upon investment and industrial growth rather than private consumption created the strongest, most successful economy in the world.

The value of strategically planned government intervention can be seen in the way Japan has consistently outpaced its competitors in manufacturing and innovation, making a mockery of the world's obsession with free markets. One of the most recent examples is the Japanese Government's decision to sponsor research into battery technology that would make possible mass transport by electric car. By comparison with free market Britain and America, Japan does not display their chronic short-termism, it does not have the same culture of high dividends, constant asset-stripping and perpetual takeovers. It relies strongly upon teamwork rather than individualism. Solidaristic group activity and collective planning, so despised by the new right, are its watchwords.

Whilst they are all different and have pursued government intervention to varying degrees, the Tiger economies are all 'guided' economies. Close linkages between banks and industry, strategic government support to the point of 'picking winners' and deployment of a variety of fiscal and monetary measures to foster manufacturing were common to all. Reviewing the experience, Keith Cowling and Roger Sugden conclude that, 'the most outstanding examples of dynamism emerging from the post-World War II Third World economy were not free market economies: as with the case of Japan, the most dramatic example of economic dynamism within the advanced industrial countries, rapid development was achieved within a "guided" market economy , in the context of a "strategic" integration with the world economy. The rules of the IMF/World Bank were violated and economic success was achieved.'

The US, often cited as an example to follow by free marketeers, is not quite what its admirers claim. The American government has been highly interventionist through its defence programme. In what William Keegan refers to as a 'proxy for industrial policy', the US government subsidised, protected and planned for its military strength. The military-industrial complex which has dominated the US economy for generations is not some creature of free market forces. It is the product of private-public collaboration.

As Michael Ignatieff graphically put it: 'Europeans like to think of the American model as *laissez-faire*, red in tooth and claw, but it is actually a form of state capitalism in which the great corporations of the military-industrial complex fatten on the largesse of the state, while the poor and the disadvantaged get a firm dose of *laissez-faire*.' The major US industries of computers, aircraft, motor cars, pharmaceuticals and biotechnology have all at one time or another been heavily subsidised by the taxpayer, principally through defence spending, but also through other forms of government support. Boeing's dominance of the international airline business is a direct product of this: it could not have succeeded in braving the winds of free market competition on its own. It is also striking that the US, even in the heyday of Reaganism, has been heavily protectionist. The Washington Institute for International Economics reported that the Reagan regime specialised in the kind of 'managed trade' that most 'restricts trade and closes markets...the most insidious form of protectionism'. A World Bank study showed that non-tariff barriers in the US covered 34 per cent of all goods compared with 9·per cent in Japan. Whether through such measures or through consistently bailing out financial capital – notably after the notorious Savings and Loans scandal of the 1980s – Chomsky's cutting comment is well-founded: 'Those who proclaim the wonders of "free market capitalism" with most vigor understand that it is to be risk-free for the masters, as fully as can be achieved.'

Cowling and Sugden show that another verity of free market mania – the need for a deregulated labour market – does not deliver the success claimed for it. The much-vaunted labour flexibility of the US is not the reason for its employment record, which appears on the face of it to be relatively good compared with the European average. Other factors, including rising population, were more important and in any case productivity was low whilst real incomes fell during the Reagan era. Employment in the US grew by 1.7 per cent annually between the business cycle peaks of 1979 and 1989. But 1 per cent of this was population growth and just 0.7 per cent *extra* jobs – a figure similar to the much despised 'protected' labour markets of western Europe. In any case part-time, temporary and casual jobs are more widespread in the US so it is not easy to make direct employment comparisons. In fact Sweden, with very high levels of trade union membership and job protection, has had a far superior employment record.

In an important report published in February 1995, the International Labour Office (ILO) fiercely attacked the conventional wisdom of the free marketeers that labour market regulations, minimum wages and job protection have caused longer dole queues. The Report argued: 'Rules that protect the income and employment security of workers can increase productive efficiency by creating incentives for competition to occur more through product market innovation and market strategy.' The real cause of world unemployment rising to the worst level since the Great Depression of the 1930s has been 'excessive deflation' caused by monetarist policies. The ILO called for a 'renewed commitment to the objective of full employment'. This could only be secured however under strong international political leadership supported by the re-introduction of an exchange rate management mechanism like Bretton Woods, more equitable trade relations and coordinated expansionary strategies.

Interventionism however is not automatically successful. There are plenty of examples of interventionist governments which have not been economically successful. Many – including state socialist ones – have been suffocatingly bureaucratic, hindering rather than enhancing development. Many of the Southern countries have regimes which are undemocratic and corruption is a serious problem.

According to Cowling and Sugden, 'The lesson to be drawn appears to be that just as we do not deny the market because of instances of market failure, neither should we deny government because of instances of government failure.' Instead the objective must be to achieve an optimal blend of the two. Specifically Cowling and Sugden advocate active labour market policies along the Swedish model, which avoids short-term industrial unemployment, together with a coherent guided industrial strategy along Japanese lines.

ALTERNATIVES

The future should therefore involve what Cowling and Sugden describe as 'a planned process, but not central planning', with markets regulated and controlled to serve communities not elites. Growth which benefits the whole of the world, protects the environment and is structured in such a way as to conquer poverty and inequality is incompatible with contemporary free market capitalism. Only socialism can offer a positive alternative to the despair, division and danger which grip the world today.

'Free trade' must be replaced by 'managed trade'. This is not a pseudonym for old-fashioned protectionism, but describes a mechanism for negotiating trade flows so as to ensure that domestic employment and industries are not wiped out, but given the breathing space either to modernise or to substitute more competitive production. As Adrian Wood points out, the countries which have been most successful in catching up on skill levels – France, Germany and the US in the nineteenth century, and Japan, Taiwan and Korea more recently – have not practised free trade. Managed trade is as much in the interest of the North as the South, which should also be allowed to benefit from reforms in the trade regime to encourage labour-intensive industrial exports. This will entail wholesale renegotiation of GATT.

Another call from the left for a radically different system of trade comes from Lang and Hines. What they term 'new protectionism' promotes maximum local trade within diversified sustainable local economies, and minimum long distance trade. They argue that regional blocs like Europe could become the focus for organising such trade relations. Their case is especially strong on environmental grounds. It also faces up to the whirlwind of nationalism which is appearing over the horizon as the workers in the North see their jobs disappearing to cheaper production areas with trade liberalisation. This is fertile ground for populist, reactionary and proto-racist protectionism. The US new right is already exploiting it: see Newt Gingrich, *Contract with America*. In *The Trap*, James Goldsmith puts the case for a fortress Europe. Against this nationalist or regionalist protectionism, Lang and Hines pose a progressive, internationalist protectionism. Whether or not their solutions are practical politics, their analysis is cogent and should be part of a debate led by the left to reform GATT.

There is also a need for an 'International Social Chapter' to protect workers' rights which have been under increasingly sustained assault from the global economy. The 1994 GATT extended free trade but made no provision for workers' rights. As the transnationals go in search of cheap and disposable labour, wages and conditions in the North are undercut, whilst workers in the developing world also lose out by being exploited. The appalling sweatshops all over China, with their dreadful safety record, are cases in point. A new social chapter in the World Trade Organisation which has replaced GATT should outlaw unfair labour practices and social dumping.

The issue is not so much cheap labour – for wages will continue to vary across the world – as naked exploitation. Workers must be given legal rights to join trade unions and for collective bargaining progressively to improve their conditions; as always, the extent to which they can make progress will depend upon the local economic environment and their own strength. An international social chapter would be an *enabling* measure to encourage conditions to be levered upward. It should also prevent national governments from deliberately undercutting workplace conditions and pay. The use of child labour (200 million children under the age of 15 work in the developing world) and denial of trade union rights should be outlawed, minimum health and safety regulations required and discrimination made illegal. These would be the price nations would have to pay to gain access to international trade.

Countries of the South should be able to trade and compete with the North, but not on the backs of their own workers whose living standards are maintained at low levels in order to be competitive. Different stages of worker protection may need to be considered: as nations become wealthier they could be required to meet higher social chapter conditions. The International Labour Organisation could play an enhanced role and its supervisory machinery could be strengthened. The United Nations and regional trade blocs like the European Union should also take enforcement action. But the principle must remain that if countries wish to sign up to trade agreements then they must respect the rights of their workers.

Investment in infrastructure should be sponsored by the IMF and the World Bank. This is critical to long-term economic success. Programmes to raise skills are also crucial. There is no point in churning out skilled people if there is no demand for them in the economy, as the lengthening queues of graduates on the dole in Britain and the US confirm. Furthermore skills investment, though vital, takes years to filter through to the real economy. Macro-economic demand management domestically and internationally is also indispensable, as are public investment and spending. The priority is to tackle the monetarism which grips the IMF, the World Bank and the OECD. It must be jettisoned forthwith and replaced with policies which use the power of government domestically and internationally to boost output and employment. International and national reflationary policies will need to be coordinated of course, but individual countries can both press for a new monetary system and initiate measures that reverse monetarism domestically.

As is argued in *Managing the Global Economy*, edited by Jonathan Michie and John Grieve Smith, the conservative notion (which has gripped many even on the left) that 'go it alone' policies are impossible in the global economy and that only international action is appropriate is based on a false premise. It is entirely possible to pursue policies on both the domestic and international fronts. And there is far more room for manoeuvre domestically than the new orthodoxy of global economics pretends. National governments typically raise and spend about 40 per cent of national income. This is a huge resource and one which can be deployed to major effect. As the British experience after withdrawal from the European Exchange Rate mechanism in 1992 showed, there is enormous scope for national economic action to generate growth if suitable macro-economic policies are pursued. We need a mix of both national and international action to ensure full employment and economic success. The proposition that we must remain locked into a deflationary spiral awaiting a favourable international environment is false. Reflationary national action can help create improved world conditions, especially if in tandem with pressure to abandon international monetarism and in the context of managed trade. Full employment must top the international agenda.

We need to reinvent the United Nations and the Bretton Woods institutions. Instead of imposing monetarism on poor countries and encouraging Western exports, these institutions should give incentives for the governments of the South and the old Soviet bloc to invest in skills, infrastructure and industry, and to adopt interventionist measures which have been successful elsewhere. They should be pursuing co-ordinated low interest rates and reflationary policies. Soft loans should be made available for public investment throughout the world, especially in the South – which should also have its crippling debts written off.

A reformed United Nations should take over economic leadership in the world. It will be necessary to institutionalise the pivotal role of the G7 industrialised countries since they are so powerful. The G7 should form the core of a new UN Economic Council, parallel to, and with equivalent powers to, the Security Council, and with adequate representation from China and the the Pacific Rim countries. The Bretton Woods institutions could then come under its wing with the aim of subjecting them to democratic political direction, instead of allowing them to continue to operate in the gift of international financiers. There is also a strong case for merging the World Bank and the IMF in a new institution under the auspices of the UN Economic Council, which would co-operate closely with the UN development programme, the World Food Programme and UNICEF. The UN's Charter already offers what could be a guide to this institutional reorganisation: 'All members pledge themselves to take joint and separate action in cooperation with the organisation for promoting higher standards of living, full employment, and conditions of economic and social progress and development.' Such an objective would make a welcome break from the dominant monetarism of today, though to secure it will also need radical reforms in the UN and a break from its stultified pattern of lowest common denominator decision-making.

But institutional reform is not enough. Effective regulation of the transnationals – including governments and international bodies taking ownership stakes – is vital. The era of floating currencies must end. There need to be adjustable bands so that currencies can move in a flexible but more predictable way. The world's leading economies need to intervene to manage and support these exchange rates. It may be that this is best achieved through the three main regional blocs – Europe, North America and East Asia. Effective regulation of international finance is perhaps the most crucial reform. The huge speculative flows in the futures and options markets must be properly monitored and regulated. Internationally agreed taxation of foreign exchange dealings to penalise short term currency speculation is essential. So is taxation on pollution and other curbs on ecologically harmful activity.

None of this will be easy to achieve. But that is no excuse for not trying. Ultimately, governments and the assertion of public power can win if the political will exists. There is an argument that the new financial instruments and the millions of financial and currency transactions which streak across the world each day have become a law unto themselves, defying regulation. But that is both illogical and defeatist. If modern information technology can facilitate such a system, then it can also monitor and police it. The real obstacle to regulation is not technological. It is political.

Without such regulation, without taming the private power of global capital and socialising it to the greatest possible extent, without managed trade which enhances employment and protects the environment, without a fairer aid and trade deal for the South which promotes self-sufficiency rather than dependence, there is no possibility of security and prosperity across the world. Not just command economics but also international capitalism has failed. A socialist alternative beckons.

CHAPTER 7

Charter for Change

Britain requires a radical change of direction in order to create a free, just and prosperous future. The scale of the challenge is awesome: nothing less than a total economic, social and constitutional transformation is needed. To embark upon this task requires a reforming Labour Government which can mobilise sufficient popular support and democratic consent to escape from the short-term fluctuations of the electoral cycle and remain in power for at least a generation.

That is a formidable challenge. It cannot be achieved by pretending to voters that we can trundle along much as before, tweaking the odd policy here, re-jigging the odd priority there and injecting a bit of decency into government. It cannot be achieved by pretending to the rich that their extravagant lifestyles can continue at the expense of the rest. It cannot be achieved by a low tax, spiv culture or by squandering resources on consumption instead of investment. And it cannot be achieved without creating an ethos of mutual cooperation rather than cut-throat competition, an ethos of constructive morality rather than destructive greed.

The opportunity facing New Labour in Britain should be judged against the recent salutory record of progressive parties gaining office elsewhere. It offers a haunting warning about the dangers of vacuous middle-way politics. The promise offered by Bill Clinton's 1992 defeat of George Bush soon expired in a series of sour retreats as his renewal agenda collapsed into directionless pragmatism, opening the way to a rejuvenated new right led by Newt Gingrich. In Canada the right's 1993 election meltdown was followed two years later by a resurgence in state elections. The experience in Europe is not much better. Without a clear strategy, determinedly underpinned by a clear and radical programme, Labour could suffer a similar fate, with a one-term Government paving the way for a revitalised, new right led Conservative Party.

People need to be engaged in a mission of renewal and reform in a way that no Labour Government has ever managed in the past. An ideological crusade is required to challenge old failed free market ideas and promote the vision of a society which empowers citizens, sustains strong communities, respects individuality and promotes equality – not just of opportunities but of resources as well. This concluding chapter is neither a mini-manifesto or a comprehensive shopping list of policies, but a socialist charter for change. It focuses upon the question of a *strategy* for a radical, reforming Labour government.

It does so bearing in mind that a Labour Government has to work within the capitalist system in order to transform it. There is literally no alternative for the *democratic* left which needs to grasp this nettle firmly. As Ralph Miliband pointed out in *Socialism for a Sceptical Age*, 'socialist democracy represents both an extension of capitalist democracy and a *transcendence* of it': socialism will not suddenly happen; there will be continuities as well as discontinuities in the process of achieving it. In many instances, he adds, 'Governments have had to save capitalism from itself'. This has important implications rarely openly acknowledged by the left. It means making strategic alliances where possible with capital – with industry and small businesses especially – and avoiding gratuitous offence to finance whilst being absolutely clear and determined about the objective of radical change. It also means maintaining popular support, even when the electorate is not necessarily converted to socialism. For instance there is widespread support for the left's agenda of high quality welfare, public services, individual rights, democracy and fairness. But they are not necessarily equated with support for *socialism*. As Miliband points out:

> The problem for socialists is to show and make acceptable the link between them, and to explain that radical demands, for democratization, for equal rights for all, for the creation of communities of citizens, can only very partially be met, if they can be met at all, within the existing structures of power and privilege,

and why their fulfilment requires the kind of comprehensive transformation which socialism signifies – yet to do this without in any way belittling the importance and value of the struggles which are conducted for immediate and limited reforms.

Such a perspective should guide Labour in power.

LABOUR IN POWER

As Sidney Webb pointed out in October 1917: 'The programme of the Labour Party is, and will probably remain, less important (except for educating the political leaders of other parties) than the spirit underlying the programme, the spirit which gives any party its soul.' Rather than simply listing policies, the Party's programme should reflect a timescale for achieving a range of objectives, themselves the product of key socialist values and attitudes which constitute the 'spirit' underlying the programme. Specific policy measures should then be selected for inclusion in the election manifesto on the basis of a clearly thought-out strategy for socialist change.

For *how* Labour governs could be as important as the programme its Ministers govern upon. The strategy an incoming Labour Government adopts could be as important as the policies pursued. However impressive an election manifesto may be, whether socialist policies are carried through depends to a considerable extent upon the thought and determination which has gone into how they are to be implemented. To that extent, debate over the practice of Labour in government is as important as the contents of the manifesto or the decisions made by annual Party conferences.

A serious strategy for taking power should have long, medium and short term objectives. The left has habitually failed to take seriously the question of socialist *strategy* and to distinguish between objectives and tactics, ends and means. It may be that to respond to short-term events or societal constraints requires compromise or adjustments to policy. This is indeed a fact of life in government. But long-term goals must be kept constantly in view to avoid being eaten up, distracted and ultimately diverted by the buffeting pressures of daily government, as occurred under Harold Wilson and Jim Callaghan in the 1960s-70s.

In order to avoid that fate, medium-term aims can assist as important staging posts.

Consider the question of devolution for example. There is a settled programme and a wide consensus in both Scotland and Wales to establish elected parliaments, with early legislation agreed. But there is no such consensus for regional government in England. The long-term objective should be re-stated: such English devolution is highly desirable on both democratic and economic grounds. It would be a goal for Labour to pursue. But, whilst there is a broad if not unanimous consensus for an elected London-wide authority, and strong support for regional government in the North of England, that is not the case in the South East, for instance. So in the short term the existing structures of regional administration – unelected and quango-like – should be made accountable through local or county councils as the case may be. In the medium term, London and the North (together with any other region strongly asserting its claim) would have elected regional authorities established. The democratic agenda would be pursued in stages. This would create a momentum in which Labour could build a consensus in other regions until the long-term objective was accomplished.

When considering constitutional reform as a whole, the issue of *priorities* needs to be faced head on. The left has traditionally been better at grand designs than at clear-headed priorities. As a result the usual course in government has been pragmatism followed by disillusionment and accusations of betrayal. Yet as Nye Bevan once said, socialism is 'the language of priorities'.

Labour is committed to a constitutional revolution. Accomplishing it will require years of parliamentary legislative time, and overcoming not a little opposition from vested interests in the establishment and the right. If undertaken all at once, almost the entire first term of a Labour government could be spent ramming through contentious constitutional Bills. The danger is that the government would be unable to deliver much less contentious legislation – on health, education, public transport, crime and jobs – which touch voters' lives more immediately, even if they are ultimately the product of the constitutional malaise from which Britain has suffered for generations.

So a step-by-step approach is necessary (see Graham Allen,

Reinventing Democracy). In the first year there should be devolution for Scotland and Wales. The right of hereditary peers to vote in the House of Lords should be abolished, pending its later replacement by an elected second chamber. There should be a Bill to incorporate into British law the European Convention on Human Rights which would establish essential civil rights and which has long been accepted by other European countries.

In the second year there should be legislation for compulsory voting and public financing of political parties: these are very important to establish the kind of hegemonic shift which the Conservatives would find difficult if not impossible to reverse, and to increase the prospects of non-Conservatives winning subsequent elections. (Compulsory voting will probably favour Labour and the Liberals since the poor tend to abstain in higher numbers and public financing will establish parity of campaigning resources with Tories.) In later years there should be a Freedom of Information Act. There should be a framework in England for establishing evolutionary regional government. There should be a referendum to decide which, if any, system of electoral reform would be supported for the House of Commons. An Executive Powers Act would be introduced to abolish the Royal Prerogative and define the limits of executive power. A full Bill of Rights would come still later, following the establishment of an all-party commission to present jointly agreed proposals.

ECONOMIC RECOVERY

Success in government will, however, stand or fall on economic policy. The case has already been made for a high skill, high quality economy as the only realistic strategy for a country like Britain. This means tough decisions. Matching up to the challenge requires a government committed to long-term imperatives rather than short-term pressures. For example, Labour cannot afford to enter government in give-away mode by aiming immediately to satisfy otherwise legitimate claims for redressing public pay inequalities or boosting consumption through tax handouts. A hard-headed, even austere, regime is required to focus determinedly upon key priorities, now that the long post-war boom, in which constant growth facilitated growing wealth and welfare, is over. In a nutshell, the priorities should be investment rather than consumption, and employment rather than pay.

Public investment instead of tax handouts is essential to rebuild the economy. Rather than increasing the existing public sector paybill, where resources are available these should generate new jobs – for instance an army of care workers to make care in the community a reality rather than a scandalous sop. Ultimately employment is the best pathway out of poverty. In the private sector, similar principles should apply, with fiscal incentives for job creation and a public campaign by government to encourage companies to promote employment rather than to increase dividends or top people's pay.

But popular support for such a programme can only be sustained if it is seen to be as *fair and just* as it can be in a capitalist society. It may be felt that something akin to the 'social contract' of the 1970s Labour Government is being advocated here. And to the extent that Labour in power must have a clear 'contract' with the people, that may be true. But there are at least two fundamental differences. Firstly, the corporatism of the 1970s cannot and should not be reincarnated: labour markets are too flexible, bargaining too decentralised and trade unions representative of too small a proportion of the workforce to sustain such corporatism. Secondly, although trade unions complied with incomes policies until they blew apart in the 1978-79 winter of discontent, the 'other side' of that social contract was never adhered to.

Top income earners broke free from pay norms enforced upon ordinary workers. (For example, companies like BOC – the former British Oxygen – tried to dodge pay norms by buying furniture and clothing for some of their senior managers.) And at the same time, cuts in public spending signalled a putative monetarism. There was no programme for empowerment: citizens did not feel it was 'their' government in power, they were not engaged, they were not given opportunities to participate in the decisions which affected them, whether in industry or the community.

An *absolute* priority must be accorded to investment in industry, infrastructure and skills, publicly financed through borrowing and taxation. This should be undertaken as part of a strategic plan to modernise the British economy and its social capital. But although such a strategy is job creating and expansionary, it needs to be acknowledged that a reflationary macro-economic stance, with a willingness to use Keynesian demand management policies, is vital to promote full employment and growth. It is also vital to ensure a 'feel good' recovery without which Labour might not get re-elected. Innovative skills schemes and interventionist supply side measures take time to feed through. Moreover they will come to nothing without additional demand injected into the economy by expansionary monetary and fiscal policies, to ensure that those trained will be productively employed.

The pessimism which has transfixed the body politic on the capacity of governments to tackle unemployment needs to be dispelled. Carefully targeted and modestly increased public expenditure can have a huge impact on jobs without incurring the inflationary ills claimed by new right apologists. The advantage of public spending is that it is more labour-intensive and less import-intensive than private spending. Such extra spending would help meet enormous social needs as well as the economic need to modernise Britain's infrastructure and skills base. Jobs can be created relatively quickly in housing, public transport, energy conservation, education, training and environmental upgrading – leaving aside the caring services.

The gross expenditure per full-time job in these areas averages at something over £15,000, which means a million jobs could be created for around £15 billion. That might sound a lot but most of its is self-financing, at least in the medium term. The cost of an unemployed person in benefit and lost taxation is about £9,000 annually. So the *net direct* cost of a million jobs is about £6 billion – less then half the headline figure. If *indirect* savings are taken into account, the amount is still smaller, for unemployment is linked to bad health and high crime. The net cost could then be around £5 billion.

This could easily be financed from borrowing, because £5 billion is less than the Treasury's margin of error for forecasting the Public Sector Borrowing Requirement; and also because a significant share of the jobs would come from a phased release of the several billion pounds of council housing capital receipt accounts. Alternatively it could easily be raised by taxing high earners more, and by other tax reforms. (For example – and it is only an illustrative example – creating a new 45 per cent tax band on income above £40,000 and a 55 per cent band on income above £50,000 would raise over £3 billion, which is only a small proportion of the £15 billion in tax cuts received annually by the top 10 per cent of earners under the Tories.) There are of course lead and lag times which front-load the costs. But these are obviously less significant in public financing than in private financing and the obstacle to Government action along these lines to create jobs is political rather than economic – a hangover from discredited free market theory.

There should be early tax reforms to encourage firms to plough back into investment a much larger proportion of their profits, instead of distributing them as dividends. In addition, new public-private partnerships need forging to mobilise the huge resources of finance capital for the funding of industrial investment programmes. As was argued in chapter four, this should be attempted by Government persuasion. The pension and insurance funds together with other financial institutions will be expected to change and to provide finance for new industrial investment banks. If they did not comply voluntarily, they would find themselves on the receiving end of an ideological campaign waged by the government – and, if that too failed, then legislation should be introduced to require their cooperation.

A contrasting example of government-private sector cooperation should be the information superhighway. Having invented fibre optic cabling which enables revolutionary inter-active communications, Britain is now in danger of falling behind other countries which are not relying entirely on the free market to create a broad band network into every home and workplace. The Japanese for instance are developing a national information infrastructure through four companies which can utilise low interest government bonds to take fibre optic everywhere in Japan by 2010. There should be a partnership with British Telecom, Mercury and any other telecommunications company interested to achieve the same thing. BT has already offered to do this without public subsidy if the government lifts its ban on the company offering broadcast services together with telephony. This ban should be lifted as soon as possible.

A progressive taxation system which redistributes from the rich to the rest is necessary for economic efficiency as well as social justice.

Early legislation to establish a statutory minimum wage is vital. A new framework of positive rights at work will help create a modern high quality economy in two main respects. It will help give workers the dignity that they are entitled to and thereby secure greater allegiance to their employer. Secondly, it will help create greater job security which means workers will be more willing to spend their incomes and take out mortgages, leading to increased demand in the economy.

THE EARLY DAYS

The immediate period after taking office will, to a large extent, determine Labour's capacity to govern strategically later on. Mistakes made in the early days can be very costly - for example in 1964 Labour ruled out devaluation at the outset only to be forced, humiliatingly, to do it three years later; and in 1974 when Labour was too quick to accept a commitment to threshold payments which automatically triggered wage rises as prices rose, helping to push up inflation to 25 per cent by 1975, and resulting in an economy spinning out of control.

It is critical that the Government establishes from the outset that it is in charge. For instance, immediately on taking office, the Governor of the Bank of England should be given a remit to make full employment rather than near-zero inflation the principal macro-economic policy objective. If necessary directions should be issued to the Governor under the 1946 Bank of England Act. Monetary policy should also be brought back into the hands of the Government, reversing the trend towards making the Bank independent.

The privatised utilities could be directed towards ends other than shareholder self-interest. Different Regulators should immediately be appointed to ensure different policies favouring the public interest rather than private competition. The Government could activate existing shareholdings where it still has them or take a small ownership stake, appoint a Director to each Board and influence policies relatively easily. Obviously, operating within the constraints of company law and its priority obligation to shareholders means that the utilities would not behave as if under public ownership. But a determined government could nevertheless exert considerable influence, with immediate and tangible results in terms of the interests of consumers and the strategic interests of the economy in areas like energy policy and telecommunications.

Another immediate step would be the phased release of local authority housing capital receipts. This would give a much needed multi-billion pound boost to the housing market, employ tens of thousands of construction workers, and make a start in tackling the chronic problem of homelessness.

There should be early legislation to lift the 'capping' controls which prevent local authorities from raising additional monies from their electors. With some 80 per cent of local council finance now funded by the Government after remorseless Conservative centralisation, the abolition of capping would not make a revolutionary difference. But it would give significant extra scope for raising council taxes to meet local needs, subject of course to the very community accountability at the ballot box which the Thatcherites effectively rendered obsolete.

The first Queen's Speech could also contain a commitment to give equal rights to part-time workers and to sign up to the European Social Chapter, bringing, for example, new employee rights to be consulted through works councils. The operation of the Child Support Agency should also be changed right away, pending its replacement, so that it no longer concentrates upon those whose benefits can be substituted by extra maintenance payments (often prohibitive for fathers in second families), and instead targets those genuinely absent parents who do not contribute any support

There is enormous potential for executive action which does not require time-consuming legislation. The ban on trade union membership at the Government's Communications Headquarters (GCHQ) should be reversed immediately. Gagging clauses in employment contracts in all public agencies should be banned, beginning with the NHS. In order to enable the Post Office to operate with commercial freedom, Treasury regulations on the Public Sector Borrowing Requirement should be altered without delay. This would enable the Post Office to borrow on the open market and invest from its own resources without it counting against the PSBR. It would also be freed to engage in joint ventures, especially in the fast growing European mail market, and to operate in an enterprising manner.

Early action could be taken to prepare for later change which needs extra resources. On child care, for example, the Government should ask every local authority to submit a feasibility study for a substantial expansion of childcare in their area. The same thing should be done with community care, to identify practical proposals which could be implemented when resources are available.

A contrasting example concerns abortion. Health Authorities could be instructed by circular to improve facilities for NHS abortions and publicise these widely. A simple administrative change to enable doctors to permit abortions on 'social grounds' under the 1967 Act would make a big difference. (In March 1981, these grounds were arbitrarily removed without prior Parliamentary approval by Departmental circular, so that doctors could only specify 'main medical conditions', thus effectively restricting the scope for abortions.)

This is not to encourage government by *fiat* instead of democratic consent. It is simply to underline how important it will be for Labour to act swiftly and with verve, especially against an economic background which will make it very difficult quickly to satisfy expectations and achieve the Party's industrial, let alone social goals. A great deal of action like this does not require substantial extra resources. Some of it indeed is costless.

A new internationalism could inform foreign policy. A positive stance on Europe is vital, building support for socialist policies such as a coordinated economic strategy for full employment. A commitment to work for a new international order which protects rather than exploits the poor South is imperative, including proposals to reorganise the IMF and the World Bank and a commitment to increase overseas aid to meet the United Nations targets. A Labour Government could initiate discussion by the G7 countries about regulating transnational companies and the international currency and financial markets. Where the Tories have dragged their feet on nuclear disarmament, Labour should support positive action to achieve a Comprehensive Test Ban Treaty and a Global Treaty to Ban All Nuclear Weapons (which means including as a minimum a British commitment to deploy no more warheads on Trident than on Polaris). Labour should also ensure that Britain is not subservient to the US on matters such as the blockade of Cuba.

Carrying forward the peace process in Ireland would obviously be critical and would depend upon the outcome of the negotiating process. It is for the people of Ireland to determine their own future. But the preferred long-term solution would be a united Ireland. This does not mean simple absorption of the North by the South which would not be agreed by the Protestant majority in the North. The solution could be a federal state or a con-federal arrangement – options explored by the New Ireland Forum Report in 1984. There could be a 'Scottish-type' solution (as suggested by the Irish Taoiseach Charles Haughey in 1984) in which the North would retain its own legal framework, with harmonisation proceeding gradually. Whichever was the agreed option, it would be essential to encourage a strong *decentralist* thrust in the structure of government and administration. For libertarian socialists this is inherently desirable. But it would also re-assure Protestants that in communities where they predominate, they will retain considerable control over local government and security.

Domestically, a radical, reforming Labour government could liberalise the impact of oppressive laws immediately, whilst planning their repeal and replacement. Discussions could take place with armed forces chiefs to lift the ban on gays. No prosecutions could be authorised under the official secrecy laws or the oppressive parts of the 1994 Criminal Justice Act (such as 'aggravated trespass' for example). The police disciplinary code could be toughened to stamp out harassment of black people or gays. Where over-zealous prosecutions were launched which clearly undermined the desire to remove oppressive laws or discriminatory practices, there would always be the facility for the Director of Public Prosecutions to take over a prosecution and then drop it. (Anyone who imagines that the judicial system is above politics is naive in the extreme.)

The system of public appointments must be reformed and subjected to transparent criteria. Pending their abolition or merger, the boards of Quangos should be reconstituted to reflect a genuine cross-section of public opinion on political, class or gender grounds, with expertise instead of Party membership being the key criterion. Positive action is needed to ensure we have more women and black magistrates and judges; as well as more non-Conservatives and individuals from ordinary backgrounds. The present upper-class right-wing bias in the judiciary and magistracy, although it has been marginally ameliorated in recent years, needs to be eradicated.

Another priority area for attention is the machinery of government. Incoming Labour Ministers will be faced with a thoroughly Thatcherised Civil Service, and they will need strong private offices. The fact that the Thatcherites have brought in outsiders from industry, leapfrogging standard civil service recruitment and promotion procedures, means a precedent has been established for appointing at a senior level individuals sympathetic to or members of Labour. Outside aides will need to be appointed with two main functions. First to monitor the implementation by civil servants of Labour's policies. Second to perform a 'campaigning' role in mobilising support for policies and providing channels of access for groups and individuals outside: parental lobbies, trade unions and pressure groups like Greenpeace, Friends of the Earth or the Child Poverty Action Group spring to mind. Much more use should be made of a government's capacity to exercise power and influence through political campaigning and public pressure, even where it may not have immediate administrative or legal leverage. The new Women's Ministry should become a model of socialist practice in Government. It should abandon Whitehall's suffocating traditions and protocol, and open itself out to establish links with women's forums at national and regional level. Perhaps on major issues Cabinet Ministers could hold open consultation 'surgeries' attended by different groups and interests, which could be broadcast live so as to involve the whole population.

Through such a strategy and by such early measures Labour could help mobilise groups and strands of public opinion behind the Government. The purpose is not to indulge in short-term gimmicks. It is to lay the foundations for establishing a new contract between Labour and the people necessary to carry through the long-term reform of society and regeneration of democracy to which socialists are committed.

ACTIVISM

But a party of the left can only win a clear mandate for change – and then help sustain a government in power – if it has undertaken a thorough-going campaign to win the battle of ideas and to support groups in society which are pressing for change in the same direction. To win popular backing for a socialist programme requires a different model of campaigning than one confined almost exclusively to national, regional or local press conferences and photo calls. It depends upon a process of engaging with local citizens through the activity of Party members and supporters. Labour will only succeed if it is a mass party and if its members are engaged in the process of persuasion and organisation needed to accomplish socialist transformation.

Political change on this scale cannot be achieved through television and the rest of the media alone. The left finds itself operating in a hostile culture largely driven by capitalist ethics and conservative values. Grass roots activity is crucial to countering this. As Antonio Gramsci showed, progressive change depends upon activity in 'civil society' – the everyday life of relationships, of community groups and networks, from parents of school children to local environmental campaigns and pensioners' clubs. It also depends upon action at the workplace through trade unions. Socialists require messengers on the ground to spread the gospel. Without the benefit of a sympathetic media, the left needs to get its arguments across directly on a one-to-one basis – in the neighbourhood, the workplace, 'non-political' groups, the family, amongst friends and acquaintances. It needs to support groups involved in progressive campaigns and struggles.

To succeed, Labour needs to be a campaigning Party with an enthusiastic army of activists and not simply a large reservoir of passive members whose only participation is to be periodically consulted by ballot or pestered by phone or mailshot for donations. Championing the role of activists is about winning elections. In *Labour's Grass Roots*, the political scientists Patrick Seyd and Paul Whiteley identified a trend entrenched in the 1987 General Election results – and confirmed in post-1992 election analysis – that Labour had relatively better results in those seats where its organisation was good and where an active campaigning strategy was pursued.

They showed that Constituency Labour Parties with above-average memberships were able to achieve above-average election swings to Labour. They further simulated the 1987 elections on these projections and concluded that if every local party had recruited an extra 100 members and had increased their 'activism' rate, then the net result would have been an increase in the Labour Party's national share of the vote to a total of 35.7 per cent instead of the 30.8 per cent it actually received. Consider what this would have meant in a number of key marginals which eluded Labour in 1992 – for example, Hayes and Harlington (Tory majority, 53, then CLP membership 318), Ayr (majority, 85, then CLP membership, 267), Bolton North East (majority 185, then CLP membership, 390), Corby (majority, 342, then membership 445) or Amber Valley (majority 712, then membership 394). Seyd and Whiteley estimated that between 1984 and 1988, some 60,000 people had left the party and that individual membership was at its lowest for 40 years. Of those remaining, four out of every ten members felt themselves to be less active than they were five years previously. Prior to and after the 1992 defeat, the Party's membership and activist base was probably less motivated than at any point in Labour's history.

There was a dramatic reverse of this decline following Tony Blair's election as Leader in July 1994. Within a year membership had surged back up by 100,000. But whether this renewal will translate itself into *activism* remains an open question. For to motivate activists requires giving them collective power which was cut back progressively from the late 1980s. This is not a left-right issue: there are both left-wing and right-wing activists and they tend to be people who are interested in policy-making, in socialist debate, in campaigning, in canvassing. If they feel they are not being involved or listened to, they won't join, they won't stay or they may lapse into passivity. If the model is of a passive membership, coming to social events, maybe the occasional rally, responding to fundraising drives, and casting the odd vote in a ballot from Labour headquarters in support of a centralised leadership, then activism will decline and there will be nobody to deliver leaflets or knock on doors in the wet and cold. In the past the Labour Party has often been led *despite* Party activists. Some appear to imagine that it can now be led *without* them, by appealing over their heads through the media to the individualised Party member or the atomised voter.

This is not to demand a return to the high noon of activist-leadership battles in the late 1970s or early 1980s. Nor is it to preach the negative oppositionalism which has often characterised (and in practice weakened) the left. Activist fervour detached from voter reality is no answer: grass roots activists may have won control of the Party in the late 1970s and early 1980s, but the country was meanwhile lost. During this period the deficiencies of 'old Labour' were exposed: a conservative political culture in an often painfully bureaucratic structure which tended to lock Party activists into a life shuffling between meetings and up and down layers of organisation. Capturing organisational positions and winning resolutions became all important – to the point where Party activity and manoeuvring took on an all-absorbing life of its own.

Labour activists often operated as if in a vacuum. Radical policies – admirable in themselves – were pushed to the point of destruction without popularising a wider socialist agenda in a way that related to the daily living concerns of Labour voters. It was easy for the Labour left to be labelled 'loony' by a hostile media when it was taking its electoral base for granted. Classic instances of this included Lambeth Council's period of left-wing Labour control in the 1980s. All manner of good causes from Nicaragua to lesbian rights were advanced whilst the Council's housing benefit system was in chaos, its homes dreadfully managed and all sorts of sharp practice reigned in its inefficient service delivery.

During the 1980s many Labour activists also made a major strategic error which reflected an absence of ideological clarity about *democratic* socialism. They found themselves – actively or by default – defending the indefensible: entryism by a Trotskyist political party, in this case, Militant. As Neil Kinnock's leadership confronted Militant head-on, left-wing activists were divided. The 'hard' left (despite having little if any time for Militant's sectarian, fundamentalist and backward politics) saw its expulsion as inviting a wider attack on the whole left. The rest of us on the left took a stand against Militant's brazenly uncon-stitutional role as a secretive, separate Party within the Labour Party. The whole episode weakened the case for an activist-led Party. On the other hand, the exit of Militant also cleansed the Party and legitimised the broad left which could no longer be tainted with actual or alleged association with Militant.

Subsequently the role of Party activists was progressively downgraded. Power started to be centralised to an unprecedented extent, with policy made from the top down, endorsement being sought through the new quarterly Policy Forum or retrospectively at the annual conference. Constituency policy motions were ignored. The 'constituency' section of the National Executive started to become a safe haven for Shadow Cabinet members with a high enough media profile to be recognised in one-person-one-vote elections for the constituency section of the ruling National Executive Committee. The otherwise admirable principle of One-Member-One-Vote (OMOV) in parliamentary candidate selections and leadership elections became part of a process which substituted indirect democracy for the direct democracy which had given local Party activists influence and sometimes power.

PARTY REFORM

The Labour Party should be a microcosm of a libertarian socialist society, pre-figuring it through its own practice, organisation and forms of participatory democracy. To secure electoral victory and – as important – sustain a Labour government in power, there needs to be a new internal Party settlement to ensure that activism is respected. The *indirect democracy* of one-member-one-vote postal balloting and a passive membership should be supplemented by new participatory structures of *direct democracy* in which each member retains the right to vote but is given the opportunity of active participation too. This is especially important in policy formulation, which is not at all appropriate for YES-NO decisions on questions which become votes of confidence in the leadership, and after debates suitably 'spun' through a media generally hostile to socialist values.

The National Executive Committee needs to be reformed. As presently constituted about half the Cabinet could be members with Labour in office. This is patently absurd: they should be busy running the country not the Party. The NEC should be made more representative of the party as a whole. Trade unions should continue to have the right to elect their own representatives who should number no more than half the total NEC, in line with equalisation of annual conference voting. There should also continue to be representation for other sections of the Party, including a new one for local government – although the separate women's section should be abolished, and replaced by quotas in the union and all other sections. The remaining sections should be elected by the ballot of the whole Party membership, but with additional built-in quotas to ensure a minimum number of constituency activists and backbench MPs.

This would secure an NEC which could legitimately speak for the Party. In government it could be an important channel for consultation with and mobilisation of Labour's grass roots. Party members could be positively involved in the tasks of government and could campaign for its policies, building maximum local popular support. They could also hold it accountable: the process would not be one-way. Because it provides the basis for mediation and consensus building between Government and Party, such a positive partnership could be successful where previously the relationship has been strained (James Callaghan once remarking that its was 'like purgatory' attending NECs as Prime Minister).

A centralised system of policy-making cannot involve members except by a right of veto through ballots, which in any case could not feasibly be conducted on every issue. Centralised policy-making does not engage with members in a way that makes them feel that, because they have participated in framing it, they 'own' the policy. This is not simply elitist: it also fails to equip members with the ability to argue the Party's case at grass roots level. New policy statements which do not go much beyond a Westminster launch cannot arm members with arguments or respond to their views. Political education in the Labour Party has been abysmal for generations; indeed there has been no real culture of policy discussion.

The whole Party needs to be positively and directly engaged in debate upon policy. Labour's relatively new Policy Forum process needs to be enhanced so that it reaches out to and involves grass roots members. It must also be more than a vehicle for the leadership to legitimise its own policy proposals: 'consultation' is not the same as 'participation'. Regional Forum meetings have started to attract large numbers, but this needs to be taken to the local level. There is a strong case for reforming the structure of constituency parties.

The present system of local branches (normally based on local election wards which send delegates to the policy-making constituency General Committee) is not working. It may have been appropriate in an era when there were more activists, when there were more delegates from affiliated bodies such as trade unions, when people attended meetings in great numbers and when transport and communications were poor. And the ward level is obviously still necessary for some purposes, such as selection of local election candidates, and in many communities, especially rural ones, it will remain the essential base for involvement and activity; similarly the General Committee needs to carry out organisational decisions and be responsible for maintaining the constitution. But both levels are clogged up with an endless merry-go-round of apologies, correspondence, affiliations, election of delegates to some conference or other, reports and organisation. The language is incomprehensible to the newcomer: all ECs, GCs, LGCs and PPCs (Executive Committee, General Committee, Local Government Committee, Prospective Parliamentary Candidate). The meetings are invariably an insult to the collective intelligence of those attending, are insufferably boring, sometimes acrimonious, dominated by a handful of obsessives and often degenerate to the point where most people wonder why they keep wasting an evening to attend. Whenever something needs to be done, a meeting is suggested to do something about it and that in turn usually decides to hold another meeting. Such institutionalised 'meetingsitis' reflects an internalised Party culture which forces members to turn inward rather than outward and divorces them from the local electorate. As John Denham MP has written, 'Power in the local party lies not with those whose contribution to the community is greatest, but whose bureaucratic endurance is longest.'

Policy discussion, if any, is confined to a one paragraph resolution tacked onto the end of the agenda and despatched to the National Executive for ritual noting. Hence a culture of 'resolutionary politics' which is no basis for either serious grass roots participation or serious policy-making. Reforms should produce constituency-wide Party meetings which *every* member is able to attend (not just delegates) to discuss and determine policy, perhaps held every couple of months, unless there is a special reason for variation, such as to meet a deadline in a national consultation exercise. The General Committee could be confined to party business, and branch meetings need not be monthly. Sympathetic outsiders could be invited to attend the Policy Meetings (for instance local GPs or school governors), to provide extra expertise and to involve the wider community in the Party. There are plenty of local people with skills, and local opinion-formers who would like to be involved and consulted; some will be Labour members or supporters who do not otherwise connect properly into the Party, and yet who could well be more influential than the average Party meeting-attender.

Constituency parties should also be encouraged to make a break from resolutionary politics, by being geared to constant campaigning. This does not necessitate attending meetings. Nor should it be confined to elections. The national Party's Regeneration Project and its initiatives to reach local campaigners, such as Active Labour, are welcome steps in revitalising Labour locally. Several practical steps could be taken. Small, task-driven, campaign committees should be established. Constituency party headquarters should be put at the disposal of local groups and trade unions, allowing use of facilities such as meeting rooms and printers. In this way Labour will be seen as the natural resource centre for the local community. Although regular local Labour newsletters are quite widespread, their content often leaves a lot to be desired. They should focus on local issues which interest residents, and encourage feedback, so that Labour councillors, MPs and Party members are seen to be accessible and to adopt an inclusive style of community politics. The latter is important since far too much 'campaigning' is simply pushing propaganda that is not read or listened to. A more empowering, inclusive style of campaigning would be a better basis for communicating Labour's politics, since it would involve listening to people.

Socialist change is not possible if pursued exclusively from on high. A Labour Government will require the support of extra-parliamentary movements (trade unions, community and single-issue groups) and a wider popular opinion if it is to overcome forces hostile to it. It also needs to be held accountable by such movements, which can provide a valuable countervailing pressure against that from the City or the civil service. So Labour should be working alongside progressive groups outside Parliament – which in practice requires activists with sufficient street credibility, and local party structures which are sufficiently empowering to build such popular alliances.

This also means a new relationship with the trade unions. The slogan 'fairness not favours' is fine. Nobody should expect Labour governments surreptitiously to favour the unions, nor to grant unjustified privileges. But equally it is nonsense to suggest that a Labour government should stand neutrally in the middle between capital and labour, between the exploitation of the market and the collective protection of trade unionism. A new Labour government should treat unions as social partners and carry through a far-reaching reform of industrial relations and establish structures for industrial democracy.

It is also important to maintain the close constitutional relationship between the Party and the unions. There is no reason to apologise for it. Labour should be proud of its heritage. Nearly a century ago the Party was set up by trade unions to gain parliamentary representation. The world has moved on since and Labour should not be speaking for trade union or producer interests alone: consumers and other interest groups also have a legitimate claim for representation through the Party. And especially in power Labour must favour the *general* interest rather than any sectional one. For instance, environmental considerations require the discouragement of opencast mining, resisting the demands of Labour affiliated trade unions representing opencast workers; and pursuing Labour's policy to phase out nuclear power is in conflict with the obligation on unions to defend their members' jobs in the industry. But workers are entitled to have a Labour Party that speaks broadly for them, not least because nobody else will do so. The unions affiliated to Labour are also entitled to maintain their influence in the Party's decision-making structures. This principle should be defended, even if reforms are made such as those already in train to individualise the block vote and to equalise voting power with constituency parties at the annual conference.

Trade union involvement is, however, not a one-way conduit. It is beneficial to Labour because it keeps the Party in touch with the views of millions of workers. It also provides the basis for a mutually supportive partnership. Labour in government will need the backing and understanding of trade unions, especially when carrying through economic policies which require a switch from consumption to investment and from real wage increases to job creation. Such support is not automatic and will certainly not be forthcoming if trade union members feel the Party has turned its back on them.

WINNING THE VOTE

Parliamentary politics world-wide appear to be facing a crisis of legitimacy, especially amongst the poor and the young. Opinion polls record burgeoning 'don't knows'. In America the 'underclass' hardly bothers to vote and total voter turnout is barely above 50 per cent. The rise of a significant third force in recent Presidential elections – Jesse Jackson on the left and Ross Perot on the populist right – indicates disillusionment with conventional politics. An important reason is that the two major parties, Democrats and Republicans, are not seen by the disaffected as different enough to warrant bothering to get down to the polling station. Their soundbite politics are a turn-off to those excluded from what J.K. Galbraith has called the 'culture of contentment'. Labour would be well advised to take note of this: unless the Party offers a radical alternative to Conservatism, it could lose some of its radical and working class support.

In Europe disaffection has also been manifest. The neo-fascist National Alliance in Italy and National Front in France have recently had significant enough votes to exert power both locally and nationally. In eastern and central Europe the former communist left has continued to be strong, confounding Western predictions. The French have identified the politics of 'exclusion' as a phenomenon affecting the young unemployed, the old, the single parents and immigrants – those looking in from the outside on mainstream free market consumerism and increasingly alienated from the politics which trap them out there.

In Britain the trends are similar, albeit not as well established. In recent general elections turnout among council tenants, those on low incomes, working-class youth and the unemployed was well below the national average, with turnout in Labour's inner-city English and Scottish seats about 20 per cent below. In 1992 Labour took *barely half* the vote of blue-collar trade unionists, council tenants, and the unemployed – its traditional working-class base.

To win, a party must motivate its core voters. That will not be sufficient for victory, but it is an essential pre-condition for victory. Although it cannot be denied that Labour's core vote is a declining share of the electorate, to make the kind of advance needed for victory Labour needs to motivate its core vote in a way that has not been possible for at least the last four general elections. Such motivation is not at all in conflict with the need to to win the progressive middle ground. On the contrary, both would be attracted by a Party that is radical and positive rather than vacuous and defensive. Both would also be won over by a credible economic policy.

In important study in 1994, *Labour's Last Chance?*, Anthony Heath, Roger Jowell and John Curtice confirm that distinctive, radical policies are needed to mobilise the enthusiasm of voters. As they demonstrate, the electorate has actually moved leftward, towards public spending on services and especially investment in infrastructure. But it needs convincing that Labour's economic programme can actually deliver rising prosperity. Labour cannot succeed by keeping its head low and hoping the Tories will lose. Heath, Jowell and Curtice say that Labour would be wrong to assume that it will be the automatic beneficiary of dissatisfaction with the government in a general election, unless it has by then convinced the electorate that it has the ideas and the ability to do better.

Some Party members argue for a programme of ideological sanitisation, driven by the belief that Labour can only win if it gives the least offence to the most people. This programme may well attract short-term plaudits from leader writers many of whom are not on the side of the left. But, come the crunch, when voters confront their choices in the privacy of the ballot box, they will want to know what Labour is *for* and not simply what it is against. Despite Tory unpopularity during the late 1980s and the early 1990s, there was still a lack of public trust in Labour. In the run up to the 1992 election, research and polling – public and private – revealed that this was because the electorate didn't know *what Labour stood for anymore.* People knew that key policies like unilateral nuclear disarmament, nationalisation and trade union privileges had been abandoned. But, beyond this, they sensed that the glitz, the televisual smile and the anti-

Tory sound-bite might conceal a vacuum. Most voters admire politicians who stand their ground and fight with a clear vision, even if they may not agree with every policy commitment. This was one of the lessons of Mrs Thatcher's success: people knew where she was coming from. They could respect her even if they detested her. The outcome of the next election could depend upon the extent to which Labour has communicated, not so much detailed policies, but a strong and clear vision.

Winning the vote through electoral pacts is not a possibility. There is no short cut to victory through a nationally agreed pact with the Liberals. It would not work for several reasons. Because of opposition from local Labour Parties (and doubtless Liberals too), it could not be enforced except at such cost that the whole Party would implode. All the polling evidence shows that Liberal voters cannot be delivered to Labour candidates. Indeed, faced with the charge of helping to usher in a Labour Government, Liberals are more likely to desert to the Tories. Similarly, soft Tories would be put off if the Liberals were seen as Trojan horses for Labour. For example, an ICM poll two days before the Newbury by-election in May 1993 – which predicted the final result to within just one point – showed that a joint Liberal/Labour candidate would still have won but with a lead over the Tory cut from the Liberals' actual huge margin of 38 per cent to just 3 per cent. In the context of a general election – as was evident from the way the Tories benefited in the final week of the 1992 campaign when Lib-Labery became an issue – that squeeze would be even more relentless. On the other hand, there is strong evidence from local elections that anti-Tory votes are being tactically cast for either Labour or Liberal candidates, whoever is the most likely to win. Whether or not this translates into general elections, it can be best progressed through independent parties.

THE WAY FORWARD

The left can only succeed if it anticipates the future rather than dwells on the past. Respect and pride in its history is one thing; being trapped in its history quite another. Whilst the old state socialists may have invited the Labour 'moderniser' charge of being 'traditionalists', the real debate on the left today is not between these two camps: instead it is between social democrats who wish to manage the free market more humanely and libertarian socialists who wish to change it fundamentally.

A libertarian socialist vision does meet the needs of our age. It offers a programme for social justice and economic success. It promotes common ownership and vigorous regulation of private power to protect the interests of the many over the few. It empowers each citizen in a participatory democracy. It guarantees individual liberty. It bans discrimination and positively promotes equal opportunities. It aims to conquer poverty both at home and abroad, maintaining equality as a socialist goal. It insists economic growth must not be at the expense of environmental protection. It puts international peace before profits and aspires to a nuclear weapons-free world.

As people become more and more aware of the failings of the free market and more disillusioned with the politics which have promoted it, they will be looking for a radical alternative. Marching in step with what Gramsci called 'the commonsense of the epoch', New Labour now has the best opportunity for at least a generation to offer such an alternative.

Selected Bibliography

Graham Allen, *Reinventing Democracy*, Graham Allen MP, 1994.

Tony Benn, *The New Politics*, Fabian Tract 402, 1970.

Aneurin Bevan, *In Place of Fear*, Quartet, 1990 edition.

Fenner Brockway, *Britain's First Socialists*, Quartet, 1980.

Noam Chomsky, *For Reasons of State*, Fontana, 1973.

Noam Chomsky, *World Orders, Old and New*, Pluto, 1994.

G.D.H. Cole, *History of Socialist Thought, Volume Five*, Macmillan , 1960.

G.D.H. Cole, *Self Government in Industry*, G. Bell & Sons, 1917.

Keith Cowling and Roger Sugden, *Beyond Capitalism: Towards a New World Economic Order*, Pinter, 1993.

Anthony Crosland, *The Future of Socialism*, Cape, 1956.

John Denham MP, *Next Business? Labour Members and the Party*, Tribune Group of MPs, 1993.

Amitai Etzioni, *The Parenting Deficit*, Demos, 1994.

Amitai Etzioni, *Spirit of Community*, Crown Publishers, 1993.

W. J. Fishman, *The Insurrectionists*, Methuen, 1970.

Newt Gingrich, *Contract with America*, Random House, 1994.

James Goldsmith, *The Trap*, Macmillan, 1994.

Bryan Gould, *A Future for Socialism*, Cape, 1989.

John Gyford, *The Politics of Local Socialism*, George Allen & Unwin, 1985.

Anthony Heath, Roger Jowell and John Curtice, *Labour's Last Chance?*, Dartmouth, 1994.

Colin Hines and Tim Lang, *Employment and the Culture of Insecurity: Time to Protect Jobs?*, Employment Policy Institute, 1995.

Peter Hain, *Neighbourhood Participation*, Temple Smith, 1980.

Peter Hain, *Proportional Misrepresentation*, Wildwood House, 1986.

Peter Hain, *Regulating for the Common Good*, GMB Union, 1994.

Nigel Harris, *Of Bread and Guns*, Penguin, 1983.

Roy Hattersley, *Choose Freedom*, Michael Joseph, 1987.

Geoff Hodgson, *The Democratic Economy*, Penguin, 1984.

Will Hutton, *The State We're In*, Cape, 1995.

William Keegan, *The Spectre of Capitalism*, Vintage, 1993.

Ruth Kelly, *Taxing the Speculator*, Fabian Society, 1993.

Tim Lang and Colin Hines, *The New Protectionism*, Earthscan, 1993.

George Lichteim, *A Short History of Socialism*, Fontana, 1975.

Martin Linton, *Money and Votes*, Institute for Public Policy Research, 1994.

Michael Meacher, *Diffusing Power*, Pluto, 1992.

Jonathan Michie and John Grieve Smith (eds), *Managing the Global Economy*, Oxford University Press, 1995.

Ralph Miliband, *Socialism for a Sceptical Age*, Polity Press, 1994.

Ralph Miliband, *Divided Societies*, Clarendon Press, 1989.

Cheryl Payer, *Lent and Lost*, Zed Books, 1994.

Michael Porter, *The Competitive Advantage of Nations*, Macmillan, 1990.

Robert Reich, *Work of Nations*, Vintage, 1992.

Sheila Rowbotham, Lynne Segal and Hilary Wainwright, *Beyond the Fragments*, Merlin Press, 1979.

Joseph Schumpeter, *Capitalism, Socialism and Democracy*, George Allen & Unwin, 1942.

Lynne Segal, *Is the Future Female?*, Virago, 1987.

Patrick Seyd and Paul Whiteley, *Labour's Grass Roots*, Clarendon Press, 1992.

Barbara Taylor, *Eve and the New Jerusalem*, Virago, 1983.

Anthony Wright, *G.D.H. Cole and Socialist Democracy*, Clarendon Press, 1976.

Adrian Wood, *North-South Trade, Employment and Inequality*, Clarendon Press, 1994.

Index

abortion, 228
activism, 230-34, 237
Africa, 182, 186
Agitators, 12
aid, overseas, 190-92, 206
Allen, Graham, 53, 221
alternative vote, 70, 74-5
Americanisation, 41
anarchism, 8, 9, 17, 32
Anti-Nazi League, 115
apartheid, 21
appointments, ministerial, 43, 229-30
arms industry, 183, 189-90, 195-98
Assisted Places Scheme,104-5

Babeuf, Francois-Noel, 100
Bank of England, 133, 165, 172, 173,
    174, 226
banking reform, 133-4
Barings Bank, 132, 207
Bell, Daniel, 6
benefits, universal,83-8
Benn, Tony, 22, 46
Bevan, Nye, 20, 99, 221
Beveridge Report, 84
Bill of Rights, 46, 47, 53, 75, 222
Blair, Tony, 4, 23, 232
Blanqui, Auguste, 10
Blunkett, David,23
Boeing, 211
Bolsheviks, 7
Borrie, Gordon, 86
borrowing, public, 148-9, 223
Brandt, Willi, 200
Bretton Woods, 198-9, 205, 212, 216

Bridges, William, 148
British Telecom, 141, 142, 225
Brockway, Fenner, 12
Bullock Report, 22

Callaghan, James, 34
Campbell, Beatrix, 117
caretakers, 108
Castle, Barbara, 67
centralism, 8, 19
Chartism, 13, 160
childcare, 87, 110, 111, 112, 113, 228
child labour, 187, 192, 214
Child Poverty Action Group, 230
Child Support Agency, 64, 227
China, 8, 10, 106, 129, 214, 216
Chomsky, Noam, 11, 184, 185, 190,
    197, 206, 211
CIA, 186
Citizens' Income, 87
citizenship, 31, 32, 53-4, 59-60
City, 34, 37, 38, 76, 103, 130-34, 237
civic education, 59-60, 61
civil rights movement (USA), 20
civil service, 24, 34, 43, 45, 50, 54, 67,
    76, 113, 230, 237
civil society, 31, 33, 54-5, 61, 231
class, 1, 6, 27, 40, 54, 76-7, 104, 117
Clause IV, 3-4, 5-6, 15, 136
Clinton, Bill, 40, 116, 197, 218
Clintonisation, 40-41
CND, 20
Cole, G.D.H., 14, 16, 17-19
command economics, 3, 26, 119, 208,
    217

communism, 3, 9-10, 11, 18, 20, 30, 239

communitarianism, 115-8

community resource centres, 58

community, 6, 115-8

compulsory voting, 60-61, 222

consumption, 119-20, 123-4, 149, 218, 222, 223, 238-9

contracting out, 50, 51

cooperatives, 9, 13, 14, 22, 136

corruption, 51

Cowling, Keith, 195, 206, 208, 210-11, 212-13

crime, 1, 25, 77, 81-2

Criminal Justice Act 1994, 24, 229

Crosland, Anthony, 20, 78

Cuba, 192, 228

Curtice, John, 240

debt, personal, 123-4

debt, world, 3, 190-92, 193

defence spending, 122, 211

Delors, Jacques, 168, 171

Denham, John, 236

dentistry, 95

derivatives, 160, 207-8

devaluation, 167

devolution, 28, 43, 47, 56-8, 65, 177-8, 221

Diggers, 12

direct action, 20, 21

disestablishment of Church, 47

education, 98-106

electoral reform, 50, 70-75, 180, 222

electoral turnout, 23-4, 61, 239-40

electricity, 19, 137, 140-45

environment, 14, 34, 55, 146-7, 193-4, 213

equal opportunities, 67-8, 108-15

Equal Pay Act 1970, 89, 109, 110

Etzioni, Amitai, 115-17

European Union,
    agriculture, 161, 162, 169, 207
    budget, 161, 165, 166, 169, 170
    Central Bank, 165-6, 172-5
    Committee of the Regions,177-8

    democracy, 176-80
    directives, 64, 65
    enlargement, 161-3
    Exchange Rate Mechanism, 122, 159, 164, 167, 168, 169-70, 215
    monetarism, 39, 40, 155, 156, 158, 166, 167, 180
    Monetary Union (EMU), 156, 162-7, 169
    Parliament, 65, 165, 176, 178-80
    poverty, 155
    qualified majority voting, 157, 162
    Social Chapter, 114, 127, 162, 227
    sovereignty, 158-60
    subsidiarity, 176-7
    unemployment, 155, 164, 168, 172

European Convention on Human Rights, 53, 222

extra-parliamentary politics, 32-4, 237

Fabians, 14, 15, 22

family credit, 81

famine, 188-90

fascism, 40, 114, 156, 239

federalism, 10, 177-8

feminism, 9, 13, 21-2, 108, 109, 113, 117

financial instruments, new, 160, 170

flexible employment, 6, 110, 121, 126, 212

food policy, 183-4, 188-90, 200-201, 207

Freedom of Information Act, 54, 222

Freeman, Richard, 90

French Revolution 1789, 10, 11

Friedman, Milton, 5, 119

Friends of the Earth, 230

Fukuyama, Francis, 6

full employment, 147-9, 153, 167, 171, 172, 175, 182, 216, 226

Gaitskell, Hugh, 5-6, 99

Galbraith, J.K., 86, 183, 239

gas, 19, 137, 140-45

GATT, 181, 185, 193-4, 195, 198-204, 213-4

gay rights, 229

GCHQ, 46, 227
General Strike 1926, 15, 166
George, Eddie, 165
Germany, 5, 39, 40, 70, 71-2, 106, 127, 133, 135, 152, 153-4, 173-4, 177
Gingrich, Newt, 214, 218
Gold Standard, 166, 174, 175
Goldsmith, James, 214
Gorbachev, Michail, 161
Gould, Bryan, 36
GP fundholding, 91-4
Gramsci, Antonio, 31, 33, 231, 242
Gray, John, 94, 100
Greater London Council, 23, 24, 49, 55, 57
green economics, 146-7, 193
green socialism, 14, 55
Greenpeace, 55, 230
Grieve Smith, John, 215
guild socialism, 14, 15, 16, 17-19
Gulf War 1991, 46, 197
Gyford, John, 16

Halsey, A.H., 13
Harris, Nigel, 188, 189, 196, 198
Hattersley, Roy, 78, 99
Hayek, F.A., 5, 119
health policy, 90-98
Hines, Colin, 193, 201, 213-14
Hodgson, Geoff, 35
Holland, Stuart, 168
homelessness, 21, 106-7, 227
hospital trusts, 90-94
House of Lords, 12, 28, 47, 48-50, 64, 222
Housing and Construction Bank, 135-6
housing, 29, 106-108, 227
Humphrey, Hubert, 190
Hungarian Revolution, 208
Hutton, Will, 35, 60, 77, 78, 103, 122, 124, 130, 208
Huxley, Aldous, 9, 208

incomes policy, 149-52, 223
industrial democracy, 13, 14, 15, 17-18, 20, 22, 23, 32, 33, 38-9, 60, 136, 152, 238
inequality, 96, 207
information superhighway, 26, 171, 225
Institute for Workers' Control, 21
intelligence services, 24, 34, 42, 69
International Monetary Fund, 170, 182, 185, 187, 191, 192, 198, 200, 211, 215, 216
International Social Chapter, 214
investment banks, 134-6
Ireland, 228-9

Jackson, Jesse, 239
Jacobin communism, 9-10
Japan, 37, 106, 125-6, 127, 133, 135, 152, 153, 197, 204, 209, 210, 213
Jowell, Roger, 240
judiciary, 12, 34, 53, 54, 69, 76, 113, 229

Keegan, William, 183, 184, 198, 211
Kelly, Ruth, 170, 208
Kendall, Walter, 18
Kennan, George, 185-62
Keynesianism, 148, 168, 175, 182, 198, 199, 224
Kinnock, Neil, 23, 233
Kropotkin, Peter, 9, 14, 31

Labour Party reform, 234-9
labourism, 21, 23
Lang, Tim, 193, 201, 213-4
Lansbury, George, 16
Laski, Harold, 177
Latin America, 186, 193
Lawson, Nigel, 107, 122, 159, 175
Leninism, 7, 10, 22, 32
lesbian rights, 109, 233
Levellers, 12, 160
Liberal Democrats, 41, 241
Liberal-Labour pact, 241
liberalism, 10-11, 31
libertarian socialism, 3, 7-41, 108, 115, 118, 125, 234, 242
libertarianism, 7, 10, 15, 20
libertarianism, right wing, 29

life expectancy, 82
Linton, Martin, 62
literacy, 83, 105
Littlechild, Stephen, 140
Livingstone, Ken, 23
local government, 24, 51, 52, 53, 57-8, 107, 177
Local Management of Schools, 101
low pay, 1, 81, 88-90, 110-11, 127, 128, 130, 145, 151

Maastricht Treaty, 46, 157, 158, 163, 165, 167-9, 170, 172, 177
MacDougall, Sir Donald, 165
magistrates, 69
Major, John, 46, 66, 157, 161
Mann, Tom, 14
manufacturing, 121, 122-3, 127, 128, 131, 134, 136, 194, 201-2, 210
market forces, 1, 3, 23, 34, 119-20, 122, 124, 126, 127, 129, 175, 205
market testing, 24, 50
markets, 34-6, 146, 208
Marquand, David, 41
Marshall Aid, 190, 206
Marxism, 10, 158
Marxism-Leninism, 7-8, 30, 31
Meacher, Michael, 36
Mensheviks, 7, 9
Mexico, 187, 191-92
Michie, Jonathan, 215
Miliband, Ralph, 30, 33, 44, 76, 219
Militant Tendency, 233
military-industrial complex, 211
Mill, John Stuart, 99
miners' strike 1984-5, 42
miners, South Wales, 14
minimum wage, 28, 88-90, 112, 151, 152, 225
modernisers, Labour, 5-6, 23, 116, 241
monarchy, 44-48
monetarism, 43, 39, 147, 166, 175, 182, 184, 199, 204-8, 215, 216
morality, 30
Morris, William, 9, 14
Morrison, Herbert, 20, 22, 139

municipal socialism, 15-16, 23

National Investment Bank, 134-5
nationalisation, 7, 10, 15, 17, 19-20, 22, 25, 38, 39, 99, 137, 138, 240
nazism, 114, 115, 156
neighbourhood councils, 51, 58-9
New Labour, 23, 218
New Left, 9, 20, 21, 23, 31
Nicaragua, 192, 233
Nolan Committee, 51, 65
Norman, Montagu, 174
North American Free Trade Area, 182
North Sea Oil, 2, 80, 119, 123
Northern Ireland, 228-9
nuclear power, 238
nuclear weapons, 20, 99, 228, 240, 242
numeracy, 83, 105
Nyerere, Julius, 185

opted out hospitals, 90-94
opted out schools, 100-102
Owen, Robert, 13, 140
ownership, 12, 15, 17, 19-20, 25, 37-9, 136-9

Pacific Basin, 3, 37, 105, 129, 153, 155, 182, 202, 216
Paine, Tom, 13, 47
Paris Commune 1871, 10
Paris May 1968, 21
parliamentarianism, 21, 23
parliamentary democracy, 54-5, 56
parliamentary reform, 63-7
participation, 16, 19, 20, 22, 59-60
participatory democracy, 13, 18, 19, 22, 26-8, 234
patronage, 43, 48
pay bargaining, 149-53
Payer, Cheryl, 191
pension funds, 37, 38, 40, 134, 135, 139
pensions, 1-2, 37, 84-6
Perot, Ross, 41, 239
planning, 15, 20, 34-6, 119, 153, 210,

213
pluralism, 26, 28, 58
political parties, finance of, 61-3, 222
pollution, 34, 146, 193, 217
Polyani, Karl, 24
Ponting, Clive, 45
Poplarism, 16
Port Huron Statement, 31
Porter, Michael, 128
Portillo, Michael, 45
Post Office, 23, 45, 138, 141, 227
post-Fordism, 26
poverty, 84, 145
price stability, 147-8, 166, 172, 173,
    174, 182, 226
private education, 76, 102-5
privatisation, 80, 119
privatised utilities, 1, 2, 29, 136-7, 139-
    45, 226
Privy Council, 45
proportional representation, 50, 70-
    75, 180
Proudhon, P.J., 10
public ownership, 38, 137, 143, 226
Public Sector Borrowing
    Requirement, 138, 224, 227

Quangos, 2, 24, 50-53, 57, 117, 229

racial equality, 113-51
racism, 1, 3, 13, 21, 40, 113-5, 156,
    180, 182
Reaganism, 5, 197, 207, 211, 212
reformist socialism, 7-8, 18
regional government, 16-17, 28, 53,
    56-7, 134, 143, 177-8, 221, 222
regulation, 37-9, 132-3, 140-45
Regulators, 140-45, 226
Reich, Robert, 129
republicanism, 47
research and development, 126, 129,
    131, 153, 196
revolutionary socialism, 7-10, 18, 32
Robinson, Mary, 48
Rochdale Pioneers, 13
Rowbotham, Sheila, 22
Royal Prerogative, 42, 45, 222

Russia, 7, 8, 9, 10, 196
Russian Revolution 1917, 7, 10

Saint-Simon, Henri de, 10
Sandinistas, 192
Sawyer, Malcolm, 139
Schumpeter, Joseph, 19
scientific socialism, 30
secrecy, official, 24, 43, 45, 54, 66, 229
security services, 69
Segal, Lynne, 22
Seyd, Patrick, 231
share ownership, 29, 33, 136
shareholders, 37-8, 63, 130-31, 133,
    139, 140, 141-2, 143, 226
Shaw, George Bernard, 156
short-termism, 119-20, 124, 126, 130,
    133, 149, 210
skills, 106, 124, 128, 129, 148, 202,
    204, 215
slavery, 13
Small Business Bank, 134-5
Smith, Adam, 24, 117
Smith, John, 23
social contract, 223
social democracy, 7-8, 9, 18, 20, 39-41
Social Democratic Party (SDP), 41
Social Justice Commission, 86
socialist feminism, 9, 13, 22, 113, 117
Solow, Robert, 127
sovereignty, 150-60, 195
Soviet socialism, 5, 8, 10, 20, 21, 32,
    119, 153, 185, 196
Stalinism, 8, 9, 21
state socialism, 3, 7-12, 14, 15, 17-19,
    28, 32, 36, 78-9, 99, 108, 196, 208,
    212, 241
statutory instruments, 64
strikes, 6, 10, 15, 22, 53, 123
student grants, 103
Suffragettes, 13, 160
Sugden, Roger, 195, 206, 208, 210-11,
    212-13
sustainable growth, 146-7, 171
Sweden, 38, 39, 82, 152, 153, 160,
    204, 212, 213
syndicalism, 10, 14-15, 19, 21

Tawney, R.H., 20, 78, 99-100
taxation, 79, 80, 85, 97, 106, 145-47, 217, 223, 224-5
Taylor, Barbara, 13
telecommunications, 137, 140-45, 225
Thatcher, Margaret, 34, 46, 49, 50, 123, 241
Thatcherism, 2, 5, 29, 119-20, 121, 122, 141, 207, 227, 230
third road politics, 55
Thompson, E.P., 20
Townsend, Peter, 86
trade unions, 6, 10, 12, 13, 14, 17, 21, 22, 40, 46, 53-4, 55, 63, 150, 160, 187, 214, 223, 227, 237, 238-9, 240
trade, free, 184, 188-9, 193-5, 198-205, 209-10, 213
trade, managed, 198-9, 209-10, 213-14
trade, North-South, 188, 189, 191, 199-200, 202-203, 206
transnational companies, 335, 160, 184, 185, 188-9, 194-5, 197, 201, 207, 208

underclass, 6, 61, 77, 112, 124, 239
unemployment, 3, 80-81, 84, 207, 212
United Nations Economic Council, 216-17

VAT, 97, 105, 145-6, 171
Vietnam War, 21, 22, 197

Wages Councils, 89, 127
Wainwright, Hilary, 229

Wales, 14, 43, 56, 57, 65, 98, 102, 177, 178, 221, 222
water industry, 137, 140-45
wealth, 82-3
Webb, Beatrice, 16
Webb, Sidney, 15, 16, 174, 220
welfare, 83-8, 116
Wells, H.G., 47
Whiteley, Paul, 231
Wilkinson, Helen, 109
Wilkinson, Richard, 82
Williams, Raymond, 20
Wilson, Harold, 22, 34
Winstanley, Gerrard, 12
Wollstonecraft, Mary, 13
women voters, 109
women's rights, 13, 21, 67, 108-13, 117, 118
Women, Minister for, 67-8, 112, 230
Wood, Adrian, 203, 213
workers' control, 10, 14, 17, 21, 22
workers' cooperatives, 22
workers' participation, 12, 22, 32, 33
workers' rights, 53-4, 150, 187, 214
works councils, 39, 150
World Bank, 170, 185, 187, 191, 192, 198, 200, 209, 211, 211, 215, 216
world poverty, 3, 185, 186, 189
World Trade Organisation, 200, 214
Wright Mills, C., 76
Wright, Anthony, 18-19

Young Liberals, 21